FORMATIVE TOOLS
FOR LEADERS
IN A PLC at Work®

Assessing,
Analyzing,
and Acting
to Support
Collaborative
Teams

KIM BAILEY   CHRIS JAKICIC
Foreword by Robert Eaker

Solution Tree | Press   a division of
Solution Tree

MW01148467

Copyright © 2022 by Solution Tree Press

Materials appearing here are copyrighted. With one exception, all rights are reserved. Readers may reproduce only those pages marked "Reproducible." Otherwise, no part of this book may be reproduced or transmitted in any form or by any means (electronic, photocopying, recording, or otherwise) without prior written permission of the publisher.

555 North Morton Street
Bloomington, IN 47404
800.733.6786 (toll free) / 812.336.7700
FAX: 812.336.7790

email: info@SolutionTree.com
SolutionTree.com

Visit **go.SolutionTree.com/PLCbooks** to download the free reproducibles in this book.

Printed in the United States of America

Library of Congress Cataloging-in-Publication Data

Names: Bailey, Kim, author. | Jakicic, Chris, author.
Title: Formative tools for leaders in a PLC at work® : assessing,
    analyzing, and acting to support collaborative teams / Kim Bailey, Chris
    Jakicic.
Description: Bloomington, IN : Solution Tree Press, [2021] | Includes
    bibliographical references and index.
Identifiers: LCCN 2021032730 (print) | LCCN 2021032731 (ebook) | ISBN
    9781951075859 (paperback) | ISBN 9781951075866 (ebook)
Subjects: LCSH: Teaching teams. | Professional learning communities. |
    Lesson planning. | Teachers--Professional relationships.
Classification: LCC LB1029.T4 B354 2021 (print) | LCC LB1029.T4 (ebook) |
    DDC 371.14/8--dc23
LC record available at https://lccn.loc.gov/2021032730
LC ebook record available at https://lccn.loc.gov/2021032731

Solution Tree
Jeffrey C. Jones, CEO
Edmund M. Ackerman, President

Solution Tree Press
President and Publisher: Douglas M. Rife
Associate Publisher: Sarah Payne-Mills
Art Director: Rian Anderson
Managing Production Editor: Kendra Slayton
Copy Chief: Jessi Finn
Production Editor: Miranda Addonizio
Content Development Specialist: Amy Rubenstein
Copy Editor: Mark Hain
Proofreader: Elisabeth Abrams
Cover Designer: Rian Anderson
Editorial Assistants: Sarah Ludwig and Elijah Oates

Acknowledgments

We would like to thank Bob Eaker, who first suggested the topic for this book. His leadership and friendship have helped us to continue to more deeply understand how best to implement the PLC process and continue to improve our own practices. We'd also like to thank the thousands of educators we've had the honor to work with as they've sought ways to improve their schools. We've learned so much from them and admire their willingness to embrace change to make things work better for their students. We are grateful to be connected with so many dedicated professionals who make student learning, as well as their own learning, an important part of their lives.

Solution Tree Press would like to thank the following reviewers:

Katie Brittain
Principal
Rose Haggar Elementary
Dallas, Texas

Molly Capps
Principal
McDeeds Creek Elementary
Southern Pines, North Carolina

Jennifer Evans
Principal
Burnham School, K–6
Cicero, Illinois

Claire Springer
Assistant Principal
Savannah Elementary School
Aubrey, Texas

Jennifer Steele
Assistant Principal
Northside High School
Fort Smith, Arkansas

Steven Weber
Associate Superintendent for Teaching
    and Learning
Fayetteville Public Schools
Fayetteville, Arkansas

Visit **go.SolutionTree.com/PLCbooks** to
download the free reproducibles in this book.

Table of Contents

PART 1

Chapter 1

A CULTURE OF LEARNING FOR ALL 15

Chapter 2

THE SCHOOL'S COLLABORATIVE STRUCTURES 39

Chapter 3

QUALITY INSTRUCTIONAL PRACTICE 73

Chapter 4

SCHOOLWIDE SYSTEMS OF SUPPORT 105

PART 2

Chapter 5

A FOCUS ON GETTING CLEAR ABOUT WHAT STUDENTS SHOULD KNOW AND DO 135

About the Authors

Kim Bailey is former director of professional development and instructional support for the Capistrano Unified School District in Southern California. Her leadership was instrumental in uniting and guiding educators throughout the district's schools on their journey to becoming professional learning communities (PLCs). She also taught courses in educational leadership as an adjunct faculty member at Chapman University in Orange, California. Prior to her work in professional development, Kim served as an administrator of special education programs and a teacher of students with disabilities.

Kim's education background spans over forty years, and her work at Capistrano has won national praise. The National School Boards Association (NSBA) recognized Kim's leadership in coordinating and implementing the district's Professional Development Academies. The academies received the distinguished NSBA Magna Award and the California School Boards Association Golden Bell Award. Kim has served on the Committee on Accreditation for the California Commission on Teaching Credentialing.

As a writer and consultant, Kim works with U.S. educators to build effective leadership of PLCs. She is passionate about empowering teams with practical, collaborative strategies for aligning instruction, assessment, and interventions with the standards so all students receive high-quality instruction.

Kim earned bachelor of science and master of science degrees in education and special education from Northern Illinois University.

To learn more about Kim's work, visit https://kbailey4learning.com or follow @Bailey4learning on Twitter.

Chris Jakicic, EdD, served as principal of Wood-lawn Middle School in Long Grove, Illinois from its opening day in 1999 through the spring of 2007. Under her leadership, the staff shifted toward a collaborative culture focused on learning and implemented formative assessment practices to shape their instructional strategies. Student motivation and performance increased. Chris began her career teaching middle school science before serving as principal of Willow Grove Elementary School in Buffalo Grove, Illinois, for nine years. At Willow Grove, she helped teachers develop high-performing collaborative teams to increase student learning.

Through her work with teachers and administrators across the United States, Chris emphasizes that effective teaming is the heart of PLCs. She also shares practical knowledge about how to use data conversations to interpret classroom information for effective instruction. She has worked closely with schools and districts that want to use the power of common formative assessments to increase learning for all students. She provides specific, practical strategies for teams who want to make the best use of their limited common planning time to write effective assessments meeting the rigor of the Common Core State Standards. Teams can use the data from these assessments to effectively provide students with exactly what they need next.

Chris has written articles for the *Journal of Staff Development* and *Illinois School Research and Development Journal* detailing her experiences with common assessments and PLCs. She has worked as an adjunct instructor at National Louis University as well as Loyola University Chicago, where she earned a doctor of education degree.

To learn more about Chris's work, visit www.chrisjakicic.com or follow @cjakicic on Twitter.

To book Kim Bailey or Chris Jakicic for professional development, contact pd@SolutionTree.com.

Foreword

By Robert Eaker

I often meet those who say, "Bob, I think the Professional Learning Communities at Work process could really help our school. I'm just not sure how to go about implementing the various processes and practices. Do you have any suggestions?" In the future my ready answer will be, "Read Kim Bailey and Chris Jakicic's new book!" *Formative Tools for Leaders in a PLC at Work* should be a companion piece for all leaders who seek to transform their school into a high-performing PLC.

As the popularity of the Professional Learning Community at Work process continues to grow, the question of *how* to implement PLC practices is more relevant than ever. However, we must recognize there is no one way to become an effective PLC. Reculturing a school into a high-performing PLC is a cyclical process, but I have found that a useful analogy is undertaking a long automobile journey. There may be more than one route. People travel at different speeds. And, more than likely, there will be obstacles along the way (Keating, Eaker, DuFour, & DuFour, 2008).

When undertaking a journey, particularly a long and complex one, it is common practice to seek advice from others who have previously undertaken the same or a similar journey. Many find a guidebook to be helpful. *Formative Tools for Leaders in a PLC at Work* is such a book. Those who are considering undertaking the journey of transforming their school into a PLC can gain significant insights from Kim Bailey and Chris Jakicic that can make the journey smoother, and, most importantly, increase the likelihood of success.

With most lengthy journeys there will be stops along the way, and the same is true for becoming a PLC. Kim and Chris drill deep into each stop on the PLC journey. They detail the why, the what, and the how to build a solid foundation of a PLC; create a collaborative culture through the use of high-performing teams; establish a focus on learning by addressing the critical questions teacher teams must address; provide effective additional time and support for students who struggle with specific skills, as well as how to extend the learning of students who demonstrate proficiency;

and provide frequent and meaningful recognition and celebration for both students and adults along the way.

The uniqueness of *Formative Tools for Leaders in a PLC at Work* is apparent in two ways: first, Kim and Chris view the journey to becoming a PLC through the lens of adult learning, and second, they recognize the power of formative assessments for team learning in order to enhance student learning.

The key to student learning is continuous adult learning. The key word in the phrase *professional learning community* is *learning,* and this focus on learning includes the learning of adults in order to improve the learning of students. Like student learning, adult learning is enhanced when undertaken by collaborative teams. Kim and Chris wisely see the leader's role as one of enhancing team effectiveness through deep and meaningful learning.

Like student learning, effective team learning requires clarity regarding *what* is essential for teams to know and be able to do. And, as with student learning, teams must address the question How will we know if our teams are learning? through formative assessments *during* the learning process. As a result of formative assessment of teams' work, leaders will discover that some teams need additional time and support in some areas, while other teams need to extend their learning.

The power of formative assessments has long been recognized. There is certainly no shortage of resources on why and how formative assessments, when developed and used properly, can have a positive impact on student learning. The breakthrough of *Formative Tools for Leaders in a PLC at Work* is that Kim and Chris had the insight to recognize that formative assessment can also be a powerful tool for enhancing team effectiveness.

For example, in a professional learning community, teams develop goals. Many leaders wait until the end of the time frame in which goals are to be completed to assess goal attainment—that is, summative assessments *of* learning. Kim and Chris emphasize the power of assessing the work of teams along the way in order to provide teams with feedback that helps teams improve—that is, formative assessment *for* learning (Stiggins, 2005).

Formative assessment of team-developed products is another example. When planning for student learning, a key question teams must address is, What would student *work* look like if students have successfully learned a particular skill or concept? The key is thinking about essential learning through the lens of successful work products—and clearly describing them. The same is true of team learning. Readers can find multiple examples of how leaders should focus their formative assessment efforts on analyzing team *products*—the work that teams produce—against previously developed standards of quality.

As a result of their training and learning, the work of teams almost always results in products. For example, teams will produce team norms, develop curriculum guides, write commonly developed formative and summative assessments, plan common units of teaching and learning, develop plans for interventions and extensions, and make plans for frequent and meaningful recognition and celebration—among many others! By including insights and examples related to the use of formative assessments of team work products, *Formative Tools for Leaders in a PLC at Work* provides a powerful template for improving the performance of collaborative teams and ultimately enhancing student learning.

Here's my advice to those who are undertaking the journey of transforming their schools into effective PLCs: buy this book! Don't skim it. Read it. I promise, if you take your time and carefully read *Formative Tools for Leaders in a PLC at Work*, you'll find a treasure trove of research-based and practitioner-based practices. More importantly, put Kim Bailey and Chris Jakicic's ideas to work and you will experience a successful journey that is doable, practical, satisfying, and inherently worthwhile.

Introduction

School leaders involved in the work of transforming a school into a professional learning community (PLC) are keenly aware that, while it's a cycle of continuous improvement in which the work never ends, there is an ongoing quest toward improvement inherent in the process. And like every worthwhile quest, those leading the charge may encounter challenges interrupting the anticipated path or flow. They may encounter detours and construction sites. They might experience difficult circumstances that prevent the journey from moving forward at the pace they first anticipated. They might have technical or structural breakdowns. What keeps those on the quest headed in the right direction, however, are the specific landmarks and milestones that let them check in and ensure they're on the right path. And based on what they're observing and the information coming from these markers and milestones, those leading the way adjust their course and decisions about what they need to do next, whether it is to make repairs, reroute the journey, or spend more time in a certain location before moving forward.

The same holds true at schools. In order to fully realize the vision of PLC at Work architects Richard DuFour, Rebecca DuFour, and Robert Eaker, school leaders must keep in mind the true definition of a PLC: "an ongoing process in which educators work collaboratively in recurring cycles of collective inquiry and action research to achieve better results for the students they serve" (DuFour, DuFour, Eaker, Many, & Mattos, 2016, p. 10). The process is ongoing and recurring, meaning that leaders need to continuously seek evidence of their context, their current location, and any challenges they are currently encountering or anticipate in the future. Leaders must take appropriate next steps while keeping an eye on the goal of improving student learning.

What we're describing here are *formative leadership practices*—in other words, leaders using key tools to gather evidence around specific milestones or markers to determine what is happening in their school. They then use that evidence to keep improving their practices and movement toward its vision.

There's a parallel between the process we're describing with formative practices for leaders and those used by teams with their students. In our work around assessment, we clarify that an assessment is formative when it's used to improve learning. Likewise, a leadership practice is formative when leaders use evidence to improve the practices in the school—in other words, when they take action to keep moving forward in order to meet the mission and vision of their school. But how can school leaders truly use these formative practices to help schools realize their mission and vision?

Leaders Can Use This Book to Truly Support Teams

In our work as educators, consultants, and authors, we have promoted formative assessment and encouraged educators to use evidence from the formative assessments they've designed to support student learning. One of the major guiding principles we share is that when educators gather small pieces of evidence, they can take informed and targeted action to further support student learning and increase the likelihood of students learning a particular set of skills. This book extends that same principle to school leaders and supports their use of formative practices. School leaders can gather evidence from their staff and teams' practices, processes, and products, using that evidence to gauge the effectiveness of a PLC and making informed and targeted decisions based on the evidence about next steps, much the same way teams would use a formative assessment. Leaders use formative tools to *assess* what is happening, to *analyze* the evidence in order to understand why this is happening, and to *act* by providing whatever time and support a team needs. Just as we expect teams to extend the learning for students who have already mastered the essential standards, we expect leaders to provide opportunities for high-performing teams to continue to move forward when they are already meeting high standards.

Throughout the book, we embed the following guiding principles, which a number of business and education researchers and practitioners have illuminated as the central tenets of the implementation and change processes (Guskey, 2000; Hall & Hord, 2006; Heath & Heath, 2007; Kotter, 2012; Muhammad & Cruz, 2019). We apply them more specifically to the work of implementing PLCs.

1. **Change is a process, so prepare for one:** School improvement, including the implementation of a PLC, is a process, not an event. Leaders must assume that there will be starts and stops and elements that require some backtracking. They can't presume that simply because teams have received training that they will be able to implement it without various levels of support. It will take time, energy, resources, and continued focus along the way. Leaders must also share this

mindset within the larger system, including the superintendent, central office, and even the school board.

2. **Emphasize the *why* first:** The phrase *begin with why*, popularized through the work of Simon Sinek (2009), recurs frequently in organizations seeking change, with good reason. If members of the school community aren't clear on the why of PLC work or any initiative requiring change—in other words, its purpose and potential impact—then that change is unlikely to happen. Our dear friend and mentor, Rebecca DuFour, always reminded us that "clarity precedes competence" (Schmoker, 2004. p. 85)—establishing the purpose or *why* of the work is the first step toward clarity. Leaders are clear on the why before building shared knowledge with their staff. They spend their time clarifying the purpose behind each element of the work, tying it back to a school's mission and vision for students.

3. **This is not a solo act:** Throughout this book, we use the term *leaders* with the understanding that the process of leading implementation is shared across all members of the school community, not just administrators. As such, any teacher who takes on a leadership role can use this book. The formative process we describe in this book cannot succeed if teachers leave leadership solely to the principal and assistant principal. Rather, the leadership must include representatives of the entire staff who work collaboratively along with the principal and assistant principal as the leadership team, sometimes known as a guiding coalition. Leadership team members may include administrators, leaders of collaborative teams—the grade-level, course-alike, or vertical teams that serve as the building blocks of a PLC—and informal teacher leaders. Individuals designated to support teachers, such as instructional coaches, have an important leadership role as well. As you consider each of the formative tools in this book, ask yourself, "Which leaders in our school could have the most positive impact using the information we gather from this tool?"

4. **Context is important:** Every school has a story. Every team has its unique composition, strengths, and areas of need. Leaders who ignore their school's story could find their efforts derailed. Acknowledging and considering the school's history, past practices, successes, and challenges provide insight into the shared knowledge that staff members need, including any emotional residue that could hinder or impede the process. For example, a school that has experienced a revolving door of administrators, all with their respective initiatives, might be wary of any new proposal. The leader of such a school must consider how best to build trust and move slowly with consideration for those individuals

who might be reluctant to try "one more thing." In each chapter of this book, we prompt leaders to consider their context in the topic of that chapter. In general, these questions or prompts will assist leaders in thinking about their context.

- What is the history of this particular topic? What is the current practice around this topic?

- What team or individual expectations for implementation related to this topic are in place?

- What challenges to implementation exist?

- What level of training and support have teams received?

- What is the teams' understanding of the why in this particular topic?

By digging into the context of a team or school, leaders gain insights about their next steps to move forward.

With all of these guiding principles in mind, let's take a moment to go over how we have set up this book. While we don't necessarily intend you to read this book from cover to cover, it does provide a comprehensive look at the implementation of a culture and systems focused on continuous improvement. Schools engaging in the PLC process are constantly viewing their efforts with what we call a *zoom-in, zoom-out* viewpoint. That is, school leaders zoom out to monitor and move forward in the areas that impact their school across teams and systems. But at the same time, they must zoom in to the work of teams and their specific efforts to support student learning. When leaders zoom in, they're looking at a more granular level with a focus on specific processes and products that impact student learning.

Effective implementation of a PLC encompasses two important characteristics: (1) shared leadership and (2) loose-tight decisions. Shared leadership assumes that to have one person lead this process would be ineffective. Instead, as mentioned, the school is led by a leadership team or guiding coalition, which makes decisions for the school, supports collaborative teams in the work, and facilitates communication among other teams in the building. Leadership teams include classroom teachers who have leadership skills but may also benefit from additional training in the areas of coaching and consensus building.

When leadership teams make decisions for the entire school, some of those decisions may be tight and some loose (DuFour et al., 2016; Sagie, 1997). A *tight* decision, one that all teams are expected to apply in the same way, might be how teams use instructional time to provide time and support for students who haven't yet mastered the essential standards. On the other hand, leaders might decide that collaborative teams should be the ones to plan the responses to their assessments. This is a *loose* decision because the collaborative teams will each decide how best to do this for their own grade levels or subjects rather than at a schoolwide level of implementation.

This shared leadership model is an example of *systems thinking*, a term that describes a way to analyze how a system's parts work together, and which comes from the work of systems scientist Peter M. Senge (2006) in his discussions of learning organizations. The model shown in figure I.1 shows the relationship between the leadership team and the collaborative teams. The leadership team guides schoolwide decisions and expected practices (what we sometimes call "tight" versus "loose") while also supporting the work of collaborative teams, and the collaborative teams provide input for those decisions that impact them. This model ensures shared leadership as well as alignment and coherence with the mission of the school.

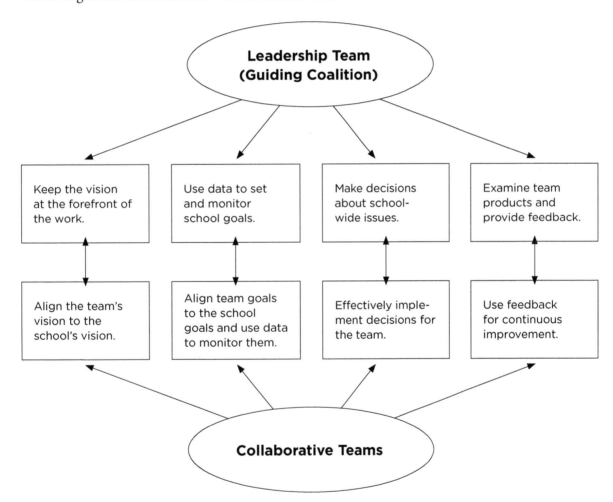

Figure I.1: Leadership and collaborative team connections to the school organization.

To acknowledge the distinction between the two parts of the system and the different approaches that leaders must take to support them, we organized the book into two parts. The chapters in part 1 address schoolwide considerations.

- Chapter 1 discusses indicators related to schools that reflect *a culture of learning* and provides tools to gauge the current reality based on evidence and nonevidence of practice.

- In chapter 2, we provide tools for school leaders to examine their grade- or course-alike collaborative team structures and the general effectiveness of collaboration.

- Chapter 3 provides tools for examining the *quality of instruction* across a school and guidance for moving forward in areas targeted for improvement.

- In chapter 4, we look at schoolwide *systems of support* for students, specifically response to intervention (RTI), and address the structures and culture necessary to ensure that *all* students learn at high levels.

Part 2 of this book provides a closer look into the work of teams as they answer the four critical questions of a PLC (DuFour et al., 2016).

- Chapter 5 examines and provides tools to gather evidence on team actions designed to answer critical question 1, *What do students need to know and be able to do?*

- In chapter 6, we look at how collaborative teams are answering critical question 2, *How will we know when they have learned it?*

- Chapter 7 examines evidence related to critical question 3, *What will we do when they haven't learned it?* In doing so, the chapter provides leaders with decision-making strategies to enhance Tier 1 and Tier 2 response to intervention within collaborative teams.

- Finally, chapter 8 provides leaders with tools and strategies as they examine and enhance the work of collaborative teams around critical question 4, *What will we do when they already know it?*

Each chapter includes a broader review of PLC concepts that may feel redundant to experienced PLC practitioners, but we feel it's important to provide a baseline. As Richard DuFour, Rebecca DuFour, Robert Eaker, Thomas W. Many, and Mike Mattos (2016) point out, redundancy can be very useful, even powerful. We provide strategies for *assessing, analyzing,* and taking targeted *action* for each chapter's topic. Embedded within the strategies are descriptions of specific practices and products (what teams produce—norms, agendas, data, and so on) related to the topic. In addition, we provide a *continuum of practice* within each chapter that provides leaders with a means of summarizing their current reality. The following questions guide the process in each area.

1. **Assess the Current Reality:** What is our current reality? This section provides concrete tools and strategies for leaders to use.

   - What are we looking for in this area? What is the desired outcome? What evidence will tell us we're on the right path in this area?

   - How can we determine our current reality? What tools might we use? How can we gather meaningful evidence to determine where our school or team is currently strong and where it needs to be strengthened?

2. **Analyze Patterns and Priorities:** What patterns and priorities emerge from the evidence? This section explains how leaders can look at the evidence they gather from the tools.

   - What is the evidence telling us about our level of implementation in this area?

   - What is the root cause of the current level of implementation? If it is not what we want it to be, does the problem arise from a lack of knowledge or skill or from a lack of clarity about expectations? Is there a positive impact taking place because of our efforts?

   - Where does the school fall on the continuum of practice? What strengths can we build upon and in what areas do we need to improve?

3. **Act on Evidence to Improve Practice:** What are potential next steps based on the analysis of evidence? This section explains how leaders can use the evidence to begin planning next steps for improvement.

   - Based on our analysis, what are the next steps we must take to further our implementation or level of use?

   - How can we strengthen the impact of our actions?

   - What support must be provided to strengthen the implementation?

   - How can we celebrate and sustain this work?

As depicted in figure I.2 (page 8), these three stages of the formative process work as a feedback loop that leaders can use to continuously improve their schoolwide and team practices.

Before we launch into the rest of the book, we want to highlight some additional insights about leading the implementation of a PLC. These insights may help leaders establish a perspective and effective mindset about the process of implementation, leading to more confident decision making and action.

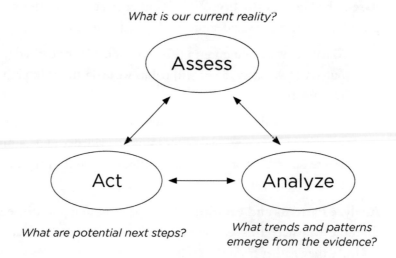

Figure I.2: The three stages of the formative process for leaders.

This Is About Leading Versus Managing

Leaders cannot approach major changes in a school's culture and mindset about student learning by evaluating others. They can't require actions from an authoritarian perspective. In other words, leaders won't accomplish true implementation through a carrot-and-stick mentality. Schools that approach the implementation of PLCs in this manner find that while they might receive compliance, they're unlikely to foster true commitment to the work. There's a sense among staff members of "We have to do this" versus "We're committed to do this for our students." Rather than requiring specific actions, leaders must first engage their staff in defining the school's mission and shared vision (DuFour et al., 2016). Through the shared vision process, leaders work with all members of the community to identify the collective commitments and goals that lead them to that vision. Remember to keep the following considerations in mind.

- **Don't wait for perfect conditions or solutions:** In our work across the years, we have never encountered a school that implemented everything in the best possible way when it first began. On the contrary, schools engaged in the work of implementing PLCs are continuously revisiting and refining their processes. DuFour and his coauthors (2016) of *Learning by Doing* based their work on this principle. The key is to analyze what leaders and staff have experienced and learn from it. To borrow a metaphor from Robert Eaker and Janel Keating (2011), schools are not necessarily putting the right things in place from the beginning but are always going back and sharpening the pencil. Leaders in these schools have the mindset of continuous learners—one of the foundational elements of a PLC. They make continual adjustments based on results and feedback on the impact of each action they take.

Things won't be perfect, but over time they grow and deepen their understanding of how the PLC process works. Increased clarity comes from experience and activating practice. In summary, this is our mantra that describes PLC work: *Learning together. Doing together. Learning more together. And making things better when we know better.*

- **Changes in experiences change mindsets:** As leaders look at the areas of change inherent in PLC work, there's a natural tendency to think that they need to first convince others to change with them, as represented on the left side of the flowchart found in figure I.3. The reality is that changes in attitudes and beliefs actually come from a different experience (Guskey, 2000, 2020), such as that depicted on the right side of the figure. After building shared knowledge through professional learning, teachers engage in collaborative work to identify clear targets for learning, gather data using common assessments, and recognize or celebrate impacts on student learning. As a result of the changed experience in student learning, leaders will see a change in teachers' attitudes and beliefs.

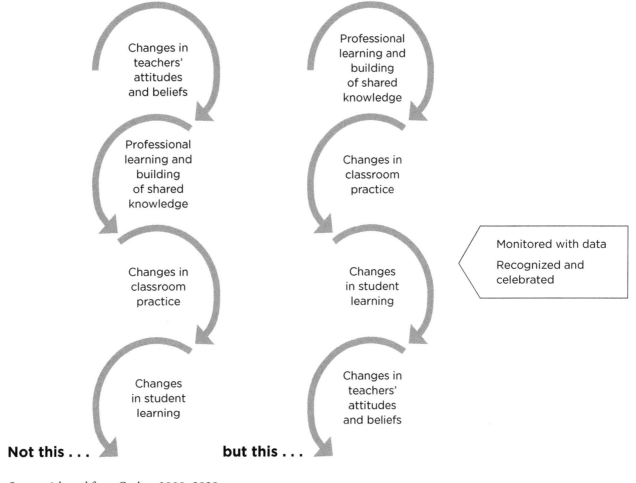

Not this . . .   but this . . .

Source: Adapted from Guskey, 2000, 2020.

Figure I.3: Changing attitudes and beliefs.

There are two important ways for leaders to lead, rather than manage, as they approach the implementation of PLCs and assess the work of teams in their schools: (1) provide support before accountability and (2) anticipate challenges.

Support Before Accountability

The actions we discuss in this book are driven by the belief that leaders can improve implementation through first building shared knowledge and skill. Put another way, leaders can't expect success if teams aren't fully clear on the why or what of the work. In his book *Transforming School Culture: How to Overcome Staff Division*, education consultant Anthony Muhammad (2018) references this premise when discussing the type of response that leaders must make, suggesting that they always start with the assumption that those not implementing necessary actions are not doing so because they are unwilling but because they simply lack knowledge or skill. In other words, leaders must clarify and build shared knowledge first, then provide support; only then can they expect success.

When determining how best to support teachers and teams, it's important to recognize that gaps in implementation stem from a variety of issues or concerns about new practices. As part of their Concerns-Based Adoption Model, Gene E. Hall and Shirley M. Hord (2006) identify seven specific stages of concern based on evidence obtained through observations and perceptions based on teacher interviews. Each stage of concern, as depicted in figure I.4, frames specific ways that leaders might see the concerns expressed by teachers and helps them look for each stage's unique root cause and needs.

General Focus of Concern	Stage of Concern	Expression of Concern
Impact	6—Refocusing	Is there anything else that's better than our current practice? (*I'd like to make some modifications to improve this practice.*)
	5—Collaboration	This new practice is working fine, but how do others do it? (*I'm curious how others are implementing this practice.*)
	4—Consequence	Is this practice worth it? (*Will the practices make a difference in my students' learning or in our work?*)
Task	3—Management	How can I master the new skills and fit everything I need to do in? (*I'm worried about being overwhelmed or not being able to manage this new practice on top of everything else.*)
	2—Personal	How does this practice impact me? (*I'm worried that implementing this practice will affect me.*)
Awareness and Self	1—Informational	How does this practice work? (*I would like to know more about this.*)
	0—Awareness	What is this practice? (*I'm not aware or concerned about the practice.*)

Source: Adapted from Hall & Hord, 2006.

Figure I.4: Stages of concern.

As leaders examine the current reality of their school along the major indicators of a professional learning community, which we will unpack throughout the book, they will analyze the evidence gathered through a number of sources, including observational checklists, interview questions, and artifacts. As they examine evidence, leaders can reference the stages of concern to base their support on what teams actually need. For example, when teams of teachers express concerns about management of a new initiative (stage 3) and their ability to "fit it all in," leaders can support them by helping teams prioritize their actions, identifying strategies for working efficiently, and providing time for them to create the products needed to support the implementation. By asking teams about their concerns and then meeting their needs, leaders set the stage for deeper implementation.

Anticipation of Challenges

It is rare that the implementation of a new initiative or program goes without a hitch. Leaders typically acknowledge and prepare for the fact that there will be occasional hiccups and challenges in this work. They can do this strategically and proactively by anticipating potential areas of challenge and then preparing for and preempting as many of those challenges as possible. While it's impossible to anticipate every challenge and concern, strategic leaders can conduct a *premortem*, or engaging key people in the school to predict the challenges that they are likely to encounter. This term comes from a *Harvard Business Review* article by psychologist Gary Klein (2007), and we often hear it from our colleague Robert Eaker. Once they have identified likely challenges, leaders can devise a strategy to avoid them or have a proactive plan in place to provide support to teachers once the problems surface.

Get Ready to Lead and Support Your Teams

We intend this book to be a practical resource for school leaders, something they can reference continually as they learn, do, and lead. It's not meant to be a complete resource that includes all that a site leader needs to implement the work of a PLC; it cannot stand alone. This book is intended to provide a supplemental set of tools that leaders can use in partnership with other resources to aid in the quest for deeper implementation of a school's PLC and its impact on student learning. These tools will help you gather relevant information about your school—information that can be analyzed and then used to support your efforts as you work to continuously improve the practices and positive impact within your PLC. Within these pages, you'll find continual references to the vital work provided by the architects of the PLC at Work process: Rick and Becky DuFour and Bob Eaker, as well as many other individuals who have expanded on the work found in their pivotal texts. Additionally, we reference many pearls of wisdom from our colleagues with "boots on the ground" leading PLCs. With the tools that we provide, as well as all this collective knowledge, we hope you find it a useful resource!

PART 1

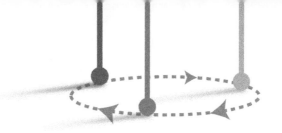

Chapter 1

A CULTURE OF LEARNING FOR ALL

In addressing this chapter's central question, Does the school culture support high levels of learning for all?, we begin with the three big ideas of a PLC: a focus on learning, a culture of collaboration and collective responsibility, and a results orientation (DuFour et al., 2016). Educators steeped in the PLC process are intensely aware of these guiding principles that schools must embrace if they hope to foster the kind of learning culture necessary for success. They also recognize that changes in a culture take place over time and require the need to keep a finger on the pulse of culture, regardless of the length of time the school has been engaged in the work of PLC implementation. In other words, leaders need to formatively gather evidence of practices and actions taking place in the school, and analyze how those reflect a collaborative culture focused on continuously improving results in the learning of all students. And, as part of that formative process, they take action to help the school get better and better. As the following scenario illustrates, teachers and teams don't always buy in to foundational PLC principles right away.

> *As Principal Kelly Philips introduces the agenda at a staff meeting, there is an audible groan from several teachers in the room. The major topic to be discussed is the establishment of school-wide practices around grading. To launch the discussion, the leadership team shares its concerns that the school doesn't have consistent practices around retakes of assessments and that students are often penalized for needing additional time and support to learn. The conversation quickly turns into a debate between two passionate groups: (1) those who feel that students who are*

*"unmotivated" or don't study shouldn't receive any special consid-
erations or extra opportunities, and (2) those who feel that students should have as many opportunities as necessary to ensure
that they learn.*

The first big idea of a PLC is that schools functioning as PLCs must demonstrate
an unwavering focus on learning. It may seem obvious that schools should focus on
their students' learning, but in some cases, teachers find themselves placing a greater
focus on their teaching rather than students' learning. Additionally, and what sets
this process apart from other approaches, is that in addition to student learning, the
focus also rests on the continuous learning of those serving the students—the educators. Members of the school staff know that their purpose is to improve the learning of their students and that in order to make that happen, they must engage in
continuous professional learning to improve their collective practices and strategies.
Teams within these schools embrace the notion of collective responsibility for the
learning of all their students, regardless of their education background, demographic
profile, or home history.

This leads to the second big idea: schools working as PLCs must create and sustain a collaborative culture. Rather than working in isolation, teachers work interdependently toward the common goal of student learning. Teachers work as part
of collaborative teams to design, deliver, and monitor the learning of their students
using the best of their collective thinking to promote higher and higher levels of
learning. Members of the collaborative teams know that they will be more successful
by pooling their collective expertise and working interdependently to achieve goals
for student learning.

Finally, the third big idea: schools that implement the PLC model must continuously examine and act upon results. It's not good enough to say they've implemented
a particular initiative or strategy—teams intentionally seek evidence through their
common assessments to monitor their impact on student learning. Most importantly,
teams continually use this evidence to guide their next action steps in order to pursue
high levels of learning for all students.

Note that these big ideas are not stand-alone concepts. Rather, they blend into a
larger picture of empowerment, representative of a school that is committed to examining its practices in order to achieve high levels of learning for its students. Creating
and enacting this picture of empowerment require that a school builds and nurtures
a specific culture. But what does evidence of this culture look like? Sound like? What
doesn't it look like or sound like? How can leaders monitor the level of implementation along these guiding principles as they are reflected within the school's culture?

This chapter will provide some considerations and tools that school leaders can use
to formatively monitor and enhance school culture so that it supports high levels of
student learning. Before diving into the tools and how to analyze and act on them,

we'll begin with some practices and products that leaders can be mindful of and look for in their schools to create a supportive culture of high levels of learning for all. These include a clear mission, a vision that drives improvement, collective commitments that guide behaviors and actions, data-driven goals to monitor improvements and actions, team culture and mindset, and the alignment of celebrations and recognition with the mission.

Understand How to Create the Culture

In our experiences of coaching schools in the PLC process, we have found that they sometimes talk the talk but don't necessarily walk the walk when it comes to culture. As an example, the scenario introducing this chapter is one we've seen far too often. A school might be structured with collaborative teams doing what's considered to be the right work, but underlying the actions is a belief system that doesn't support the mission. So how do schools establish the type of culture that walks the talk, one that puts into action a clear focus on preparing students for their next level of school? When do they make sure that the behaviors they demonstrate are consistent with a culture of learning for all? One that embraces the notion that the school will do whatever it takes for its students to ensure that they're learning, even when they need additional time and support? One that encourages educators working interdependently with colleagues to reach the goal of learning for all students?

First, a school must have a strong foundation to anchor this culture—in other words, a clear mission and vision for the school, collective commitments from its members, and specific goals to drive their work in support of students. Let's examine each element and define what leaders must look for within their schools.

A Clear Mission to Solidify the School's Purpose

One of the first steps a school must take in building its culture of learning is defining its mission. A school's mission relates to its overall purpose—its reason for existence. Leaders can ask the question, "Why do we exist?" to stimulate thinking about formulating the mission. While a school's purpose may seem obvious, this is an important conversation to have with staff. What do you hear when you ask staff members what their purpose is? Is it to teach students? Or is it to ensure they are learning? Leaders can't sidestep this conversation or make assumptions, because the school's mission is the core of the work. The mission is more than a jargon-filled banner on the website or plaque in the hallway of the school. Additionally, it's not something that should be merely handed down to members of the school community without input from or clarifying conversations with the school's staff.

To illustrate this concept, compare and contrast the two following mission statements.

1. The mission of School A is to teach students within a safe and caring atmosphere so they can reach their potential and become lifelong learners.

2. The mission of School B is to ensure that all students learn the knowledge and skills they need to be prepared for their next level of education and life.

What words jump out within each of the two statements? When we examine School A's mission, we see the words *teach*, *reach*, and *potential*. School B uses the words *ensure*, *learn*, and *prepared*. Which school's mission statement is focused on learning for all? We would assert that School B's statement has student learning as its focus. While we recognize that having a quality mission statement doesn't necessarily guarantee that a school has a culture focused on learning, it becomes the strong base on which the remaining foundational pieces of a PLC are established. A school's mission serves as a lighthouse that guides all efforts and keeps them headed in the right direction.

Understanding the origin and intent of a school's mission can reveal a great deal of the school's culture. This initial set of reflective questions will help leaders, whether they are veterans or new to the school, get a sense not only of how it was established, but more importantly, its focus and how it serves to sustain the behaviors and actions of the school community.

A Vision That Drives Improvement

The next foundational piece that builds on a school's mission is its vision. While a mission defines a school's purpose, the vision defines what will actually be happening at the school when it accomplishes its mission. A school's vision answers the question, What attributes would describe the school we are trying to become? A well-conceived school vision describes the ideal end that a school is working to create through its actions. It should be descriptive enough to drive the actions of a school. A key question that leaders can pose to their school community is, "How would you describe the school you would want your child, grandchild, niece, nephew, or neighbor to attend?" Further questions to help the community articulate their vision could include, "What would be happening in such a school? Not happening? What if that student is a struggling learner? What if the student is not a native English speaker?"

A school's vision is more than a slogan. Think about a vision statement like "We'll lead the nation in student achievement." While this statement might describe the aspiration of the school to reach the pinnacle of student achievement, it does little to drive a school's action. A vision statement can describe considerations for each aspect of the school, but a good way to look at it would be to engage staff members in describing their ideal picture of interactions between:

- Teachers and students

- Students and their curriculum and instruction

- Teachers and their curriculum and instruction

- The school and parents or the community

Following is an example of a vision from Eastside Elementary School (n.d.) in Greenbrier, Arkansas, that considers all of these variables.

> Working in partnership with the community, Eastside Elementary will provide all students:
>
> - A collaborative team of professionals who are committed to improve their practices, so that all students learn at high levels
>
> - A safe, positive, and inviting learning environment
>
> - An engaging and challenging curriculum focused on essential academics and life skills
>
> - Individualized and timely support that provides students with what they need to succeed

The development of a school's vision is just the beginning. Its role is to serve as a beacon or lighthouse toward which all actions point. In a school focused on continuous improvement, every action should bring it a step closer to its vision. The school should reference and renew it on a regular basis.

Powerful school visions that guide the work of continuous improvement are established by members of the school—not delivered down to the masses by those on high. Because they have input into that future, staff members have clarity as well as a commitment to work toward that future. In other words, members of the school must own the future they're trying to create.

Collective Commitments That Guide Behaviors and Actions

Once a school community has a clear vision for the future it's trying to create, and a school shifts its focus to student learning, that community will need to commit to aligning its behaviors and actions in accordance with its mission and vision. It's this step that is so crucial. Having a mission and vision is absolutely important, but unless staff members commit to acting in alignment with the belief that they'll do whatever it takes, and to ensuring that all students are valued and supported so that they will learn at the highest levels, then they are simply words on a piece of paper. Living a school's mission and vision is what changes a culture. Behaving in accordance with a school's mission and vision is what brings them to life and completes the circle of accountability.

We suggest that leaders directly engage their school community in the development of collective commitments. To arrive at collective commitments, they can begin by posing the following questions: *If we believe that our job is to ensure that all students learn at high levels, what behaviors must we consistently demonstrate? To what actions will we commit so that we can reach our vision for all students?* While there is not a specific number or limit on the collective commitments, we have observed that having major categories to consider is helpful and will ensure that members of the school community are considering the critical aspects of their work. Activities can be designed around collecting input via sticky notes or digital tools, and then the input can be organized into categories. Input from all staff can then be drafted into commitment statements by the leadership team, and then brought back to the whole staff for final review.

Here are Eastside Elementary School's collective commitments:

- We commit to intentionally seek and share best practices with colleagues.
- We commit to building wide collaboration to keep our work student focused.
- We commit to using data and evidence to improve student learning.
- We commit to respecting all students and meeting their diverse needs: academic, social, and emotional.
- We commit to setting goals to ensure continued student success.
- We commit to engaging parents in their child's education and making them feel welcome in our school.
- We commit to celebrating all success, large or small. (M. Dunlap, personal communication, October 19, 2020)

Eastside's commitments clearly describe how its members commit to act in order to achieve its mission. These commitments reflect a school that will work collaboratively and systematically to support the learning of all students, and celebrate their achievements along the way. All the proverbial bases are covered; in other words, the culture that leaders, teachers, and teams create when they meet these commitments is one that truly supports high levels of student learning for all and embraces the entire school community.

Data-Driven Goals to Monitor Improvements and Actions

Schools that support high levels of learning for all students use evidence to make decisions and instructional adjustments. Using that evidence, they set incremental goals toward improvement. Schoolwide goals are developed in SMART terms (that is, strategic and specific, measurable, attainable, results oriented, and time bound) and monitored on a regular basis using data from ongoing sources, such as common assessments, benchmark assessments, and other tools that align with the targeted outcomes (Conzemius & O'Neill, 2013). At least once a year, teams develop SMART goals that focus on improving in areas of need, as well as those for each unit of study, using common end-of-unit assessments as data for their measurement. We provide more detailed support in the area of SMART goals in chapter 2 (page 39).

Team Culture and Mindset

The work of collaborative teams is the power behind a clear schoolwide mission, vision, collective commitments, and specific goals. Schools know that they are successfully on the road to having a school culture that supports high levels of learning for all when the beliefs reflected in these foundational pieces begin to permeate conversations about students, professional learning, use of data, and the actions members will take to improve student learning. For instance, the culture within a team will progress from a group of individuals meeting around a table focused primarily on how they will teach their students to an interdependent team of teachers focused on a shared outcome of student learning and that is willing to examine and change their instructional practices to meet the needs of their collective students. They demonstrate a growth mindset not only about students, but about themselves as continuous learners. In other words, teams are living the mission, working toward the vision, and keeping their commitments to ensure all students are learning at high levels. In the never-ending cycle of improvement that a PLC represents, leaders can look at the behaviors of their teams to gauge their progress.

Celebrations and Recognition Aligned With Mission

Another source of evidence that reflects a school's culture is its celebrations. What does the school actually celebrate, and how do these celebrations connect to the school's mission? Does the school only celebrate the academic achievements of elite students, or are there celebrations for students who have grown significantly in their achievement? Perhaps celebrations focus only on athletics or awards. What other outcomes can be celebrated on an intentional basis? How are the efforts of teacher collaborative teams recognized and celebrated? Are there celebrations focused on all members of the school community? Does the school recognize teams' growth in their implementation of quality practices as well as the impact of their work on student learning? Does the school celebrate the closing of gaps because of the schoolwide focus on improving learning for all?

Knowing that recognition and celebrations can take multiple forms, we suggest that schools examine their practices to ensure two things: (1) alignment with the school's mission and (2) intentionality of implementation. Celebrations and recognitions that are aligned to a school's mission reflect balance and equity in who and what is celebrated—a PLC celebrates not only those achieving at high levels, but those closing the gap and meeting goals. PLCs recognize the collective efforts of collaborative teams as well as individual staff members making a difference in student lives. PLCs celebrate academics as well as other schoolwide accomplishments, including school-related activities.

All of these facets of school culture are important for leaders to understand their schools' current context. As we shared in the introduction of this book (page 1), our purpose is to provide leaders with tools to gather evidence around the implementation of PLCs. To that end, the next section of this chapter provides tools to examine the school's culture and whether it reflects a focus on learning for all.

Assess the Current Reality

Before planning changes on a schoolwide level, leaders must first consider their school's context. Doing so not only enables them to build on the school's strengths and prior implementation efforts but also provides insights into potential obstacles, which means school leaders can plan future efforts using careful and thoughtful navigation. Figure 1.1 shows some guiding questions that leaders can reference when considering the context of a school.

Guiding Questions	Leadership Reflection
What is the history of this school? What potential past experiences related to previous initiatives or implementation should we consider?	
What background knowledge do teams have regarding the guiding principles of a professional learning community?	
What is the school's status regarding its mission, vision, collective commitments, and goals?	
What is the overall climate of the school? How are members demonstrating or not demonstrating a collaborative mindset? What resistance has there been, if any, to changing practices?	
What is the sense of schoolwide ownership of learning for all?	

Figure 1.1: Guiding questions to consider a school's context around culture.

Visit go.SolutionTree.com/PLCbooks for a free reproducible version of this figure.

After reflecting on the context, leaders can use the tools in this section to gather evidence of their school's culture from a variety of perspectives. These tools include:

- Reflections on the School's Foundations
- School Culture Survey for Educators

- Collaborative Team Observation
- Walking Survey
- Student and Family Focus Groups and Surveys

The question to focus on when using these tools is, What is our current reality? Leaders can use the tools individually or in combination to create a clear picture of their school's culture and related practices.

Reflections on the School's Foundations

School leaders can use the tools in figures 1.2–1.4 to reflect on the elements of the school's foundations, including their communication regarding its mission, vision, and collective commitments to stakeholders. The purpose of these tools is to examine and gather evidence about how the foundational elements are reflected on a day-to-day basis across the school, guiding leaders to seek information beyond any assumptions or what is in place on written documents.

Figure 1.2 presents some guiding questions leaders can use to examine their school's mission.

Guiding Questions	Current Practice and Evidence
What is your school's current mission? How was it defined? By whom? Did all members of the school community have input? Does it focus on learning?	
What professional behaviors are present that are consistent with the school's mission? What incompatible practices are present?	
How frequently is the school's mission referenced or revisited? What opportunities might exist to re-examine and gather input from the staff?	

Figure 1.2: Guiding questions for a school's mission.

Figure 1.3 (page 24) offers some guiding questions related to a school's vision that leaders can use to consider the current design and use of a schoolwide vision.

Building on the reflection about the school's mission, this tool provides questions that give insights about the origin of a school's vision and whether it's used as a living document. Leaders can note their observations using the tool, and later discuss implications for action with other members of the leadership team.

Figure 1.4 (page 24) offers guiding questions related to the collective commitments.

Guiding Questions	Current Practice and Evidence
What is your school's current vision? Have members of the school and community developed it so that it describes the future school that everyone is working toward? How recently has the school examined this vision?	
How often does the school reference this vision to guide the next actions that it takes?	
How often is the vision updated with input from the school community? When was the last time that staff examined and reflected on the vision?	

Figure 1.3: Guiding questions for a school's vision.

*Visit **go.SolutionTree.com/PLCbooks** for a free reproducible version of this figure.*

Guiding Questions	Current Practice and Evidence
How were the staff involved in developing the collective commitments?	
How does the school communicate these commitments to parents and students?	
How often does the school reference these commitments in the day-to-day work of the school?	
How well does the school confront incompatible practices (that is, those practices that oppose the school's collective commitments)?	

Figure 1.4: Guiding questions to consider a school's collective commitments.

*Visit **go.SolutionTree.com/PLCbooks** for a free reproducible version of this figure.*

Again, leaders can gain a lot of insight by taking some time to reflect on this foundational element of school culture.

School Culture Survey for Educators

Leaders can use the survey tool in figure 1.5 with staff at various times to examine the alignment between a school's vision for student learning and the current culture or reality. By using this tool on an intermittent basis, leaders gather evidence from the staff on an individual basis and use that evidence to paint a picture of the school culture over time.

Please rate your perception of each statement as it relates to our school culture:

Descriptor	Rating: 3—This is us! This statement reflects the culture at our school. 2—We're getting there! This describes an area of growth in our school's or team's culture. 1—Not Yet! This does not reflect our school or team yet.	Comments or Description of Evidence or Nonevidence
1. Members of the school community are clear on the school's vision (the school we are trying to create).	3 2 1	
2. Members of our school share a strong commitment to ensure that all students learn at high levels.	3 2 1	
3. All students in our school are known and valued.	3 2 1	
4. Members of the school community embrace the notion that we must collaborate to ensure our students learn at high levels.	3 2 1	
5. Members of the school community are willing to change their practices to help students learn more.	3 2 1	
6. The school has a culture of high expectations for student learning.	3 2 1	
7. Members of the school community work collaboratively to empower all students and ensure they receive the support they need to learn.	3 2 1	
8. We use results and evidence of learning to monitor our goals and continuously adjust our instruction and support.	3 2 1	
9. The school celebrates and communicates growth as well as achievement of our students and staff.	3 2 1	
10. Input from members of the school is sought and valued.	3 2 1	
11. Our school views our work with a growth mindset, in other words, we may make mistakes but we learn and improve.	3 2 1	

Figure 1.5: School culture survey for educators.

Visit go.SolutionTree.com/PLCbooks for a free reproducible version of this figure.

Note: This survey can be accessed at http://bit.ly/Schoolculturesurvey as a Google Form. It can be an online survey, or staff members can complete it during a staff meeting. Alternately, leaders could write each descriptor statement on a poster and participants could put a colored sticky note on it to represent their rating. For example, they can use green to represent a 3 rating, yellow for 2, and pink for 1. They can write reasons or evidence on the sticky note to support their rating.

Collaborative Team Observation

Figure 1.6 is a tool to analyze indicators of a culture that supports high levels of learning. Leaders can use this form to record their observations of teams during their collaborative meetings. The purpose is to gather evidence and gain insights about the culture that exists within collaborative teams. For each cultural indicator, the tool provides both evidence and nonevidence, or behaviors incompatible for the desired indicator. Leaders can use this tool for all collaborative teams, and they can analyze the evidence they gather to get a general sense of the culture across teams.

Walking Survey

The purpose of a walking survey is for staff members to gather authentic evidence from their school about a particular topic. For example, a school might want to gather evidence about the level of engagement of its students, or the use of digital tools in the classroom. This tool focuses on the question, What do we see throughout our school that reflects a culture of high levels of learning for all? The entire staff can engage in this activity, which can be structured to take place during a collaborative team's meeting time or a specific time during the day, such as an off-duty period. To begin this activity, staff members first determine the major categories of the school's culture on which they will gather evidence. Those collecting evidence should refrain from associating evidence with a particular staff member, keeping it objective and nonjudgmental and not specifying anyone by name. As members walk around the school, they record evidence and take pictures of artifacts that support various aspects of the school's culture. If this is taking place during a staff meeting, leaders can provide a brief overview about the goals of the activity, engage teachers in brainstorming the major categories related to the school culture, and then walk the school to gather evidence.

Following the evidence collection, the staff members come back together to share and review all input and look at patterns that emerge. One way they can do so is to use posters to display the evidence, with staff members adding sticky notes with their comments and observations of the patterns. The outcome that the staff aim for in these conversations is a summary of the school's strengths and areas for continued growth.

To the observer: As you sit in on collaborative meetings, what evidence (or nonevidence) of a culture that supports high levels of learning do you note?		
Evidence of Culture That Supports High Levels of Learning for All	Nonevidence	Notes
☐ Members collectively define learning outcomes for all of their students.	☐ The work of the collaborative team is not focused on building clarity around student learning. It is driven by individual preferences or adherence to a textbook.	
☐ Members collect evidence of learning by skill and by student.	☐ Team focuses on averages. ☐ Teachers make excuses or blame external factors for students who are learning at low levels.	
☐ Members examine evidence to identify effective practices.	☐ Members show little to no interest in learning from others or changing their practices.	
☐ Members identify areas of strength and weakness without judgment and use the data to improve their professional practice and their students' learning.	☐ Members are reluctant to examine data together for fear of judgment.	
☐ Members appear to work together in a psychologically safe fashion and express differing viewpoints in a constructive manner.	☐ Interactions within the team seem stilted. Opposing views are not valued.	

Figure 1.6: Collaborative team observation.

Visit go.SolutionTree.com/PLCbooks for a free reproducible version of this figure.

Figure 1.7 (page 28) is a sample recording sheet that can help staff look for and document the evidence they gather during their walking survey. Note that the categories listed are suggestions; these may vary depending on the input of the staff. In this instance, we adapted the walking survey to focus on schoolwide culture.

In this example, the staff first discussed the major categories of the school's culture about which they would gather evidence around their school. As a team, they created the shared template so that all staff members could contribute. The template works well as a paper-and-pencil document or a shared electronic document. Note that there is also a column for staff to indicate any nonevidence or incompatible practices that they observe.

Evidence of a School Culture That Supports High Levels of Learning for All

Category	Evidence at Our School (include artifacts and observations)	Nonevidence at Our School
Focus on learning (versus teaching)	Learning targets are posted for daily lessons.	When we asked students what they were learning, many couldn't tell us.
Actions aligned to our school's mission and vision	We're using small groups to provide additional time and support. We just added an intervention block to our schedule.	
Goals and data to monitor improvement in learning	SMART goals are posted on the walls in the staff room. Students are keeping track of their progress in some rooms. Teams are using common assessments.	Most rooms didn't have evidence that students were monitoring their progress.
Celebration of learning (staff and student)	The newsletter and the school's Facebook pages share mostly information about students in sports or those that win academic awards.	There aren't really any celebrations that focus on teams or even individual teachers. We don't really celebrate growth, only excellence.

Figure 1.7: Walking survey recording sheet.

*Visit **go.SolutionTree.com/PLCbooks** for a free reproducible version of this figure.*

Student and Family Focus Groups and Surveys

One of the most powerful sources of information about a school's culture is those who directly experience that culture: the students. What is their perception of the school's culture? Faculty and staff may perceive that they are sending messages of equity and support, but would the students agree? Consider the value of collecting evidence through the voices of students (Colburn & Beggs, 2021). A student focus group is a great way to get a sense of how they perceive the culture of their school. The composition of the focus group should represent the school community; leaders will not get an accurate sense of the culture by selecting only students who are highly successful and active in school functions, such as student council members. When inviting participants to a focus group, consider the following questions.

- Are we considering participation from each student group, including those students who may be receiving services for their special needs or who may be new to the school?

- Are we seeking input from students of all genders and ethnic groups?

- Are we intentionally seeking input from students who may struggle in school or who may be marginalized, such as students learning English or those with an individualized education program (IEP)?

The purpose of a focus group is not to solve a problem but to gather feedback and input. To that end, we suggest designating an impartial facilitator, such as a counselor or staff member who doesn't interact with students on a daily basis, to facilitate and ask the focus questions. Establish the norms, or ground rules for the discussion, up front, explaining that the information stays within the room and that it will be used to keep improving the school. For example, the facilitator should share that students are not to mention specific names of teachers and to help clarify their points with examples. As the facilitator poses the questions, the students can take turns responding. The facilitator can take notes on a laptop or notepad during the session but should explain that student responses are anonymous and that student names will not be in the notes. Facilitators should also refrain from responding to comments made by students, although they can ask follow-up questions to clarify or get additional examples. The intent is to collect evidence in an objective fashion so that it can be used to improve the school.

Following are some questions that facilitators can pose during the session (note these can be adjusted to be age-appropriate).

- How does the school (including teachers) help you feel like you belong or matter?

- How does the school help you be successful?

- How do you know what you're supposed to be learning?

- What are some ways that you get feedback in classes?

- What happens when you are struggling with a skill or concept or need help to learn something?

- If you could describe the school with one word, what would it be and why?

Students' families can also help shed some light on the culture through focus groups as well as online surveys. The invitation to participate in a family-member focus group should follow the same guidelines for inclusion as with students, with all parent groups represented in the selection of participants. For example, if the school has a significant number of English learners, their parents should be represented in the focus group. Likewise, there should be parents of students with special needs, or those who are considered to be economically disadvantaged. Some key questions may include the following.

- What is your overall sense of the culture of the school?

- In what ways does the school ensure that your child learns?

- How do you perceive that students are supported when they struggle in school?

- As a parent or community member, do you feel that there is an avenue to share ideas or concerns?

- In what ways is our school welcoming?
- Are there any areas that can be strengthened?

Leaders can also use paper-based or online surveys to gather input and feedback from parents and the school community at large. The example in figure 1.8 shows how a survey sent home to parents and others in the school community might look.

Dear School Community,

As part of our continued effort to improve our school, we are seeking feedback from you. Please share your perspective by indicating with a checkmark your level of agreement with the following statements. There is also space at the end for you to share any comments or suggestions.

Indicator	Agree	Not sure	Disagree
The school is welcoming and supportive.			
The school climate is positive.			
The school communicates general information to parents in a timely fashion.			
The school staff communicate information about my child's learning on a frequent and timely basis.			
When additional support is necessary, the school works to make sure my child receives it.			
If I have questions or concerns about my child, I feel comfortable asking the teacher or other staff.			
Do you have any feedback to help us improve any areas you feel aren't strong at our school?			

Figure 1.8: School community perception survey to assess a school's culture.

Visit go.SolutionTree.com/PLCbooks for a free reproducible version of this figure.

Analyze Patterns and Priorities

After gathering evidence, the next stage of the formative process is to analyze it to determine the school's current reality. As leaders and teams examine the evidence on the school's current culture and its focus on learning for all, they will likely identify some trends. At this time, leaders should focus on the question, What patterns and priorities emerge in the evidence? They can reflect on the following questions, using evidence to identify areas of strength as well as areas to consider for support.

- Have all members of our school community been involved with the creation of the school's mission and vision? Do these drive our actions as a school?

- Have staff members engaged in identifying collective commitments? Are they meeting the commitments in their day-to-day actions?

- Is there evidence that the culture of our school aligns to our mission, vision, collective commitments, and goals? Are there any incompatible practices that don't align?

- As we examine evidence, what are the written and unwritten expectations for student learning? Do they reflect equity and inclusiveness? Are the practices and behaviors consistent with our school's commitments?

- Is there evidence that our school culture promotes a growth mindset for staff and students?

- Do parents perceive that they are informed and engaged in what happens at school and with their children? Is our mode of communication effective in establishing a partnership between school and parents or community or is it one-way in nature?

- What do we celebrate? Whom do we celebrate? Are our celebrations intentional and part of our continuous improvement system?

Additionally, leaders can use the continuum in figure 1.9 (page 32) to provide a big-picture view of their school's foundations, culture, and celebrations, and enable teams to identify areas of strength as well as those that need support to deepen implementation.

The continuum is helpful to reflect on and analyze school culture at multiple points in time, updating strengths, areas of growth, and potential areas to improve. Using this continuum analysis as well as other evidence gathered around the school's culture, leaders can complete the next step of the formative cycle: acting on the evidence to improve practice.

Act on Evidence to Improve Practice

In the course of analysis, leaders may have identified specific areas in their school's culture that they consider strengths as well as some that they would like to enhance or improve. At that point, it's time to determine how to move forward. Following are some general strategies for enhancing specific areas that leaders can reference depending on the needs they have identified at their school: build shared knowledge about the PLC process, enact the process of building or refining PLC foundations, activate and employ the leadership team, expect alignment of behaviors, and celebrate the work.

Knowledge and Practice	Level of Use or Implementation			
	Limited	Emerging	Established	Strategic
Schoolwide foundations	The school has not collaboratively established its foundational elements. Teaching, rather than learning, is the focus. Decisions, allocations of resources, and actions are not tied to the school's mission and vision.	Members of the school community can articulate the school's mission and vision but haven't yet translated them into actions; collective commitments aren't yet in place.	The school's mission is clear and embraced by all members of the school community, and the school's vision reflects the mindset of all students learning at high levels. Members of the school embrace the notions of collaboration, an unwavering focus on learning, and seeking continuous improvement in results.	Educators are beginning to ask questions, dig deeper into issues surrounding school culture, and innovate in alignment with their school's mission and vision and to close any gaps or challenges with equity. The school continues to focus on improving the culture to ensure engagement of the larger school community.
Team culture and mindset	Teachers are primarily working in isolation or limit their collaboration to sharing of teaching tools and activities. Staff members do not express a sense of urgency to address the needs of students who are struggling or may only be concerned with their own students.	Teachers have been formed into collaborative teams and are beginning to focus on student learning. Teams are beginning to have a sense of urgency and mindset to address the needs of all learners but may not feel empowered to make a difference yet.	Collaborative teams keep student learning as the focus of their meetings. They recognize that by improving their practices, they also improve learning outcomes for their students. Teams hold the mindset that they will work to impact the learning of all students and that they will collectively take responsibility for providing support when needed.	Teams not only use their collaborative work to ensure student learning but they are continually challenging themselves to impact the entire school system, making vertical connections and committing to explore new practices in order to tackle challenges in student learning.
Celebrations and recognition aligned with mission	Celebrations are not fully in alignment with the school's mission.	The school is beginning to examine its practices and focus on celebrations.	There is an intentional and balanced feel to celebrations, with clear reflection of the school's mission.	The staff actively and creatively seek opportunities to celebrate actions and results aligned with the school's mission.

Figure 1.9: Continuum of practice for school culture.

*Visit **go.SolutionTree.com/PLCbooks** for a free reproducible version of this figure.*

Shared Knowledge About the PLC Process

For schools that haven't yet had the opportunity to engage all members in learning about the PLC process, we suggest that the leadership team find a way to give the benefit of shared knowledge to all. We've often observed school leadership teams that attend a multiday professional development institute and return to school with a fire in their bellies to get the work going. What might happen, however, is that the majority of staff remains behind in their general knowledge about the work while the leadership team is well ahead. In their enthusiasm, leaders may not take the time to first build awareness and establish baseline knowledge *before* starting to change structures and expectations for teachers. To prevent this information gap within the school, leaders can ensure a general baseline of knowledge by providing an introductory overview of the process and give teachers a chance to engage in conversations, see models, and examine the why behind the work. In addition to the pivotal resource *Learning by Doing* (DuFour et al., 2016), *Make It Happen* (Bailey & Jakicic, 2019) provides tools leaders can use to share information with staff. We also consider Anthony Muhammad's work around schoolwide culture and learning as highly valuable in building schoolwide mindsets consistent with the mission of a PLC. Chief among his resources are the second edition of *Transforming School Culture* (Muhammad, 2018) and *Overcoming the Achievement Gap Trap* (Muhammad, 2015).

There are a number of ways to actively engage all members of the school community and build shared knowledge. School leadership can design activities such as the following to empower members of the school community with knowledge about the why of the PLC process and give them an opportunity to reflect on the information in light of their school's context.

- Blog, article, or book shares
- Video clips of credible experts from the field
- Personal testimonials of teams engaged in the work
- Leadership team presentations

At the center of building shared knowledge is the belief that those responsible for implementing a particular practice need to be empowered with the knowledge that sets the stage for moving forward with building or refining the foundational elements of a PLC.

The Process of Building or Refining PLC Foundations

As an extension of the shared knowledge discussed in the previous section, all school members need to be part of the process to develop a schoolwide mission and vision. Far too often, we've seen these statements simply handed down to the teams—something we call the Moses approach. When initiatives are handed down without engaging those who are responsible for implementing the work, we typically see compliance but not necessarily commitment to the work. By actively engaging members of the school and soliciting all voices in the process, leaders ensure the staff's inherent ownership of the work, which then extends to the development of collective commitments and school goals.

As members of the school work together on these foundational pieces and their connected nature, they constantly hear and revisit their beliefs about student learning. For example, we hear many schools ask, "What would we want for our own children? Would any parent want less for their child?" to evoke a continued focus on the work of ensuring high levels of learning for all students.

Activation of the Leadership Team

We see the role of a school's leadership team as critical for clarifying the work, building expertise across teams, and helping monitor and support them. The leadership team is the guiding force behind the school's journey. Members of the leadership team should collaborate on the following actions.

- **Promote a schoolwide culture of learning:** They continuously reference the school's mission and vision and set clear expectations for the behaviors that are aligned to the culture.

- **Create and refine structures and supports so teams can do the work:** They ensure that all teachers are members of meaningful collaborative teams that have embedded time to collaborate.

- **Clarify and ensure alignment of the work:** They build shared knowledge across the entire staff and empower them with the tools to do the work.

- **Model best practices:** They lead the way through their actions and help facilitate growth in collaborative practices.

- **Monitor and provide input to support continuous improvement:** They are always gathering data to monitor both implementation and impact as well as set goals for continued improvement.

- **Celebrate progress:** They intentionally celebrate staff and student learning, implementation of processes, and impact on achievement across the school.

Alignment of Behaviors

Schools develop collective commitments to clarify expectations for school members as they work to achieve their mission. Members continuously reference the commitments to empower each other and expect that team members will hold each other accountable for their behaviors. They should also confront behaviors that are incompatible with the collective commitments. Although teachers are frequently reluctant to call out a colleague, seeing correction as the responsibility of the principal, leaders can ask teams to identify strategies to reinforce accountability. That's what we mean when we talk about using formative tools to identify teams that need support and provide resources to help them improve their practices. Shared leadership is an essential part of the PLC process. All team members are responsible for making sure everyone follows through with the commitments they've made to each other. This means that the process of building collective commitments *begins* the journey for *all* teachers to take responsibility for any behavior that gets in the way of high levels of learning for *all* students.

The reality of this work is that it's unlikely that an entire staff will buy in to the PLC process at the beginning. It's common to encounter resistance. Some teachers resist because they don't know *why* they're doing it that way. Some resist because they don't know *how* to do it and may not want to admit to that. But others resist because they see themselves as very successful doing things the traditional way. Generally, the way to overcome resistance is to identify what is getting in the way of a colleague embracing these practices and then respond accordingly. For instance, if resistance is the reaction of a teacher because of not being clear on *why* leaders are bringing a particular initiative or practice to the table, then it's the leaders' responsibility to share the research behind the work to help build shared knowledge. PLC practices are research based, as we will show in each of the subsequent chapters of this book.

When leaders see that some of their colleagues aren't sure *how* to complete a process—perhaps how to write good assessments or use the data to plan next steps—it's their responsibility to provide support for these teachers, just as it's teachers' responsibility to provide support to students who are struggling in reading or mathematics. In *Learning by Doing*, DuFour and colleagues (2016) discuss how important it is that leaders have reciprocal accountability with teachers. This builds on education professor Richard Elmore's (2006) assertation that to expect someone else to perform at a certain level means providing that person with the capacity to meet that expectation. If leaders expect teachers and teams to implement the PLC process, they must provide the support and resources teachers and teams need to effectively do so. If shared knowledge has been built, and teachers have been supported to learn new processes, then it's reasonable to expect that teachers will behave in alignment with expectations.

Although shared leadership is important, school leaders still need to be prepared to set an example. Periodically, leaders hear what others say, often in the context of a larger group, and they must ensure that their responses reflect consistency with the school's commitment to working collaboratively with a focus on achieving high levels of learning for all students. If the mission is important and the collective commitments mean something, then it's critical to confront behaviors of both individual staff members and teams when they are counter to those commitments. Depending on the situation, a leader (teacher or administrator) might simply restate the comment so that it aligns with the school's mission. For example, if a teacher says, "These kids are just lazy. No wonder they're failing my class," the leader can then restate it by saying, "You're clearly frustrated by the difficulty some students are having. Remember how we said it's our job to make sure all students are successful? Let's work together to figure out how we can help them learn."

In other circumstances, such as when the problem is recurring, the leader might need to have a *crucial conversation* with the teacher, or a talk with high stakes, differing opinions, and emotional weight (Patterson, Grenny, McMillan, & Switzler, 2012). We dig deeper into crucial conversations in chapter 2 (page 39). Keep in mind that resistance is not necessarily negative; it's an opportunity to learn and move forward. Chris recalls, for example, how she knew that the culture of the school where she was principal was really changing. A teacher leader said at a meeting, "I like resisters because they make me think more deeply about why what we're doing is so important!" It was an unexpected and welcome insight.

One proactive practice we suggest is for leadership teams to anticipate potential challenges or questions that could arise with the implementation of a new dimension of the work. We call these anticipated challenges "Yeah, buts. . . ." For example, when moving into the realm of interventions, one challenge the team might anticipate is "Yeah, but what about the kids who aren't motivated?" As a leadership team, discuss how to respond to such a challenge. This process helps leaders avoid being caught off guard and without a response in group discussions. It also ensures consistency of messaging across the leadership team.

Celebration of the Work

Earlier in this chapter, we discussed the role of intentional celebrations that align to the school's mission. We suggest that leaders solicit input from the entire school staff about the celebrations they feel would align with the school's mission and vision. Recognizing the staff's efforts to support high levels of learning for all students is one of the most important areas of celebration. As Robert Eaker has shared, letting teachers know they are appreciated is often an underused tool (R. Eaker, personal communication, March 11, 2020). Schools have gotten quite creative with social media as well as special awards to honor the work of teams. For example, there may be a team of the month post on Facebook to recognize a particular grade level's impact in the area of reading and highlight the fact that the team exceeded its goal for student learning. Leaders can also use things like newsletters to highlight best practices happening at the team level. Leaders can solicit school staff for suggestions about specific teams that have gone above and beyond in a particular area to impact their students' learning or invite specific teachers or teams to share their successes. In *Learning by Doing* (DuFour et al., 2016), the authors offer four keys to effective celebrations.

1. **Make explicit why celebrating is so important:** Without celebrations, it would be hard to sustain the PLC process. It's not only OK to acknowledge this; it's preferable. Schools should encourage every collaborative team to celebrate its successes as a way to keep everyone focused on the right work and motivated to continue.

2. **Ensure celebrations are everyone's responsibility:** In a traditional environment, a school may have a committee to plan celebrations, or the role may fall to an administrator. In a PLC, everyone must be attuned to recognizing colleagues who have been helpful or effective, especially at the team level.

3. **Celebrate values:** Moving from only recognizing a teacher of the year to also recognizing a team of the year celebrates the importance that the school is placing on collaboration. Celebrating academic growth when that growth signifies closing the learning gap reminds everyone that the organization expects high levels of learning for all. Because continuous improvement is a hallmark of the PLC process, schools should recognize the successes of their collaborative teams.

4. **Create lots of opportunities for recognition and celebration:** Celebrating once or twice a year at a formal event is far less effective than having regular shout-outs and recognitions at team meetings and schoolwide gatherings.

Too often, the day-to-day demands of running a school distract leaders from building in specific recognition and celebration. Given its importance to a school's culture, we suggest that leadership teams keep an item on their agenda at all times for celebration and recognition so that it remains in the forefront of the team's focus and planning.

When leaders are intentional and celebrate not only results but the mindsets and learning that take place through the work of teams, they are reinforcing a culture that values both students and staff. They are reinforcing the notion of collective efficacy and strengthening the commitment to work collaboratively on behalf of all students.

The Process Gains Momentum

When embarking on the implementation of a PLC, school leaders quickly recognize that the culture within a school can work for or against the school's mission of achieving high levels of learning for all. As leaders, examining the evidence that paints a true picture of school culture is an imperative step for moving forward and creating the conditions that allow this mission to be accomplished. Leaders know that each school brings its own history and context to the table, and they would be naïve to think that there's a single approach to shifting beliefs. Using the evidence collected through formative tools can guide leaders to take specific actions, whether it's to build shared knowledge, revisit or strengthen foundational elements, or reach consensus on collective commitments. By implementing these actions, the process begins to gain momentum, and practices continue to improve. In the next chapter, we describe how leaders can formatively examine the collaborative structures and processes in place at their school.

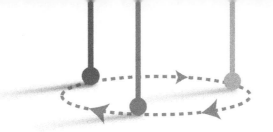

Chapter 2

THE SCHOOL'S COLLABORATIVE STRUCTURES

Collaborative teams have been described as the engine that drives the PLC (DuFour et al., 2016) and, as such, deserve special attention from the leaders in the school and district. While high-performing teams can make a huge difference in successful implementation, underperforming teams can make things go terribly wrong. The following example scenario helps illustrate the difference between high-performing and underperforming teams.

> *Jason, an elementary school principal, visits the third-grade team during its collaborative time in the morning and the kindergarten team in the afternoon. The third-grade team brings the most recent results of a common formative assessment it had given with the intent to plan its response. Team members come prepared with their students' work, and the team quickly begins using a protocol (such as "Protocol for Analyzing Common Assessment Data," on page 143 from* Make It Happen, *Bailey & Jakicic, 2019) to determine which students need additional learning time and support. The common formative assessment evaluated two learning targets coming from their fraction standard in mathematics, and the team is easily able to develop the plan for the next day when the teachers will provide support (review the targets with visual fraction models) and enrichment (working with fractions with denominators other than 2, 3, 4, and 6) for their students.*
>
> *The kindergarten team, on the other hand, seems to be stuck in a discussion about when and how it should begin assessing*

its students for the upcoming report card. Two team members are having a separate conversation about one of the students on the team and how to best manage behavior issues. When Jason enters the room, they all look to him to tell them what to do.

"How can two collaborative teams in the same school function so differently?" Jason asks himself.

How effective collaborative teams are in their work together can have a significant impact on student learning. The third-grade students in the previous scenario will likely benefit from the specific instruction their teachers have planned based on the results of a common formative assessment. The kindergarten team, without the benefit of sharing strategies and new learning, will likely respond to their students just as they have in the past.

One constant we've noticed when working with collaborative teams is that no teams in a school are ever in the same place in the process. One would think that if all teams start at the same time with the same actions, they would be at the same place. However, there are so many different issues, personalities, and situations that impact team functions that this doesn't typically happen. Consider, for example, a team composed of several senior teachers and one teacher new to the profession. This team may experience difficulty if the senior teachers aren't comfortable trying out new strategies. The new teacher may be reluctant to speak up in meetings where her teammates have so much more experience. Another team in the same school may have mostly inexperienced teachers. This team might struggle just trying to figure out what its members are supposed to be doing during their collaborative team time. In both situations, team members are all working hard to make sure students are successful, but they've experienced that collaboration isn't as simple as just coming to a team meeting.

The collaborative process is the lifeblood of a PLC, and leaders must intimately understand it and know what effective collaboration looks like when they support collaborative teams. We'll discuss each of these considerations in this chapter before moving on to how leaders can assess, analyze, and act to help their teams improve.

Understand the Collaborative Process

In PLCs, collaborative teams must have a common goal or goals and work together interdependently to achieve those goals. We know that *no* one teacher, working in isolation, can possibly have all the skills and time to ensure each student will learn at high levels. Instead, teams of teachers take on this responsibility for all of the students they are working with.

In schools, for the most part, these teams are organized so that the members teach the same content. For example, the first-grade team members all teach first-grade curricula. In small schools, such as one where there is only one sixth-grade science teacher, the collaborative team might consist of all the science teachers. This means that most schools don't allow teachers to decide which team they want to be a member of or who will be on their team with them. As a result, teammates could be good friends, colleagues, or even teachers who haven't gotten along in the past. In any case, it is important that they can successfully work together to achieve their goals despite any personal differences.

Not all teams start out as high performing. Psychologist Bruce Tuckman (1965) describes how a typical team evolves through four stages as it works together: (1) forming, (2) storming, (3) norming, and (4) performing. His foundational model of team development begins with the forming stage, which is when the team members are optimistic about their future but look to the leader to make decisions and keep them moving forward. The team then enters the storming stage, a time when they may feel overwhelmed and frustrated. During this stage, conflicts often get in the way of the team's goals. During the third stage, norming, the team becomes much more functional as members understand their roles in the process. Finally, the team reaches the performing stage, in which it has become highly functional, interdependent, and capable of accomplishing its goals. The Tuckman model continues to be implemented and reviewed by researchers and practitioners because it accurately describes the ways that teams work together (Jones, 2019; Tuckman & Jensen, 1977).

Author Patrick Lencioni (2002), in his work on team evolution, considers five dysfunctions teams face: (1) lack of trust, (2) fear of conflict, (3) lack of commitment, (4) avoidance of accountability, and (5) inattention to results. Major organizations continue to embrace his work to ensure their teams are functioning effectively (Timms, 2020), and our experience shows us that schools and education agencies make daily use of his work. Lencioni (2002) theorizes that teams must overcome each of these dysfunctions to be high performing. He suggests the order in which teams must resolve these dysfunctions is linear; a team must overcome each of these dysfunctions before moving on to the next. For example, team members must first learn to trust each other before they face and overcome a fear of conflict. This impacts the work of the team because a team that fears conflict likely avoids discussing ideas that might lead to disagreement, thus not likely getting better at its work. According to Lencioni (2002), leaders who use some specific tools such as developing strong group norms, using effective consensus strategies, and making collective commitments, can help teams move through these dysfunctions to become high functioning.

In study after study (D'Costa, 2018; Friedman, 2014), it becomes apparent that collaboration isn't something that comes easily to adults. Principals and school leaders must provide training on effective practices as well as support to teams that are struggling if they want collaboration to work. First, let's dig into how schools can structure their teams and then into how to help them function effectively.

Assignment of Teachers to Teams

First, all staff members in a PLC must be members of at least one collaborative team, and this team must be given collaborative time during the school day to work together. If some teachers are allowed to opt out of collaboration, leaders send the message that collaboration isn't that important. As we discussed in chapter 1 (page 15), the leadership team must make sure that everyone is assigned to a team that makes sense and will allow for meaningful partnerships. Most teachers work best on teams where everyone teaches the same content or grade level (DuFour et al., 2016). In a typical elementary school, this means that all fifth-grade teachers are on a team. In a middle school this might mean that the seventh-grade science teachers form a team. In a high school, all of the teachers who teach algebra are on a team.

When a school is small, there aren't always multiple teachers teaching the same content. When a teacher is the only one in a school who teaches a grade level or course, we call that person a singleton. For these teachers, being on a collaborative team is still important, but it's often more difficult for them to see how best to do their work. One common configuration for singletons in small schools is to create vertical teams (DuFour et al., 2016). In an elementary school this might include the kindergarten, first-grade, and second-grade teachers. In a middle school, this might mean the sixth-, seventh-, and eighth-grade ELA teachers. In a very small high school, all mathematics teachers might form a team.

Another configuration for singletons would be an interdisciplinary team (DuFour et al., 2016). This is a team composed of all the teachers who work with a group of students. For example, a middle school seventh-grade team might include an ELA teacher, a mathematics teacher, a social studies teacher, and a science teacher. These configurations work well with small middle schools and high schools in particular. One very small high school we worked with had only one ELA, mathematics, science, and social studies teacher for all four grades. They worked effectively in their interdisciplinary team configuration.

Teachers who teach the same content but who are assigned to different schools can also work together in electronic teams (DuFour et al., 2016). For example, in a district with several elementary schools, the art teachers for each of those schools might form a team. This team may meet electronically or in person depending on their locations and meeting times.

Schools also must decide how to integrate into teams their specialists, special educators, second language experts, and other staff members who have responsibilities across the school using what DuFour and his colleagues (2016) call logical links. A *logical link* is a connection between a collaborative team and the specialists who serve the students on the team. A common example is the special educator who serves students in grade 4 meeting with the fourth-grade collaborative team. Coaches should have regular access to the teams they coach so that they are able to be a part of the collaborative process. One thing we've learned in our work is that the more these folks are able to be a part of the collaborative team, the more effective they will be. For example, if special educators participate in such a way that they have only one or two grade-level or content-area teams to plan with, they can be extremely effective for their students as well as their teammates. Because they work so closely with the team, they are able to make sure the students they serve are proficient on all of the essential standards. They know what proficiency looks like because they have been included in the discussions the team has about proficiency. According to education administrators Heather Friziellie, Julie A. Schmidt, and Jeanne Spiller (2016), "Collaborative teams may take many forms, but regardless of their structure, they must include both general and special educators to support all students' learning" (p. 28). If they don't include these important members, students with an IEP may not be expected to learn at the same levels as other students.

As the school becomes more effective in its work, issues might emerge when teachers begin to question the status quo of team configuration. Consider, for example, an elementary school that has two teachers at grade 5. In the past, one was assigned to be the reading and social studies teacher and the other the mathematics and science teacher. While this configuration may have been in place for years, one or both teachers might raise the question of whether it's better to have both teach all four subjects so they can collaborate around the four critical questions for each of the subjects. This issue often emerges in middle schools that structure their interdisciplinary teams around a group of teachers who teach a specific group of students but all teach different content. As they get more deeply involved in this work, they see how they might be more effective if they work with teachers who teach the same content they do. As with any major change, changing team structures will require support from both the leaders and the teachers to be successful. In the example of two fifth-grade teachers who are now going to teach all four subjects, the leader may find that the teachers feel more supported if they can receive more than the standard planning period to work together. Another support that may help is to arrange to have one of the teachers observe the other in a lesson the first teacher may not feel comfortable teaching.

Protected Time

One of the first actions the leadership team and building principal must take in becoming a PLC is to develop a master schedule that allows for protected time for collaborative teams to meet. In some schools this requires teachers to see the differences between time that was previously designated as personal planning time and time that is now required as collaborative team time. For collaborative team time, all team members are expected to meet to carry out the work of answering the four critical questions. We call the time protected because leaders should guarantee that team members will be able to develop agenda items without receiving added paperwork to do. Effective teams typically need a *minimum* of forty-five to fifty-five minutes per week to do their work. With more time than that, teams can accomplish much more during the school year. Typically, this time comes when all of the team members' students are in electives or specials such as art, physical education, or technology. In other cases, the district schedules late-start days or early-release days to accommodate this common meeting time.

Effective Collaboration Drives a PLC

Many people who choose to engage in the PLC process don't know exactly what the work of the collaborative team is. As evidence of this, when we coach teams, we often see that they are struggling to know how to build agendas for their meetings because they don't know exactly what their team should be doing during this planning time. However, once we focus them on the four critical questions, they see how this new collaborative process is likely very different than any teamwork they've done in the past and will bring better results around student learning.

The four critical questions are the central questions provided by the architects of the PLC process, which they believe teams must answer as they do their work (DuFour et al., 2016).

1. What do students need to know and be able to do?

2. How will we know when they have learned it?

3. What will we do when they haven't learned it?

4. What will we do when they already know it?

Leaders will know if teams are engaged in the right work if their agendas and products are aligned to these four questions. Part 2 (page 133) details the expected actions and products for teams when they answer these four questions. In addition to the specific products created as teams answer the four critical questions, the team will likely develop such products as SMART goals, norms, and data that enhance their collaborative practices. *Norms* are behaviors the team agrees to exhibit to make their work together more effective. It's important for teams to establish these norms early so that the team can build trust with each other. For example, teams might consider what norms they need to write around their use of data. A data norm might say, "We will value data for what they tell us to do next and will not make excuses about them." We discuss these products in more depth later in this chapter.

When teams are unsure about what they're supposed to be doing during their collaborative time, it can help to remember that the work goes in cycles (DuFour et al., 2016). One step in the process easily leads to the next step and so on. Teams plan, do, study, and act (PDSA) in recurring cycles. Typically, these recurring cycles begin and end with a unit of instruction. The team starts with *planning*. During this step team members look at the essential standards they will teach in the upcoming unit, unwrap them to identify the specific skills and concepts students must learn to master a standard, and discuss instructional plans and possible assessments. The next step is actually *doing* the work—implementing the instruction and using common formative assessments to gather data about student learning. In the third step, they are *studying* the results of their assessments to determine which students still need additional time and support to learn the essential standards. The final step is *acting*, as they implement the response they've planned so that every student is successful in learning. This cycle starts again with the next unit of study. Figure 2.1 visualizes this cycle.

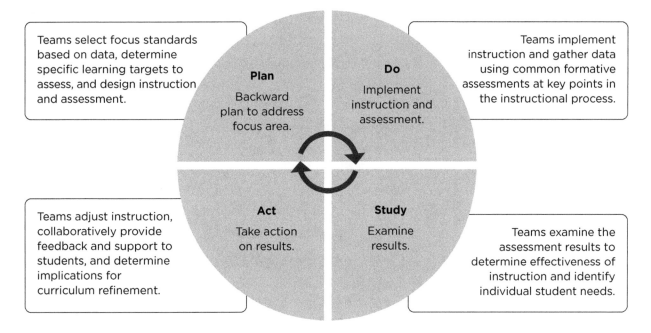

Source: Bailey & Jakicic, 2019, p. 13.

Figure 2.1: PDSA cycle.

When teams truly understand this cycle, they can easily build their agendas at the end of each team meeting. If they've finished *planning*, they move to *doing*, and so forth. Teams sometimes need to see this process in action and may benefit by observing a team that has figured out how the cycle works for them. When teams put the cycle into practice, they can create agenda items that flow from each other, as shown in figure 2.2 (page 46).

Teams can also use the PDSA cycle as they think about how to answer each of the four critical questions in their work. Figure 2.3 (page 47) shows how each of the questions is related to part of the cycle.

Stage	Likely Agenda Items
Plan	• Review essential standards in upcoming unit and associated learning targets. • Develop or review the unit plan with consensus on the timing of lessons and assessments. • Discuss and write the end-of-unit assessment and common formative assessments.
Do	• Discuss effectiveness of lessons, especially those related to the SMART goal action plan for the unit. • Review timing of lessons and assessments and make adjustments as needed. • Administer and score common formative assessments in preparation for data meetings.
Study	• Conduct data meeting to identify, by student and by target, which students need support. • Plan responses using student work. • Plan extensions for students who have mastered essential learning targets.
Act	• Carry out planned responses. • Reassess targets to identify students who still need additional time and support even after this extra help.

Figure 2.2: Likely agenda items for teams effectively using the PDSA cycle.

Depending on the content and the grade level the team is responsible for, it may go through one or two full cycles for each unit of instruction. We've seen teams with multiple weekly collaboration times go through a full cycle in a week, and we've seen a team take up to three weeks to finish a cycle when it meets weekly. Teams should evaluate where they need to stop to give a common formative assessment and for which learning targets when they are doing their unit planning.

We also know that one way to help teams stay on track in doing their work is to use protocols that are designed to provide step-by-step directions on how to do this work. Many protocols also include suggestions about how much time each step might take as well as products that will result from this work. Throughout this book we offer many different protocols to support teams in this process. We will discuss protocols in more detail and list those we offer in this book in the Act on Evidence to Improve Practice section of this chapter (page 65).

SMART Goals Promote Interdependence

In chapter 1 (page 15) we introduced the ideas of SMART goals as we discussed the third big idea of a PLC—to be results oriented. A results orientation means the staff use data to guide their decisions. The process starts when the school sets SMART goals for the year after gathering and analyzing various data points including information about student achievement, attendance, behavior, demographics, and professional learning. The term SMART is an acronym for the characteristics of these goals: strategic and specific, measurable, attainable, results oriented, and time bound (Conzemius & O'Neill, 2013). The leadership team examines the data

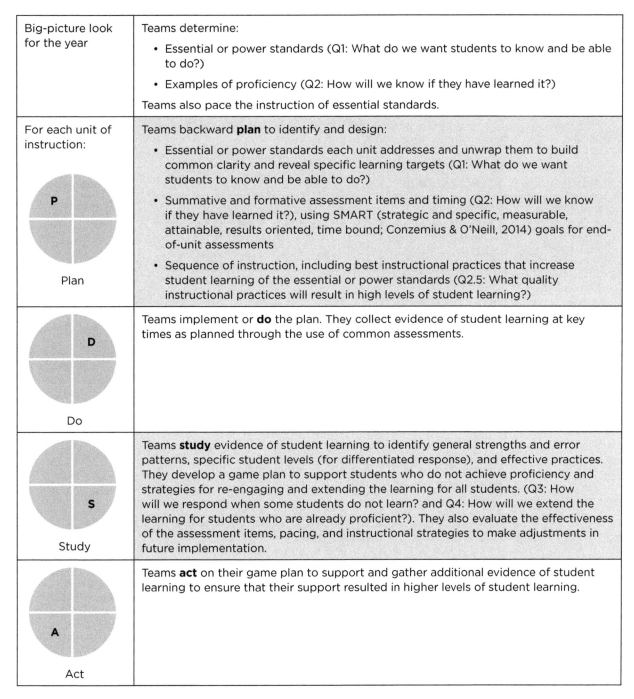

Big-picture look for the year	Teams determine: • Essential or power standards (Q1: What do we want students to know and be able to do?) • Examples of proficiency (Q2: How will we know if they have learned it?) Teams also pace the instruction of essential standards.
For each unit of instruction: **P** Plan	Teams backward **plan** to identify and design: • Essential or power standards each unit addresses and unwrap them to build common clarity and reveal specific learning targets (Q1: What do we want students to know and be able to do?) • Summative and formative assessment items and timing (Q2: How will we know if they have learned it?), using SMART (strategic and specific, measurable, attainable, results oriented, time bound; Conzemius & O'Neill, 2014) goals for end-of-unit assessments • Sequence of instruction, including best instructional practices that increase student learning of the essential or power standards (Q2.5: What quality instructional practices will result in high levels of student learning?)
D Do	Teams implement or **do** the plan. They collect evidence of student learning at key times as planned through the use of common assessments.
S Study	Teams **study** evidence of student learning to identify general strengths and error patterns, specific student levels (for differentiated response), and effective practices. They develop a game plan to support students who do not achieve proficiency and strategies for re-engaging and extending the learning for all students. (Q3: How will we respond when some students do not learn? and Q4: How will we extend the learning for students who are already proficient?). They also evaluate the effectiveness of the assessment items, pacing, and instructional strategies to make adjustments in future implementation.
A Act	Teams **act** on their game plan to support and gather additional evidence of student learning to ensure that their support resulted in higher levels of student learning.

Source: Bailey & Jakicic, 2019, p. 14.

Figure 2.3: The work of collaborative teams.

to identify strengths and weaknesses and develops three to five school goals for the year. Collaborative teams are then expected to write one or more SMART goals to support their roles in ensuring the school can meet the goals it sets. For example, if an elementary school sets a goal to improve reading achievement, each of the grade-level teams should set its own reading goal linked to the current student achievement level. When the collaborative team aligns its goal to the school goal, it meets the first

SMART criterion—strategic. Figure 2.4 is an example of how a collaborative team might write that goal along with the action plan it's putting in place to accomplish it.

School: Maple Crest Elementary School

Team Name: Third Grade

School Goal: By the end of the 2021–2022 school year, we will have increased the number of students proficient in ELA by 10 percent as measured by the state test.

Team SMART Goal	Strategies and Action Steps	Responsibility	Time Line	Evidence of Effectiveness
Our reality: This past year we had 76 percent of our students proficient on the state test. **Our goal:** By the end of the school year we'll have 86 percent of students proficient on that test.	We will identify the essential standards we know that all students must learn in our curriculum.	All team members	Draft list developed during our opening school workshop	The list will align with the REAL criteria (readiness, endurance, assessed, and leverage) and represent approximately one-third of our curriculum.
	We will develop common formative assessments and use the results of those along with our benchmark and progress-monitoring tools to improve our interventions and extensions.	All team members	Updated lists of students receiving support	We'll monitor students every three weeks to determine if they are making progress or need more support.
	We will implement our new vocabulary program across all content areas.	All team members	All year	We will monitor this using our quarterly benchmark assessments with the word analysis score.

Figure 2.4: SMART goals worksheet.

*Visit **go.SolutionTree.com/PLCbooks** for a free reproducible version of this figure.*

In addition to being strategic, the goal must be measurable. In the example in figure 2.4, the team is using quarterly benchmark assessments, progress-monitoring tools, and the state test to measure its effectiveness. It must also be attainable; the likelihood of the goal being reached is high but does require the team to work together for success. It must be results oriented—that is, it must have an impact on student learning. And, it must be time bound, meaning teams set time limits for the goal to be reached.

To make sure a team doesn't spend a whole year working on a goal to find out after the state test at the end of the year that its plan was ineffective, we recommend the team set some interim goals or specific times to gather data to monitor its progress.

Leaders Can Support Collaborative Teams

We specifically used the term *formative tools* in the title of this book to ensure that leaders, such as principals and assistant principals, see the importance of separating their evaluative role from the important role they play in supporting the work of collaborative teams in the PLC process. When we use the term *formative assessment* with students, we are describing ways that teachers determine whether a student has learned an essential learning target yet or whether that student needs additional time and support in order to be successful. We suggest that leaders take this same view with their staff. Are staff members effective yet, and if not, what support will they need to become effective? For this work, we recommend that leaders think about collaborative teams as their unit of support. Leaders should ask themselves, "Where is the team currently, and what can I do to provide them with the time and support they need?"

How Leaders Offer Mindful Support

When teams struggle, it usually happens for one of two reasons. The first is that the team needs specific support in the area of professional learning or instructional design. Members might not know *how* to do the work. For example, a team may be attempting to unwrap its essential standards without understanding how to do this work. In these cases, support might mean some specific training, an opportunity to observe another team in action, or even having a facilitator work with them to model what good team practices look like. The second reason teams may struggle is that one or more members don't behave in a way that allows the teams to operate effectively. For example, some participants may not speak up in meetings, and others may dominate the meeting or take the discussions off the agenda topic. Sometimes the other team members recognize this is happening but are unwilling to call out a peer for his or her behavior, and so the behavior continues, derailing the work of the team. Not all teams are willing to admit when they are experiencing difficulty with team dynamics, and some teams may not even realize this is happening. Consider, for example, a team whose members are unwilling to risk conflict for fear of retribution. Team members might simply go along with the leader so that they can get their work done and survive to the next meeting. We've seen teams where one person does most of the work so that the team appears to be productive despite the personal disagreements of some of the members. While this team does create products, those products don't have the benefit of multiple ideas and points of view.

School and district leaders, then, must consider how each of the teams in their school are functioning at any given time. The tools we suggest allow leaders to gather evidence through direct observations of teams as they work by examining products of collaboration, as well as by interviewing and using perception surveys from teams as a whole or from individual team members. We offer the formative tools in this chapter to gather evidence about how well teams are collaborating so that the leaders can provide additional support. When a team is struggling, team members might be very willing to share their frustration about their team's behavior with leaders, hoping that the leader can help solve the problem. In other cases, however, team members might be unwilling to share their feelings, as many teachers are uncomfortable challenging one of their peers. We've purposely developed ways to gather information from more than one source of evidence so that leaders can gather a complete picture about what's happening with their collaborative teams.

I remember a specific situation when I was a middle school principal. Two relatively inexperienced teachers came to me about a problem they were having on their team with a team member we'll call Ann. They described Ann's behavior at team meetings, which clearly sent the message that she didn't want to work collaboratively and saw team meetings as a waste of time. Early in the PLC process, Ann came late to every meeting giving different excuses—for example, "I had to call a parent immediately. It was an urgent situation" or, "I needed to work with John after class as he's been absent so much and needed to catch up." Rather than confront this behavior, the team moved its meeting location to Ann's classroom, hoping this simple solution would make a difference. However, she continued to demonstrate her unwillingness to be an effective team member and most recently raised her voice at these two less experienced teachers, saying they were naïve in their thinking that their team could ever get all students to succeed. Wow! My first reaction was to tackle this issue myself, but I soon realized if I took on this problem it would likely make things worse rather than better. Instead, I worked with the two inexperienced teachers to have a crucial conversation with their colleague. We planned out the script and role-played various ways the meeting could go. While neither of the teachers was excited to confront their more experienced colleague, both also believed that things weren't going to get better without something drastic happening. While I can't say things went from disaster to perfection overnight, this team moved on from the problem and continued its journey and capably helped students learn at high levels.

—Chris Jakicic

The lesson Chris learned as a building leader was that making sure teachers know how to handle team dysfunction is an effective way to solve problems. The first step was to review norms to see if teachers in teams needed to add a norm for a behavior they were seeing. It's not uncommon for teams to write generic norms. However, high-performing teams are intentional about the norms they write. If they are aware of specific problems they face, they make sure they have agreements about that behavior. Consider, for example, a team whose members know they tend to let discussions dissolve into complaints that take away from the time they need to get their work done. This team needs a norm such as, "We will all be aware of and willing to call time out when our discussions become complaint sessions." Consider how different this norm is than the more generic "We'll keep our meetings focused on positives." When teams are new to collaboration, they may not know up front what issues they'll face when working together. This is why it's so important that teams regularly look at their norms to make sure they cover any emerging issues.

Another lesson learned was to make sure all teachers understood the phrase "care enough to confront" (Kanold, 2011, p. 108). This means that the team has ownership of their time and their behavior. Members must believe that their work is important enough to overcome the reluctance to call out a peer if his or her behavior is interfering with the work of the team. The best way to empower teachers to do this is to discuss—before issues emerge—what members may do when a norm is violated. The answer may be as simple as holding up a hand and calling for a time out. Then the team member would name the problem and remind team members of the norm. Finally, the team can move quickly back to its work. This keeps members' attention focused on the behavior (not the teacher).

If these strategies aren't effective, the idea of a crucial conversation—teammate to teammate—is an important skill. As we work with teams across the United States, we regularly run into teams who are afraid to confront behaviors that aren't productive on their teams. Members say that only an administrator can challenge a colleague's behavior. As Chris's vignette suggests, if the building leader steps in, the conversation could be perceived as evaluative. While the conversation leaders have with their colleague may be uncomfortable, the result is usually a far more productive team. "Groups that ignore inappropriate member behavior in an attempt to avoid conflict decrease their ability to solve problems that are often conspicuous. Avoiding conflict frequently results in hostility and reduced performance" (Wolff, Druskat, Koman, & Messer, 2006, p. 230). In fact, conflict may be necessary for the health of the team. Education author and speaker Casey Reason (2018) suggests, "Conflict is a signal that a growth opportunity is just around the corner." It's important, however, for leaders to show teachers how to have those crucial conversations.

In their work on crucial conversations, management experts Kerry Patterson, Joseph Grenny, Ron McMillan, and Al Switzler (2012) explain one important thing to know about them: "When it comes to risky, controversial, and emotional conversations, skilled people find a way to get all relevant information (from themselves and others) out into the open" (p. 23). To do this, it's important to plan out this conversation in advance.

Patterson et al. (2012) suggest that effective crucial conversations consider the following actions.

- It's rare that one event triggers a conversation. The teacher initiating the conversation should take some time to put together the supporting information—to consider what has led him or her to realize the necessity of this conversation. For the teacher who has violated the norm, receiving a list of specific behaviors and issues that have occurred will help him or her understand what he or she is doing to undermine the team's work.

- Prior to asking for the meeting, choose a safe place for it to happen. In schools, that will likely be in the classroom of the teacher who violated the norm. At the end of the meeting, the initiator can leave and the teacher is in his or her own territory.

- The initiator should clarify what he or she hopes to happen as a result of this conversation. It's also important to discuss what both parties have in common. What's their ultimate goal in working together; what is their mutual purpose?

- Be careful to make sure the teacher doesn't feel ganged up on. The entire team doesn't need to participate. Provide an opportunity for and listen carefully to the teacher's thoughts and perceptions about the way the team is working.

- The initiator should keep the focus of this conversation on the behavior he or she is hoping to extinguish and summarize the anticipated outcomes at the end of the meeting.

As a leader, be mindful that it is difficult for teachers to challenge a peer's behavior. Role-play the conversation. Develop plans for different reactions from the teacher. Focus on the fact that the only way all students can learn at high levels is if collaborative teams function effectively.

When Leaders Should Attend Team Meetings

In some schools, the principal and other leaders are considered members of each team. A principal might believe he or she must attend all the team meetings to make sure each team is focused on the right work. The principal may even think, "I want to show the teams how important I think this work is. How will they know that if I don't go to their meetings?" Unfortunately, what the principal views as support, the teams may view as control. They may see the attendance of the principal as evidence that the principal doesn't trust them to do their work. Sometimes having an administrator at the meeting forces the team to behave differently than if the principal wasn't there. However, it would be equally ineffective if leaders simply put their staff on teams and told them to collaborate on the four questions with no further input or support.

Instead of either of these choices, the leadership team should regularly monitor the products of collaboration. That is, each team representative brings an assigned product to the leadership team meeting to share with the other members. For example, a few weeks into the school year, teacher leaders bring a copy of their team's SMART goals. They each share their goals and the action plans. During this time, teammates may ask questions, probe for ideas, or offer feedback. Leaders should take care to be supportive rather than evaluative. As the leadership team builds trust, team leaders who are experiencing difficulty on their teams will feel more confident being honest about what's happening and more willing to ask for advice from other leadership team members.

This isn't to say that administrators shouldn't ever attend meetings. We believe there is a balance that leaders should achieve; they should attend when they want to engage with the team, solicit information from team members such as with the tools from this book, and share professional learning or coaching ideas. But be careful not to take ownership and responsibility from the team members.

Assess the Current Reality

In the introduction (page 1), we talked about how important it is for leaders to consider the context of their schools as they take stock of their practices. When assessing collaborative structures, the important aspects of context to evaluate include the history of collaborative practices, connections between the school and district, and evidence of previous shared leadership practices.

Leaders can use the following guiding questions in figure 2.5 (page 54) to reflect on their current context.

Guiding Questions	Reflection on Context
What is the history of collaborative practices in your school?	
How much collaborative time is built into the master schedule for each team?	
Are teams expected to use common pacing, or do individual teachers assess for proficiency when they think their students are ready?	
What is the role of the team leader in your school? How are leaders chosen?	
Are special educators members of general education teams?	
How are teams configured for singleton teachers?	

Figure 2.5: Guiding questions to consider a school's context around the collaborative process.

*Visit **go.SolutionTree.com/PLCbooks** for a free reproducible version of this figure.*

Leaders should consider the history of collaborative practices in their school. Many schools have organized teachers into teams and provided common planning time for them to work together prior to embracing the PLC process. These schools would expect that teachers use this common *planning* time to talk about the curriculum, instructional strategies, student issues, and parent communication. But this structure means that it's unclear whether this planning would lead to common expectations. These groups might be called collaborative teams, but their purpose is quite different than teams in a PLC. This previous experience often leads to what's called PLC lite—planning together rather than learning together (DuFour et al., 2016). However, in a PLC, collaborative teams intentionally work to agree on common expectations for student learning as well as to plan how to respond together to support their students. If teams are moving from a PLC-lite environment, leaders need to keep it in mind to ensure that teams are fully realizing the potential of the PLC process.

The difference between common planning and common pacing is an important distinction for teams in this process. In a PLC, there is no expectation that all teachers will teach a concept the same way. This means that leaders do not expect them to use the same lessons on the same day. However, it *is* important for teams to use the same pacing. They must agree on the total number of days a unit will take, as well as the dates of any common formative assessments that teams will administer in that unit. This is an example of loose and tight leadership; leaders are *loose* on some things, like how teachers teach individual lessons, but *tight* on others, like pacing (DuFour et al., 2016). This means that pacing guides that teams used prior to determining essential standards and common formative assessments will change as a result of the differences in how instructional time is used. If a district has an expectation about pacing that isn't aligned with this process, it will be important for leaders in the school to communicate between teams and the district office.

Consider the recommendation education researcher Robert J. Marzano (2017) makes based on the analysis of research about what works in education: teachers should focus on unit planning as opposed to lesson planning. While he isn't specifically addressing the work of collaborative teams here, the point he's making is that daily lesson plans can and should be flexible and reactive to what students demonstrate they need. Those plans should fit into a unit of instruction, and the outcomes of the unit will affect decisions teachers make during daily lessons. Putting this notion into the context of collaborative teams makes sense. Collaborative teams identify explicit outcomes (learning targets) and then develop common formative assessments to gauge whether students are learning the essential targets. They set common dates to administer the assessments, and develop common expectations for proficiency—that is, common answers to assessment items and common rubrics. Individual teachers make their own choices for lessons but share results when they discuss their assessments. In this way, they learn together what works best for each of their students.

Another context that's important to think about is who is considered a leader in the school. As explained in the introduction, we purposely use the term *leader* to include administrators, coaches, team leaders, and informal school leaders, as one of the hallmarks of a PLC is the importance of shared leadership. The leadership team consists of multiple teacher leaders who collectively make decisions and guide this work, along with the more formal leadership of the principal and assistant principal. If there has been little history of teacher leadership in a school, it will likely take some time for everyone to feel comfortable with this new model. Deciding what will be loose (individual or team choice) and what will be tight (the same for all teams) will be very important early in the process. When teams aren't sure what they are allowed or expected to do, they may be reluctant to move forward.

The tools in this section help leaders answer the question, What is your currently reality? Notice that they are designed to solicit information from a variety of perspectives—those of team members, a leader observing meetings, and from the products the team is creating. This can help leaders make accurate conclusions about the strengths and weaknesses of the team.

- Staff's Perceptions About Collaboration Tool
- Team Observational Checklist
- Monitoring the Products of Collaboration Tool

- Team Reflection Tool
- Team Reflection Tool for Singletons

Staff's Perceptions About Collaboration Tool

Sometimes teams struggle with collaboration without knowing exactly what is wrong. For example, a member may be happy to agree to disagree about a decision when that action itself avoids something important the team is deciding. The survey in figure 2.6 asks teachers to look at a series of statements to determine which one most closely reflects their thinking. The results can give leaders insight into the members' perceptions about collaboration.

	This survey should be completed by all members of the team. For each category, team members should read the three statements and put an *X* in the last column for the statement that most closely reflects their feelings.	
	Belief Statement	
1.	Most of the time our meetings are a waste of time.	
	Our meetings are OK, but it takes longer to get things done than if I did it myself.	
	Collaboration time is extremely valuable. Our products are much better when we work together.	
2.	When we spend time talking about a student assigned to another teacher on the team, it makes me tune out.	
	When we talk about students together, we often share good ideas with each other.	
	All of us take responsibility for all of the students on the team.	
3.	When making decisions, we tend to agree to disagree or take a vote.	
	We don't have a specific plan for making decisions, but it usually works out OK.	
	We effectively use consensus to make important decisions.	
4.	We tend to share opinions and use them to complete our work.	
	We know it's important to build shared knowledge but often fall back into sharing opinions.	
	We build shared knowledge in order to do our work effectively.	
5.	We aren't very comfortable with using data and often make excuses when it exposes issues for us.	
	We understand that we should use data but don't always see how it helps us get better.	
	We view data as information to guide our work. If the data reveal undesired results, we figure out how to fix the problem together.	

Figure 2.6: Staff's perceptions about collaboration tool.

Visit **go.SolutionTree.com/PLCbooks** *for a free reproducible version of this figure.*

Team Observational Checklist

While figure 2.6 provides perceptual information about team processes, it is important to couple that with direct information about actual practices. Leaders can use the observational checklist in figure 2.7 to note the presence or absence of effective team behaviors, help isolate individual team problems, and develop a plan to support any teams they identify as needing additional support.

Read the following behaviors and place a checkmark in the column that corresponds with how well the team exhibits each.

Team Behaviors	Yes	No	Unsure
The team has an agenda and uses it to guide its work.			
The team stays on topic during the meeting.			
All team members participate in the meeting.			
Team members are respectful to each other.			
Team members use norms during the meeting when appropriate.			
Work Completion	**Yes**	**No**	**Unsure**
The team makes effective use of its time.			
Team members identify and complete specific tasks during the meeting.			
The team knows how to use protocols to keep its meetings moving forward.			
Members organize the products of team meetings in such a way that all members have easy access.			
Debate and Disagreement	**Yes**	**No**	**Unsure**
The team can discuss, debate, and disagree in a respectful manner.			
Team members listen to each other during discussions and debates.			
Team members are willing to change their minds when they see effective evidence for another choice.			
Decision Making	**Yes**	**No**	**Unsure**
The team uses consensus when appropriate.			
Once the team has made a decision, members willingly move forward to implement it effectively.			

Figure 2.7: Team observational checklist.

*Visit **go.SolutionTree.com/PLCbooks** for a free reproducible version of this figure.*

Monitoring the Products of Collaboration Tool

A second method for gathering evidence of effective team behaviors is to look at the products of collaboration—norms, agendas, SMART goals, and data. The quality of these products can provide some insight into how well collaboration is going on a team. In the introduction we discussed how teams use student work from assessments to understand what support will benefit students. In figure 2.8, the products of collaboration serve as the work of the team in the same way. Leaders can use the scale to assess one or more of the following: norms, agendas over time, SMART goals, and data. As leaders examine the product, they should consider which level on the continuum best describes the team's product as evidence of its effectiveness. If a team starts at the Learning level on the continuum, leaders can consider specifically what steps can help the team move forward.

Product	Underperforming	Learning	Effective	High Performing
Norms	Norms are generic and represent typical meeting expectations such as being on time and coming prepared. The team hasn't discussed what will happen when a member violates norms.	The team has norms in place and regularly reads and refers to them. While members may be reluctant to call out a team member who isn't following the norms, they make references to the expected behaviors.	Team norms are in place, and members review them regularly. Members wrote the norms to reflect the behaviors they're committed to displaying. When they were developed, they were written around issues the team anticipated they would face in their work.	Team members take collective responsibility to make sure everyone follows norms so that they are effective in their work. They add norms when issues arise that aren't already covered. Meetings run smoothly with everyone engaged in the work.
Agendas over time	The team might not have agendas, or its agenda items might be unfocused. Some items may look more like announcements than steps in the process.	Agendas are in place, but the team doesn't always follow them. Sometimes the team gets caught up in discussions not related to an item on the agenda. Team members add agenda items during the meeting.	Agenda items flow from meeting to meeting, and the team members build the agenda for the next meeting at the end of each meeting because they know where the team left off.	The team's embrace of the PDSA cycle is apparent in its work. Items have an anticipated beginning and ending time to keep members from veering off topic during discussions. Team members use protocols when appropriate.

SMART goals	The team has written its SMART goals from a model the school or district provided rather than creating their own product. Team members are concerned about the accountability these goals will bring to their work. They worry about what will happen if they don't make progress throughout the year in accomplishing their goals and tend to set low expectations for themselves.	The team sets SMART goals for the year and uses the action planning to develop the steps they will take. The team typically looks at its goals a few times a year when it receives fresh benchmark data.	The team sets SMART goals for the year and regularly checks in with its action plan to monitor its progress. When team members see that they are not making anticipated progress, they revise or adjust their action plan.	The team uses short-term SMART goals in their work. Team members are comfortable setting high expectations because they are confident that they are able to improve student learning as they collaborate. They use the goal-setting process to make their team more effective.
Data	Team members know they are expected to use data in their work but don't always know what data to use and how to analyze them for their purposes. For example, after each benchmark they look for trends but aren't sure how to use this information in their work. These discussions invariably fall back into talking about students who need help but don't provide insight into what help they need. Teams also tend to use a cut score to discuss student performance on common formative assessments rather than student work.	Team members are getting better about using student work from common formative assessments to plan effective responses, but they often group all students who are not yet proficient together for the response. They know the importance of using their benchmark data but are most comfortable when someone prints the reports for them and helps them understand what they are seeing.	Team members are comfortable moving from facts to inferences in their data. They know what data to use to identify students who need extra time and support and have practices in place to track student learning. When they are struggling with an aspect of student learning, they know how to dig deeper into their results to learn more. They see data as helpful rather than threatening.	Team members seek out data to provide them the information to help their students. They dig deeply into benchmark and diagnostic data to get answers to their questions about student learning. They look at data for what the data can tell them rather than seeing them as a judgment of their quality as teachers.

Figure 2.8: Monitoring the products of collaboration tool.

*Visit **go.SolutionTree.com/PLCbooks** for a free reproducible version of this figure.*

Team Reflection Tool

Using the tool in figure 2.9 provides leaders with feedback from team members about how they believe their team is functioning. The Team Reflection Tool is designed to encourage open-ended feedback so that members can be honest about what they perceive is happening but without anticipating what they might say. It can be completed during a team meeting or handed out so team members can fill it out individually.

Please consider each of the following areas of collaboration and provide feedback about your team. The purpose is to understand how your team currently works and provide any support you might need to become more effective.	
Collaborative Practice	**Feedback**
Effective meetings: Our meetings run efficiently, and we are able to be effective with our work.	
Trust: We trust each other and can ask for help when needed.	
Interdependence: We accomplish more together than what we would be able to accomplish individually.	
Decision making: We make decisions in different ways but know how and when to use consensus.	
Data: We know how to use achievement data and common formative assessment data to plan next steps.	

Figure 2.9: Team reflection tool.

*Visit **go.SolutionTree.com/PLCbooks** for a free reproducible version of this figure.*

Another way to use this tool would be to interview the entire team at one time so that they might share ideas and provide more details as they brainstorm the answers together.

Team Reflection Tool for Singletons

Because teams composed of singleton teachers face different issues and problems than traditionally configured teams, we suggest the following reflection in figure 2.10 for their use.

Collaboration within singleton teams can be very different than with typical collaborative teams in a PLC. They may face different problems (finding meaningful partnerships) and often do their work differently. For example, since each team member teaches a different grade level or course, choosing essential standards requires all

	Collaborative Practice	Feedback From Team

Please consider each of the following areas of collaboration and provide feedback about your team. The purpose is to understand how your team currently works and provide any support you might need to become more effective.

Collaborative Practice	Feedback From Team
Team configuration: We are able to have meaningful partnerships with our current team members and are able to complete purposeful work together.	
Allocated time: The time we've been allocated for collaborative meetings is effective for our work.	
Collective responsibility for students: We see all of our students as belonging to us collectively and are effective in helping them achieve at high levels.	
Team organization: We all have easy access to the products from our meetings as well as the data from our students.	
Interdependence: Our members believe that they are better as a result of working together.	

Figure 2.10: Team reflection tool for singletons.

Visit go.SolutionTree.com/PLCbooks for a free reproducible version of this figure.

team members to first choose the standards for their course or grade level, and then the team works to vertically align them.

Analyze Patterns and Priorities

Just as effective formative assessments help teachers perceive which students need extra time and support as well as impart insight into the time and support those students need, formative tools such as effective surveys and observations yield data that help leaders see the specific support teams need. The purpose of the Staff's Perceptions About Collaboration Tool (figure 2.6, page 56) is to provide some insight about the feelings individual team members have about their teams. Of course, leaders always want all of their staff to choose the third option for each belief category when using figure 2.6, but it's important to remember that new teams and other teams that might be having difficulties with the collaboration process are unlikely to feel that way. The continuum tool in figure 2.11 (page 64), however, can help leaders understand more deeply what's going on with teams. Is it a matter of not believing the time spent together is worthwhile, not supporting the way decisions are made, not committing to taking collective responsibility for all students, or being reluctant to use data in decision making? If members have negative perceptions about collaboration in more than one area, leaders can use the tools in figure 2.7 (page 57) and figure 2.8 (page 58) to get more precise information.

While the Staff's Perceptions About Collaboration Tool asks teachers to react to statements in order to tease out team members' perceptions about collaboration, figures 2.7 and 2.8 intentionally use observations and products to understand the effectiveness of team practices. Using the Team Observational Checklist in figure 2.7, a leader can determine which areas a team is struggling with: team behaviors, work completion, debate and disagreement, or decision making. While observing a team during a regular meeting, leaders might not see all of these categories. For example, the leader may not see debate and disagreement because the team is engaged in developing a product that comes from a common belief. On the other hand, the leader may not see debate and disagreement because teams are worried about looking dysfunctional to the observer. Therefore, there is no hard and fast rule about how many marks on the checklist a team should exhibit during a particular meeting. However, the observation tool should provide an insight into how the team functions.

Using the Monitoring the Products of Collaboration Tool in figure 2.8, leaders can see evidence about collaborative practices from the actual work products of the team. We advocate that the leadership team should conduct this process for all of the collaborative teams in the school. The leadership team members themselves can provide ideas and support to any of their colleagues who are concerned about the quality of their products. However, for leaders who have identified a team that needs help using either the Staff's Perceptions About Collaboration Tool (figure 2.6, page 56) or the Team Observational Checklist tool (figure 2.7, page 57), the tool in figure 2.8 can be a way to triangulate the data about what help a team needs.

The Team Reflection Tool in figure 2.9 (page 60) helps teams reflect on their own work to encourage buy-in for whatever help and support the teams may need. When analyzing the feedback, leaders should look for confirmation from more than one team member or from more than one tool. For example, this tool asks about effective meetings, but leaders can also see evidence about this in the Team Observational Checklist tool (figure 2.7, page 57) as well as by looking at the agendas through the lens of the Monitoring the Products of Collaboration Tool (figure 2.8, page 58). The actions a leader might take would likely be the same either way.

The Team Reflection Tool also asks about trust. Leaders can also verify members' trust in one another in the Team Observational Checklist (figure 2.7, page 57), which looks at how teams debate and disagree. If this is an issue, teams can overcome a lack of trust by establishing norms that allow members to be vulnerable with each other. For example, the team may want to add a norm to its list that relates to debate and disagreement, such as "When making decisions, we are willing to listen to everyone's ideas before we seek to reach consensus." Or, "Instead of relying solely on opinions to make decisions, we will first build shared knowledge." These experiences (when positive) will develop higher levels of trust among members. On the other hand, we've worked with teams that have never built trust in which the members see any discord or disagreement as lack of respect. This leads to some teachers being unwilling to engage with the rest of the team. Trust is vital to effective collaboration. When considering interdependence, a leader might consider responses on the Team Reflection Tool as well as evidence of how team members work together to accomplish their SMART goal when looking at the Monitoring the Products of Collaboration Tool (figure 2.8, page 58). The Team Reflection Tool also asks teams for feedback about how they make decisions. Confirmation of the responses can be made from observations via the Staff's Perceptions About Collaboration Tool (figure 2.6, page 56) in the category of decision making. Finally, in using data, leaders can confirm results by also looking at the way the team collects and uses data in the Monitoring the Products of Collaboration Tool (figure 2.8, page 58).

The Team Reflection Tool for Singletons in figure 2.10 (page 61) is a variation of the Team Reflection Tool designed for teams of singletons. This tool helps teams focus specifically on issues that singleton teams face; they can use it either in writing or as a team interview. The benefits of using it as an interview are that hearing from multiple members at the same time might allow members to build on each other's ideas, which can be especially helpful when initiating new practices and solving problems collaboratively. The tool solicits feedback for each of five topics. Leaders might need to clarify their expectations for some topics. For example, some singleton teams might feel that all team members must participate in all discussions. However, if a science teacher and a mathematics teacher are collaborating on a concept they both teach, not all of the members of the interdisciplinary team necessarily have to participate. On the other hand, if an interdisciplinary team is working on an ELA standard about developing strong arguments, it makes sense that all teachers will be involved because students can apply this skill in multiple content areas.

As leaders consider other areas that singleton teams provide feedback about in the Team Reflection Tool for Singletons, the leader may be responsible for finding a solution. For example, if there are issues with time allocation that involve the master schedule, a solution might not be possible until a new master schedule is developed. Therefore, leaders must ask themselves what they plan to do with the data they get from the interview and must be ready to seek out solutions.

In this step, leaders should focus on the question, What patterns and priorities emerge in the evidence? Using the evidence gathered from the previous tools, they can use the continuum in figure 2.11 (page 64) to chart the current reality of their teams.

As we discussed earlier in this chapter, we expect that teams likely go through many steps as they become more effective in their collaborative practices. And many things can impact team collaboration, such as new members, a new curriculum, new testing systems, and new master schedules. Leaders can use this continuum to stay up to date about teams that need additional support.

Knowledge and Practice	Level of Use or Implementation			
	Limited	Emerging	Established	Strategic
Teachers see the value of collaboration in allowing the team to take responsibility for all students learning at high levels, solving problems, and learning together.	Team members may skip meetings because they don't feel a responsibility to their teammates.	Team members attend meetings because they are held accountable by leaders or because they enjoy the camaraderie of their teammates.	Team members value collaboration time. They see their teammates as assets as they work together to help all students be successful learners.	Team members value collaboration time and seek out ways to become even higher performing. They seek out new learning when faced with a problem and know that their collective wisdom far exceeds each other's individual knowledge.
Teams implement collaborative practices that lead to meaningful partnerships and effective products.	Teams haven't yet recognized the collaborative practices that will improve the quality of their meetings and products.	Teams are aware of effective collaborative practices but don't always use them effectively in their work.	Teams are knowledgeable about effective collaborative practices and use them effectively so that they have meaningful partnerships and effective products.	Teams function at high levels of collaboration, routinely take stock of the effectiveness of their practices and products, and serve as models to other teams.
The products collaborative teams create (norms, agendas, SMART goals, and data) will likely lead to improved student achievement.	Teams haven't been able to create quality products either because they haven't had the time or they don't yet understand what those products should look like.	The quality and quantity of products teams have produced are limited, but teams are more knowledgeable about how to produce them.	Teams have created quality products and are using them to improve student achievement.	Teams have created quality products and used them to improve student achievement. They use data to monitor the effectiveness of their products.
Teams engage in a continuous improvement cycle by reflecting on their practices and planning ways to get better at their work.	Teams haven't had time to reflect on their work or don't see the importance of doing so.	Teams talk about and see the importance of continuous improvement but aren't sure exactly how to make it work for them.	Teams regularly reflect on their work and see how important continuous improvement is to student learning.	Teams have an explicit cycle they engage in for continuous improvement. It drives their work.

Figure 2.11: Continuum of practice for collaborative teams.

*Visit **go.SolutionTree.com/PLCbooks** for a free reproducible version of this figure.*

Act on Evidence to Improve Practice

To plan how to act on all the evidence they've gathered, leaders should consider the question, How do we move forward? As we discussed in the Analyze Patterns and Priorities section, after using the Staff's Perceptions About Collaboration Tool (figure 2.6, page 56), leaders should identify teams that show negative perceptions about collaboration. Using the Team Observational Checklist (figure 2.7, page 57) and the Monitoring the Products of Collaboration Tool (figure 2.8, page 58), a leader can diagnose where collaboration is breaking down. These tools are designed to move away from perception to gather concrete information about practice.

If the Team Observational Checklist indicates that the team is struggling with *team behaviors*, leaders can use each of the items in the checklist to be more specific about which area the team needs help with. For issues related to norms and agendas, the leader might want to work directly with the entire team to show how to develop agendas, keep minutes, or write effective norms. The leader may also want to share the idea of assigning roles to members so that there is a sense that the work belongs to everyone. If the issues identified have to do with everyone participating in the meeting or team members being respectful to each other, the leader might want to work specifically with the team leader to teach and practice facilitation skills. Leaders sometimes forget that teachers don't typically learn how to work this way with adults. One excellent resource for building high-performing collaborative teams is *The Handbook for SMART School Teams* by Anne Conzemius and Jan O'Neill (2014).

For teams that are struggling with *work completion*, the solution might be as simple as having someone set up shared folders on the team drive and make sure that the team members all know how to easily access the documents they're creating. We've seen many teams wasting collaboration time trying to find documents that were created in a previous meeting because no one remembers where they were saved. Another support the team might need is awareness of specific protocols that they can use to complete tasks. Rather than have the team struggle to determine next steps, protocols can list the steps and an estimated amount of time each step should take. There are many protocols in this book that are specific to the tasks collaborative teams are responsible for. Figure 2.12 (page 66) lists the options.

For collaborative teams just getting started in the work, protocols can be especially helpful. We recommend using protocols that are specific to this work (as those listed in figure 2.12) because they help keep the team on track to effectively answer the four critical questions. Often these protocols are specific enough that they need little or no training to use.

Protocol	Figure
Protocol for Identifying Norms	2.13
Vertical Unit Review Protocol	3.13
Protocol for Choosing Essential Standards	5.1
Protocol for Unwrapping Standards	5.2
Protocol for Analyzing Assessment Results	6.2
The Design Process	6.8
Team Intervention Planning Protocol	7.4

Figure 2.12: Protocols for collaborative team tasks.

Teams that struggle with *debate and disagreement* may be under the false assumption that high-performing teams always get along. Conflict isn't a sign of a dysfunctional team. Recall from Understand the Collaborative Process (page 40) that Lencioni (2002) lists five team dysfunctions and suggests that teams typically overcome them in a specific order. The first is absence of trust. Lencioni (2002) suggests that many teams begin with little or no trust, which makes it hard to create interdependence for their work. The second characteristic is fear of conflict. Teams that are unwilling to discuss and debate important decisions get stuck in the status quo, never getting better at their work and never solving tough problems that arise.

Leaders may find it helpful to show teams struggling with disagreement how to build shared knowledge about issues and problems they are facing. Some teams tend to get stuck sharing their opinions with each other; this usually results in one side winning and the other side losing. Instead, if the team gathers research and best practice information, members will likely find it easier to come to a satisfactory resolution. Another strategy a leader might share is how to do reflective listening, which involves the team members using clarifying questions, summarizing what another member has said before adding their own input, and paraphrasing a statement to check accurate understanding. While these strategies often feel contrived when teams first practice them, they are welcome solutions later on during tough conversations.

Teams who find *decision making* difficult may not have any tools other than putting decisions to a simple vote. For these teams, some understanding of what consensus decisions are and some ideas about how to build consensus may be all the team needs. In a PLC, we say consensus occurs when the following two criteria are met (DuFour et al., 2016).

1. All points of view have not merely been heard but have been actively solicited.

2. The will of the group is evident even to those who oppose it.

The first action a leader might take is to make sure teams know when and how to use consensus in their work. Teams should understand that not all decisions have to be made using consensus—the process is time consuming and only necessary for substantive decisions. For example, when teams are choosing essential standards, it's important that they build consensus on their final product by making sure all members have had input and a chance to share their thinking.

The second action that a leader might take is to teach the team leaders how to facilitate the process of coming to a consensus decision.

- **Step 1: Clarifying the decision to be made**—During this step, the team develops a collective understanding about both the problem being solved as well as the issues that are related to the problem. It is important that, during this first step, all members keep an open mind and willingly ask questions for clarification.

- **Step 2: Engaging in discussion**—During this step, all team members must contribute to the discussion about the problem. As members move into this next step, they can identify possible solutions based on the ideas and information from the early discussions.

- **Step 3: Examine the pros and cons of any decision being considered**—During this step, the team members discuss each proposal to determine how it will work for them and whether it will achieve the desired outcome.

- **Step 4: Amendments made to make solutions better**—During this step, members suggest ways to make the solution or solutions stronger and more agreeable to the group members. If there is more than one possible solution, all members consider each one.

- **Step 5: Check for agreement**—During this step, the group uses the fist to five strategy (DuFour et al., 2016) to see what the level of agreement is—members indicate a range of reactions from full agreement (holding up five fingers) down to opposition (holding up a fist). If the team feels that it has reached consensus (the will of the group is evident, even to those who oppose it), the decision is accepted. If not, the group goes back to step 4 to determine what amendments could be made to satisfy the blockers.

Consider the following example of a team using this process to reach consensus. A middle school team is considering how to make changes in its grading practices. Currently members are giving students a zero for work that isn't turned in by a specific date, and they want to come up with a different solution to this problem. During step 1, they discuss the problem they are trying to solve (a grade so severely impacted by missing work that students give up) as well as the issues that solutions might raise (students not turning in work until the end of the grading period or turning in sloppy work just to get some points). In step 2, they discuss the problem and possible solutions more thoroughly, trying to clarify anything that is ambiguous. For example, will the student get full credit or partial credit when turning in late work? Can students redo an assignment which earned a C and get a higher grade? As they begin step 3, team members list the pros and cons of the various thoughts they've had about changes in grading practices, encouraging all team members to participate with all solutions. Before they move to step 4, the team agrees to take some time to explore some information from books and other resources concerning what other schools have found successful and the research behind changing grading practices. During step 4, team members share what they've found and are particularly interested in the idea of having students sign a social contract (Schimmer, 2016) that lays out the expectations by teachers about students having to try their best on the first attempt if they want a second attempt. This solution alleviates some of the teachers' concerns about students waiting until the last minute. They work together to put all of their ideas about grading into a document that they can share with students as well as parents. Once the document is complete, they conduct a fist to five to make sure they have all members on board.

For work products, there are a number of ways leaders can act to support teams in making improvements. Here we present tools and criteria that leaders can share with teams to hone their work on norms, agendas, SMART goals, and data.

Norms

Shortly after the school year starts, teams should be prepared to share their *norms*. The characteristics the leaders should look for include the following.

- Norms are written as behaviors rather than as aspirations. For example, instead of, "We believe that all opinions should be respected" the team uses, "When making decisions, we will make sure all members have shared their thinking."

- Norms are few in number and focus on problems the team may encounter in doing its work. Five to seven norms are usually sufficient for teams.

- Included in the norms is an agreement about how the team will respond when a member violates one of the norms. For example: "When a team member violates a norm, we will identify the problem and move quickly to solve the problem."

Because every team make-up is unique, different teams may find the need for different types of norms. For example, if a team sees that one member is reluctant to contribute to the discussions, it may include a norm such as, "We'll solicit feedback from every team member when discussing new ideas."

If teams are finding it hard to create effective norms, we suggest the protocol in figure 2.13 from our book *The Collaborative Team Plan Book for PLCs at Work* (Bailey & Jakicic, 2020).

Step	Action
1.	Make sure that the team members understand why they are writing these norms and how they will use the norms to make their collaborative practices more effective. Remind the team members of areas to consider as they write their own norms: decision making, participation, time management, response to conflict, and confidentiality.
2.	Ask team members to reflect on teams they've been on before or have observed in their work. What were the negative behaviors that prevented them from functioning at high levels? Members should write each of these behaviors on a sticky note. Make sure teachers do this step individually and without discussion.
3.	Collect and review all the sticky notes, asking for clarification if needed. Cluster any similar behaviors together.
4.	Ask team members to consider successful teams they've been part of. What positive behaviors did these teams engage in? Again, have members write these behaviors on sticky notes. These sticky notes should be a different color than the sticky notes from step 2.
5.	After collecting the sticky notes from each team member, cluster any similar behaviors together, and seek clarification on those that are ambiguous. As a team, take some time to link the positive behaviors to the negative behaviors that would diminish the positive ones if implemented. If a negative behavior doesn't have a corresponding positive one, the team should discuss and develop a positive action to diminish the negative behavior.
6.	Initiate an open discussion about which of the positive behaviors the team members want to include on their final list of norms.
7.	If there is disagreement about a norm, allow time for discussion about how the norm would help the team in its work. After thoroughly discussing the norm, use the fist to five strategy to see what the consensus is for that norm. To use this strategy, each member holds up the number of fingers that represents his or her confidence in this product. Five fingers represent 100 percent agreement; a fist represents complete disagreement. Teams must ensure all members hear from any dissenting voices. Learn more about this strategy in *Learning by Doing* (DuFour et al., 2016).
8.	The team members need to agree how they will handle situations when a team member violates one of the agreed-on norms. Suggest that the team members must be willing to take responsibility for the way the team works together and that they must care enough to confront.
9.	Capture the final set of norms in writing and publish them for use at all team meetings. Start each meeting with a review of the norms, and plan to revisit them twice a year.

Source: Bailey & Jakicic, 2020; DuFour et al., 2016.

Figure 2.13: Protocol for identifying norms.

*Visit **go.SolutionTree.com/PLCbooks** for a free reproducible version of this figure.*

Agendas

The second product that leaders should monitor is the *agendas* a team develops. While some schools have a specific template that teams are to use for their agendas, other schools expect each team to choose an agenda template that works best for their team. When monitoring agendas, the leadership team should look for the following attributes.

- The team uses agendas to focus its meetings and keep records of its decisions.

- Agendas are focused on the work of answering the four critical questions.

- Agenda items should pick up where the team left off at the last meeting.

- Agendas should consist of a reasonable number of items that teams can complete in the typical team meeting time.

There are many different templates for teams to use to create agendas. We offer the following one in figure 2.14 that provides space for important information and that teams can also use to capture the decisions or minutes of the meeting.

Date:			
Members Present:			
Estimated Time	**Agenda Topic**	**Lead Person**	**Outcome or Decision**

Figure 2.14: Team agenda template.

*Visit **go.SolutionTree.com/PLCbooks** for a free reproducible version of this figure.*

SMART Goals

Leaders should also look at team *SMART goals*. These goals are few in number and represent what the team expects to accomplish as a result of its collaboration. These goals ensure that the team is interdependent—that *no one* teacher is responsible for students or for results. With SMART goals, the leadership team should look for:

- Goals that fit the SMART acronym—strategic and specific, measurable, attainable, results oriented, and time bound (Conzemius & O'Neill, 2014)

- Goals that require the team to operate interdependently
- Action plans that focus the team on the right work to accomplish its goals

At least as important as the goal itself is the action plan the team writes that lists the strategies and steps they will take to achieve the goal. In addition to strategies and steps, the team should specify who is responsible for each item and how and when they will measure them to ensure success.

Often the leadership team can help a team that is struggling with writing its goals. Depending on what criteria the goal is missing, leaders can provide ideas and examples of how the team can revise what it has developed. Consider, for example, a team that writes a goal such as, "We will implement the new reading curriculum with fidelity." Leaders can remind teams of the SMART criteria; this isn't a measurable goal. Rather, the goal might be, "We will increase the number of students proficient on the state reading test from 65 percent to 75 percent." If a team is reluctant to set high expectations, seeing how other teams are writing goals can be helpful.

Data

One additional product leaders should monitor is collaborative teams' use of *data*. These data include benchmark and annual test scores, as well as their own common assessment data. As collaborative teams begin PLC implementation, it's not uncommon for them to worry about accountability when using data. These teams are often used to seeing data as an unmoving roadblock in their work. They may feel that way especially when all teachers are working hard but pursuing different solutions for student learning. However, when a team sets a SMART goal and interdependently focuses on solving problems, the data usually take care of themselves. The leadership team should look for the following criteria.

- The data are easily available to team members in a form that makes them user friendly.
- The team regularly uses its data to guide its work and decisions.
- The team uses the right data for each of the discussions it has and each of the problems it's working to solve.

The Team Reflection Tool (figure 2.9, page 60) and Team Reflection Tool for Singletons (figure 2.10, page 61) will help teams take ownership of their own practices. When we talk about continuous improvement, the concept often refers to gains in student achievement. However, keep in mind that high levels of learning are not only the goal for students; everyone in the organization can learn and improve. High-performing teams are always looking to find ways to improve their collaboration. Whether that improvement comes from team members gaining better technical skills or from encouraging better team behaviors, this focus on improvement is vital to strengthening teamwork.

Leaders Can Be Vulnerable, Too

When considering collaborative structures, leaders should always be willing to consider their own behavior and beliefs about trust and conflict. One important writer on this topic, Brené Brown (2018), has swept the field of leadership with her research and thinking. One important conclusion she's drawn is that in order to develop trust, a person has to be willing to be vulnerable rather than expecting the other person to be vulnerable. Leaders can model vulnerability, making it more likely that teams are willing to be vulnerable. In fact, admitting that they don't have all the answers can work in their favor. When Chris was first helping her teachers have a conversation with a difficult teammate, she pulled the *Crucial Conversations* book by Patterson and his colleagues (2012) off the shelf and admitted she didn't know the steps in the process by heart. They worked through them together. Sometimes the best thing a leader can do is ask the question, "What does support from me look like?" (Brown, 2018, p. 38). When teams have input into the PLC process, they are usually more willing to embrace it. Don't be afraid to be vulnerable, because it can really bring teams on board, allowing them to collaborate effectively and focus on instruction, which is the subject of the next chapter.

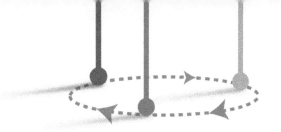

Chapter 3

QUALITY INSTRUCTIONAL PRACTICE

When we look at the four critical questions teams are tasked with answering in a PLC, there is no question directly tied to instruction. In fact, this was, as shared by Dr. Rick DuFour at a PLC associate retreat, intentional (R. DuFour, personal communication, August 2, 2008). The rationale behind *not* adding a specific question about instruction, he explained, was that it might lead teams to skip over or spend too little time clarifying outcomes in student learning and the evidence that would indicate students reached those outcomes. In his observations, if teams skipped the crucial conversations around *learning*, there would be no clarity about these outcomes among members and the conversations would quickly devolve to the comfort zone of talking about *teaching*. Despite the lack of a specific critical question, however, quality instruction *is* important in this work. A major premise of the PLC process is that educators get better results when their professional practices improve (DuFour et al., 2016). In fact, we encourage teams to examine what we call critical question 2.5: What quality instructional strategies will result in high levels of student learning? Teams can embed this question as part of their backward planning of instruction process, but keeping in mind the wisdom of Rick DuFour, *only after* they are clear on questions 1 and 2. This helps keep conversations focused on the right work but allows members to be proactive and determine any instructional strategies they feel will bring about high levels of learning while teaching a particular unit of study (Bailey & Jakicic, 2019). When working with teams in this area, leaders should focus on the questions, What is the schoolwide quality of instruction we provide students? And what practices will bring about high levels of learning?

The following scenario highlights a common challenge in schools.

> *For over two years, Sheila, the principal at Lakeview Elementary, has discussed the need to increase student engagement. In her observations and those of others visiting the school, too many students are not actively interacting with their teachers or fellow students and appear detached from what they are meant to be learning. As part of their school improvement plan, staff members sat through professional development activities in which specialists shared strategies for increasing student engagement. Some teachers implemented a few of the strategies and informally shared that they did find them helpful in engaging their students. However, despite these isolated bright spots, Sheila's observations during her subsequent classroom walkthroughs still reveal a general lack of student engagement in the majority of classrooms, low student interest and participation in the learning activities, and limited meaningful interactions between teachers and students. In addition, she notes evidence of students being confused about what they were supposed to be doing. She also observes that there is disproportionately less engagement by male students compared to female students.*

If schools are to meet their mission and vision, leaders must examine the quality of instruction across classrooms. While collaborative teams may be using strategies for improving learning in a particular unit of study, there may still be pervasive schoolwide practices that impact the overall quality of instruction and student learning. Issues around ineffective practices may be obvious to those walking through classrooms, yet others may be subtle in nature and only recognizable to those intentionally seeking evidence and providing feedback based on a clear vision of effective instruction. For example, a walk through one school may reveal that students are sitting obediently in their seats during a lesson, but they may not be interacting with other students or the teacher around meaningful learning tasks. Teachers might spend significant class time ensuring quiet compliance, while a closer examination of the evidence reveals minimal academic discourse. They conclude that they're facing that common challenge: students, while perhaps compliant, are not actively engaged in the learning process.

Schools often use professional development activities to target key instructional strategies, as in the scenario about Sheila's school and lack of student engagement. However, these activities may not directly align with the specific needs of a school, and schools may place them in the midst of multiple initiatives taking place at the same time. This constant feeling of changing the channel, diluting the focus of professional learning, often results in spotty or minimal follow-up to clarifying expectations or providing support for actually implementing the strategies. This typically results in a low level of systemwide or schoolwide implementation.

So how might leaders, including team leaders, coaches, and administrators, ensure that the quality of instruction is continuously improving on a schoolwide basis? How can these improvements be systematically supported and focused on specific areas of need? How might Sheila, in our example scenario, help her school's teams improve student engagement? In this chapter, we discuss how leaders can formatively assess the quality of schoolwide instructional practices and then use the evidence they gather to support all teachers and teams toward a shared vision of effective instruction.

It's important to note that the tools we discuss in this chapter are intended for gathering data about schoolwide instructional practices that leaders can use to plan and provide systemic and focused support leading to improvement. Although there may be similarities, we want to clarify that the purpose of these tools is not to be confused with those tools used by school leaders for evaluative purposes. We advocate that leaders use the formative tools in this book to gather evidence in order to *improve* instruction on a systemwide basis. They can use the evidence to analyze and then identify specific actions to systematically improve the practices. They are not intended to be used for formal evaluations of teachers' instructional practices.

When they assess the work of teams around instruction, there is much that leaders need to know and look for. Here we'll discuss what evidence of quality instructional practice is, what these practices look like, how teams align content to standards, and how to prioritize the examination of schoolwide implementation. Then we'll focus on tools that will help leaders assess, analyze, and act to support teams.

Understand Quality Instructional Practice

By definition, a PLC works on collectively improving its practice in order to impact student learning. The specific focus on which teachers are improving their practice is based on the specific needs of students. While individual teachers have their unique teaching styles, PLCs work under the assumption that all team members will commit to sharing and using the instructional practices they identify as effective. Over time, they build a repertoire of shared practices that consistently yield high levels of learning, many of which are supported by research, such as ensuring that students are clear on learning targets, providing timely and effective feedback, and providing graphic representations of concepts (Hattie, 2012; Marzano, 2017; Wiliam, 2018). By ensuring these practices for quality instruction on a schoolwide basis, schools move closer to ensuring a guaranteed and viable curriculum for all students, meaning student learning is not dependent on which teacher they happen to have, and all teachers have time to teach the identified essential content and skills (Marzano, 2017).

In other words, all staff are committed to use high-quality instructional practices to *guarantee* that all students learn the skills and concepts that are deemed as essential.

As they identify and examine the quality practices for instruction they want to ensure across all classrooms, leaders should consider the following categories and clarifying guiding questions.

- **Equity:** Instruction is culturally responsive and takes into consideration the needs of students to ensure that all students have certain access to core instruction and gain the skills needed to be successful. This does not simply mean that students are in the room while core instruction is taking place; core instruction is designed to ensure that it is comprehensible and relevant for students who are economically disadvantaged, learning a second language, or culturally diverse.

    ○ Are all students, regardless of their cultural, socioeconomic, or educational background, learning at high levels?

    ○ How do the design and delivery of instruction intentionally support the instructional needs of all students, including those who may be traditionally marginalized?

    ○ Are low-performing students who need additional time and support receiving it?

- **Expectations:** Instruction is aligned to clear and rigorous expectations for learning, which teachers make visible to students.

    ○ Are expectations for learning the same for all students, including students of color, those with identified special needs, and English learners?

    ○ Are students clear on the expectations?

- **Efficiency:** Instructional time is structured to maximize learning and minimize wasted or "down time."

    ○ Do teachers maximize time for learning in each classroom?

    ○ Are transitions between activities efficient, or do students end up with a lot of down time?

- **Engagement:** Instruction actively engages students in the learning process.

    ○ Are students clear on what they're learning and why?

    ○ Does the instruction hook students and actively involve them in the learning process? Are some students disengaged?

    ○ Is there evidence of students being in a learning partnership with the teacher within a culture of mutual respect and trust?

- **Effectiveness:** Instruction embeds strategies that support high levels of cognitive understanding.
  - Do teachers structure lessons to support student achievement of high-level concepts?
  - Do they support dependent learners' building cognitive skills in order to attain higher levels of thinking?

These general categories provide a framework of the indicators that leaders can reference while looking at the quality of instruction on a schoolwide basis. Later in this chapter, we provide specific tools leaders can use to gather evidence in order to paint a picture of schoolwide quality instructional practice.

Leaders Can Support Quality Instructional Practice

When looking at quality instruction on a schoolwide basis, two key areas emerge: (1) classroom culture, routines, and structures and (2) design and delivery of instruction. Following is a brief overview of the key elements within each area.

Classroom Culture, Routines, and Structures

All teachers set a general culture or climate in their classrooms, and that culture serves to define the types of relationships that will develop between the teacher and students as well as among students. For instance, when leaders can see evidence of positive relationships within the classroom, that's a strong indicator of a positive classroom culture. Teacher-student relationships can be *instrumental* in nature, meaning that they are intended to motivate students to comply with teacher direction and completion of tasks, or they can be *reciprocal* in nature, which means teachers invite students to interact with them and their peers to grapple with content and learn together (Theisen-Homer, 2018). An indicator of reciprocal relationships is a classroom culture where students feel valued and heard. When teachers take time to learn more about their students' interests or go to after-school activities like athletic events or artistic performances, this helps build positive relationships. In schools that are experiencing attendance issues, behavior issues, or even motivation issues, building these positive relationships can make a huge difference (Marzano, 2017).

In her book *Culturally Responsive Teaching and the Brain*, instructional designer and educational coach Zaretta Hammond (2015) discusses the power of effective relationships and meaningful connections in raising the achievement of culturally and linguistically diverse students—traditionally those students who fall into the achievement gap. Among practices outlined in her Ready for Rigor framework are those that enhance the relationship between students and teachers so they can work as partners to raise achievement. Mutual trust and respect create an environment that is socially and intellectually safe for students to stretch themselves and take risks (Hammond, 2015).

Another indicator of an effective classroom culture is classroom expectations being clear to all students and setting the stage for high levels of learning. Tied to these expectations are classroom management techniques that assure all students the opportunity to learn and build ownership of the learning process. Students are clear on the established routines and procedures.

Just as important as culture is having systems in place to provide structure and organization within the learning environment, which can refer to the physical structures in a classroom or the structured use of time during instruction. Here are some indicators of structures associated with effective classrooms.

- Physical environments are inviting but orderly and enhance student focus and independence in the learning process.

- Student spaces are structured to allow for a variety of collaborative interactions among students (for example, teams, pairing, or centers).

- Visual spaces highlight artifacts that enhance and promote the learning process, including the display of student work.

- Systems for transitioning students from one activity to the next maximize instructional time and allow for bell-to-bell teaching. As a result, students are actively engaged and in learning mode, as opposed to waiting mode, for the majority of the time.

When every classroom evidences a positive culture, and students have clear routines and structures that provide them with an environment that supports learning, it sets the stage for high levels of learning for each and every student.

Design and Delivery of Instruction

The field of education has an endless amount of literature focused on quality instructional practices. Some researchers have poured their efforts into focusing and quantifying those practices (Hattie, 2012; Marzano, 2017; Saphier, 2017; Wiliam, 2018). One of the most widely known meta-analyses is John Hattie's (2012) *Visible Learning for Teachers*. In his work on instructional practices and their influence on student learning, Hattie (2012) "considered more than 800 meta-analyses of 50,000 research articles, about 150,000 effect sizes, and about 240 million students" (p. 1). Using a scale of effect size, which is a measure of the impact of teachers' instructional efforts, he looks at the relative impact of these efforts on student achievement in comparison to a typical classroom experience. The average effect size is 0.4, which represents gains owing to typical teacher actions and students' own maturation. We would consider anything greater than a 0.4 effect size as having a positive impact. The idea is that educators can see which influences are most powerful and choose to use them in their classrooms. For instance, a team may historically spend a lot of time teaching students test-taking skills. However, the effect size for this practice is 0.3, well below the hinge point of 0.4. Given this knowledge, the team members learn that their assumptions about what works may in fact be less effective than they thought. However, they note that feedback is actually correlated with a 0.7 effect size. Using that information, the team can strengthen its approach to ensuring that students get timely and specific feedback.

Another source of information related to instructional practices comes from Marzano (2017) in his book *The New Art and Science of Teaching*. While he discusses forty-three elements of instruction in the book, he cautions readers in the introduction that one can't simply adopt one new strategy and expect all students to learn.

> Specifically, I note that no single instructional strategy can guarantee student learning for a number of reasons. One is that many factors other than the use of instructional strategies affect student learning. Another is that instructional strategies work in concert or sets and should not be thought of as independent interventions. Still another is educators have to use strategies in specific ways to produce positive results. (p. 1)

Leaders can reference Marzano's (2017) statement to help clarify the intent of any efforts to support the development of quality instructional practices. The individual strategies are not guaranteed as stand-alone "silver bullets" that will magically bring about high levels of learning but work in conjunction with other quality practices to strengthen the likelihood that students will find greater success in learning.

Some professional organizations provide direction about instructional strategies for specific content areas. In its publication *Principles to Actions*, the National Council of Teachers of Mathematics (2014) identifies eight teaching strategies that promote student learning in mathematics:

1. Establish mathematics goals for learning.
2. Implement tasks that promote reasoning and problem solving.
3. Use and connect mathematical representations.
4. Facilitate mathematical discourse.
5. Pose purposeful questions.
6. Build procedural fluency from conceptual understanding.
7. Support productive struggle in learning mathematics.
8. Elicit and use evidence of student thinking. (p. 5)

Similarly, the National Science Teaching Association (NSTA) partnered with other stakeholders in developing the Next Generation Science Standards (NGSS), which have been adopted by twenty states and whose framework has been used by twenty-four additional states to develop their own standards (NGSS Lead States, 2013). The NSTA (http://nsta.org) has developed materials for schools that are transitioning to these standards and the instructional strategies that support them, including a number of curated instructional resources available through its website.

In light of the potential overload of information regarding quality instructional practice, educators need support from instructional leaders to select new instructional strategies and connect any new focus on them to their purpose in response to specific areas of instruction that need strengthening. In other words, leaders need to ensure that they and the teachers are clear on why particular strategies have been selected for use, and how those strategies relate to the big picture or vision for student learning. For example, if there is evidence of a schoolwide need to increase student engagement at a higher level of critical thinking, leaders should focus on building schoolwide strategies specifically targeting that outcome, such as constructing probing questions, using Socratic seminars, or designing inquiry-based lessons, all of which serve to enhance critical thinking. Teams would then design their instruction and as appropriate, embed the newly learned strategies so that students engage in deeper levels of academic discourse and critical thinking, collectively noting whether the strategies resulted in better results in student learning. Conversely, if leaders ask teams to learn or adopt a revolving door of strategies without a strong connection to an identified need, then they may view the strategies as the "next shiny thing" they need to do to be in compliance, rather than a vehicle to meet a need in student learning.

Align Content to the Standards

In tandem with quality practices is the need to align instruction to the adopted content standards for student learning. School leaders, including the leadership team, continually affirm that instruction is aligned with the standards, and in particular, those standards deemed essential by staff. In other words, there should be evidence in every classroom that students are learning grade- or course-level standards that have been collectively determined as essential. There should be evidence that not only is instruction aligned to the standards but also that the level of learning teachers target is at an appropriate level of rigor. For example, the heightened emphasis on argumentation in ELA and other content areas means that the evidence should show that students are exposed to more complex texts, learn how to evaluate sources of information, and receive guidance on drawing accurate conclusions using explicit evidence and inferences from the text. In mathematics, aligned instruction means that students are expected to solve real-world problems, explaining their reasoning and critiquing the reasoning of others. Science instruction has moved away from focusing primarily on the content to expecting students to investigate and explain phenomena they see. The inquiry arc in social studies requires lessons that no longer focus on dates and facts and require students to make connections and use reasoning (Marzano, 2017).

Prioritize Areas for Examining Schoolwide Implementation

Over time, school leaders can examine schoolwide quality of instruction in multiple areas ranging from broad categories to specific strategies. However, for purposes of gathering initial insights on the general effectiveness and quality of schoolwide instruction, we suggest examining the following five fundamental clusters or elements, each of which reflects research-based practices of effective and culturally responsive teaching.

1. Classroom climate and management (Marzano, 2017; Saphier, 2017)

2. Clarity and alignment of learning targets (Dean, Hubbell, Pitler, & Stone, 2012)

3. Lesson structure and delivery (including pacing; Marzano, 2017; Saphier, 2017; Zwiers & Crawford, 2011)

4. Questioning and feedback (Dean et al., 2012; Marzano, 2017; Saphier, 2017; Zwiers & Crawford, 2011)

5. Student engagement (including interactions between teachers and students and among students; Dean et al., 2012; Marzano, 2017; Saphier, 2017; Zwiers & Crawford, 2011)

Before leaders examine these elements across the school, it's important to clarify what constitutes evidence and nonevidence of effectiveness. In other words, leaders need to identify the look-fors for each element and any evidence that would be incompatible with effective practice for that element. Figure 3.1 (page 82) offers some ideas for these look-fors (evidence of quality practice) and incompatible practice descriptors (nonevidence or incompatible practices), but we suggest that leaders engage with staff to generate input and establish common criteria for their observations.

Site leadership can use these descriptors, or ones that they develop and clarify, to gather initial evidence about the school's overall quality of instruction in a consistent fashion. Ultimately, however, there should be schoolwide agreement about what constitutes effective instruction—a shared vision. Later in this chapter, we share ideas for ensuring that all educators in a school are clear about their vision for effective instruction.

Assess the Current Reality

Before moving forward with considering their current reality, we highly recommend that school leaders consider their context as it relates to the quality of instruction. The best place to start is to consider how leaders and teams in their schools

Element of Instruction	Evidence of Quality Practice	Nonevidence or Incompatible Practices
Classroom climate and management	Established routines, procedures, and evidence are in place to ensure that students are clear on expectations for class behaviors and processes. Climate promotes respect for all cultures and viewpoints and fosters a growth mindset for learners. Well-organized physical spaces and materials facilitate learning and collaboration among students.	The classroom focus is on compliance rather than a focus on learning. Routines or procedures are unclear.
Clarity and alignment of learning targets	Daily and unit-level targets for student learning are in place, and the class references them frequently. Students are clear on what they're learning and why. Targets align to the essential standards for the grade level or course.	Students are unclear about what they're learning and why. Learning targets may be posted, but no discussion of them or how the class meets them takes place.
Lesson structure and delivery (including pacing)	Lessons employ scaffolding and actively engage students in learning. The teacher naturally moves between direct instruction and facilitation. Lesson design and delivery provide students with opportunities for meaningful collaboration and reflection.	Students are expected to learn everything on their own. Lessons center on busywork. Lecture is the dominant instructional strategy.
Questioning and feedback	Questioning fosters complex thinking around content in alignment with the standards, with consideration for what students are capable of doing with and without guidance. Students are engaged in giving and getting actionable feedback in order to improve their learning. Students know where they are in relation to the targets for learning, including their strengths, and specific strategies that they can use to improve.	There is only low-level questioning that is not aligned to the rigor of the standards. Feedback is evaluative or solely focused on a grade and raises the feeling of threat (instead of empowering students with strategies for moving forward). The focus is on grades, not on learning; feedback is infrequent and doesn't drive improvement.
Student engagement (including interactions between teachers and students and among students)	Students are actively engaged in meaningful activities and have frequent opportunities to interact with teachers and fellow students. Teachers promote academic discourse and use strategies to support higher-order thinking. Student choice is embedded, and there are supports for students to become confident learners.	Students are inactive or disengaged in learning activities. Student interactions are discouraged. Low-achieving students are exempted from activities that promote higher-order thinking.

Figure 3.1: Sample evidence and nonevidence statements to gauge quality instructional practices.

make decisions about instructional practices. Some schools or districts have a pre-scribed lesson-delivery model, such as the example in figure 3.2 from Hot Springs School District in Arkansas, which reflects its focus on Marzano's (2017) *New Art and Science of Teaching* framework.

HSSD Instructional Model 2019–2020		
Areas in parentheses are tied to Marzano's *New Art and Science of Teaching* (NASOT) framework. Staff members should refer to their NASOT chart to make references to best instructional practices.		
Should See and Hear Daily	**Might See and Hear**	**Should Never See or Hear**
Capturing students' hearts (3, 31, 41)	Tracking mastery of learning (2, 3)	Unsupervised students
Clear learning targets and academic language (6, 12, 16, 21)	Reteaching and intervention (11, 13, 17, 19, 43)	Non-engaged teachers (at desk)
Consistent procedures and behavior expectations (33, 36, 37)	Common formative assessments (5)	Exclusion of students based on labels or classifications
Culturally responsive environment (31, 39, 40, 41)	Learning engagements beyond the classroom (27, 32)	Student assignments unrelated to learning targets (busywork)
Well-balanced questioning (using Depth of Knowledge strategies; 14, 16, 17, 19, 42)	Community involvement (27, 32)	Screen time not relevant to learning targets
Standards-based teaching and learning (1, 6, 7, 20)	Digital collaboration (28, 32, 35, 39)	Putdowns and cultural insensitivity
Assessments (4, 5, 43)	Academic games (30)	Wasted instructional time
Engaged students (23, 25, 27, 32)	Direct instruction (6, 7, 8, 9)	Personal phone usage during instructional time
True rigor (1, 11, 12, 14, 42)	Extension of learning (11, 12, 14, 21, 39)	Disrespectful or inappropriate dialogue among staff or students
Student voice and ownership (1, 2, 19, 21, 31, 32)	Student and teacher reflection (19)	Low expectations of students
Collaboration and intentional grouping (22, 23, 34, 39)	Lesson adjustment (4, 7, 18, 19, 24)	

Source: © 2019 Hot Springs School District. Used with permission.

Figure 3.2: Sample lesson-delivery model.

Some districts select curriculum materials and expect teachers to use them with fidelity, with little latitude on the adjustment of pacing or strategies. Whatever the context, leaders need to get an accurate picture; figure 3.3 (page 84) provides some guiding questions for capturing that picture.

In this section, we provide school leaders with tools to gather evidence about the implementation of quality instructional practices. The question leaders should keep in mind throughout these efforts is, What's our current reality? Although we provide tools to gather evidence on specific areas, such as classroom management, most tools are flexible in their use—in other words, they aren't geared to a specific strategy or component of quality instruction. Rather, the following tools provide a structure for

Guiding Questions	Reflection on Context
What initiatives related to the enhancement of quality instruction have taken place in the recent past? What triggered those initiatives, and what was the outcome?	
What quality-instruction needs has the school identified in the past? What specific activities have taken place, and what is the level of implementation?	
Are there districtwide expectations for elements of instruction? Are they tied to the evaluation process? What professional learning or support is available to support teachers' growth in these expectations?	
How aligned are curriculum or instructional resources to the expected practices? What tools do these resources provide teachers that are compatible with the practices?	
What do informal observations reveal about the quality of instruction on a schoolwide basis? Is there a particular element that emerges as a priority for improvement?	
Has there been a clear expectation set for the level of implementation of particular practices across the school? Are teachers clear on what is tight versus loose in how they implement these practices? How is this implementation being monitored and supported?	

Figure 3.3: Guiding questions to consider the context of quality instructional practices.

*Visit **go.SolutionTree.com/PLCbooks** for a free reproducible version of this figure.*

gathering evidence to gain insight into any of those components and can be adapted accordingly based on a school's priorities.

- Instructional Impression Walkthrough Recording Form
- Checklist for Standards-Based Instruction
- Analysis of Physical Indicators and Artifacts
- Look Who's Talking Checklist
- Collective Reflection and Analysis of Artifacts
- Teacher Interview Questions

Instructional Impression Walkthrough Recording Form

Leaders can use the recording form in figure 3.4 to organize evidence of quality practices observed during classroom walkthroughs. As leaders use this tool,

Date of Walkthrough:	Observer:		
	General Impressions		
Element of Instruction	**Evidence of Highly Effective Practices**	**Evidence of Effective Practices**	**Evidence of Ineffective Practices**
Classroom climate and management			
Clarity and alignment of learning targets			
Lesson structure and delivery (including pacing)			
Questioning and feedback			
Student engagement (including interactions between teachers and students and among students)			

Figure 3.4: Instructional impression walkthrough recording form.

*Visit **go.SolutionTree.com/PLCbooks** for a free reproducible version of this figure.*

they simply place a tally mark representing each classroom observed to reflect their general impressions about the elements of instruction. Using this tool across classrooms, school leaders can put together a visual, at-a-glance picture to gauge the level of instructional quality for the entire school. Several observers can use this tool more than once over a period of time. This tool can help prioritize areas of need or improvement as well as celebrate those areas in which there has been growth or overall high quality.

Leaders can conduct walkthroughs even in virtual classrooms by sitting in on instruction that teachers deliver synchronously and asynchronously. They can collect evidence around the quality of the instructional design and delivery just as they do in a physical classroom. A list of elements similar to the ones we've provided in the tool can be used with added considerations for virtual learning. For example, in the realm of lesson structure and delivery, leaders might seek evidence of an appropriate balance between direct instruction versus student-directed learning through independent work.

Checklist for Standards-Based Instruction

Teachers and leaders can use the checklist in figure 3.5 periodically. The purpose is to make sure that instruction is aligned to the standards assigned to a grade level or content area. Additionally, the checklist helps make sure that teachers create formative assessments to match learning targets based on essential standards, and to ensure sufficient time to teach, respond, and reteach when necessary.

Classroom	Yes	No
The teachers have posted learning targets for students that connect to standards for this grade or course.		
Learning targets appear in student-friendly language that keeps the original intent of the standard.		
Students can identify the learning target for a lesson.		
Unit Plans	**Yes**	**No**
Unit plans include the grade-level or content-area standards.		
The unit plan identifies essential standards.		
The teacher aligns class activities to learning targets from the standards.		
Assessments	**Yes**	**No**
Assessment items are linked to specific learning targets.		
Learning targets are included on assessments.		
Teachers and teams can use data to identify learning targets that students haven't mastered.		

Figure 3.5: Checklist for standards-based instruction.

*Visit **go.SolutionTree.com/PLCbooks** for a free reproducible version of this figure.*

While there may be times a teacher is not actively demonstrating one of the pieces of evidence on this list, these indicators should be embedded in all classroom instruction. Leaders can also ask questions to determine whether the practice is in place. As with the Instructional Impression Walkthrough Recording Form, leaders can easily adapt this checklist to examine instruction in virtual environments.

Analysis of Physical Indicators and Artifacts

Walking the halls is a great strategy for gathering evidence about the culture of classrooms and the school in general. Is student work posted? Does posted work change frequently to demonstrate an ongoing focus? What is posted on the walls in the classroom? What is the type of work in which students are engaged? Does the quality reflect progress toward grade-level expectations? Is there evidence of students' interaction with their learning in the form of learning reflections, data notebooks, or other self-monitoring?

Look Who's Talking Checklist

School leaders can use the checklist in figure 3.6 to categorize the nature of instruction and interactions during walkthroughs or classroom observations.

Date: _____   Time: _____

Classroom: _____

Teacher Is:	Most Students Are:
☐ Lecturing	☐ Interacting with content as part of a whole-class activity
☐ Reviewing lesson learning targets	
☐ Engaging students in academic discourse (whole group)	☐ Listening to the teacher
	☐ Working with peers to complete a task
☐ Working with small groups	☐ Actively but independently engaged in task completion
☐ Working with individual students	
☐ Reading aloud	☐ Engaged in silent reading
☐ Facilitating collaborative groups	☐ Off task or disengaged
☐ Not engaged or sitting at desk	☐ Gathering materials or transitioning to another activity

Additional notes:

Figure 3.6: Look who's talking checklist.

*Visit **go.SolutionTree.com/PLCbooks** for a free reproducible version of this figure.*

Leaders can convert this checklist to an electronic form (such as a Google Form) that they can access on a portable device and easily submit for each classroom observed. If leaders use the paper-and-pencil version, they can tally the data on a master sheet and review for emerging patterns. Electronic versions would automatically time stamp the data and make it easy to retrieve a summary of the results. Regardless of the tool format, leaders should conduct walkthroughs multiple times and on multiple occasions before reaching any generalized conclusions.

Collective Reflection and Analysis of Artifacts

Another way to gather feedback about how frequently or effectively teachers are using a new strategy or innovation is to ask them to bring an artifact from their own classroom related to the strategy or innovation to a staff meeting. These artifacts might include student work, learning targets, instructional materials, or even interviews with students.

Leaders ask teachers to form two lines facing each other and have them share their experiences using the following questions.

1. What was your experience like using this strategy or innovation? Please share the artifact you brought.

2. What did you learn when you tried the strategy out?

3. Did your students learn what you wanted them to learn from this lesson? How do you know?

4. What would you do differently the next time you use this strategy or innovation?

5. What help or support do you need to learn about to improve on using this strategy or innovation?

Leaders should give the paired teachers enough time for both to answer one question—usually three to five minutes. After each question, one of the lines of teachers will move to the next person to form a new pair to answer a new question; the person who drops off at the end can circle back around to rejoin the line.

After teachers have been through the process of answering the questions with different people, have them go back to the first person each participant met with and share what they heard. Finally, ask each team to generate two sticky notes—one with what's going well and one with what additional help teachers and teams need. Leaders can use these notes with the guiding coalition to develop their next steps.

Depending on the strategy being initiated, teachers will likely provide a variety of different kinds of artifacts. If the strategy is increasing dialogue in mathematics classes, for example, a teacher may bring a sample lesson and the questions planned for students to discuss. If the strategy is teaching explicit vocabulary, the teacher may bring a student's vocabulary notebook. It will be important to note if a teacher doesn't bring an artifact, as it's possible that the teacher doesn't yet have the support needed to try the strategy out. The most powerful data will come from the sticky notes generated by teams. What they list on their *what's going well* notes can be used for celebrations and to help determine what teachers are finding effective. The notes indicating the *additional help needed* can help leaders prepare the next training or support sessions that teams will need.

Teacher Interview Questions

In the introduction we discussed the work of Hall and Hord (2006) as it relates to understanding how teachers implement change. Hall and Hord (2006), authors of the Concerns-Based Adoption Model (see figure I.4, page 10), suggest what they call "one-legged" interviews as a way to gather information from staff. Their research suggests that facilitators or leaders take opportunities for brief interviews with teachers asking how the implementation is going as well as what they are doing or thinking of doing. Possible interview questions might include the following.

- Can you share what you've learned as you tried out this strategy or innovation?

- What feedback do you have for the guiding coalition about the current action plan?

- Is there any specific support you need that you haven't gotten?

The responses to these three short questions can provide insight into teachers' perceptions—both positive and negative—regarding implementation. More importantly, they can lead to actions that will increase implementation. For example, some responses to the interview questions may reveal a lack of awareness about how to implement a particular strategy or a general lack of confidence in attempting the strategy without support. This feedback implies that those teachers need additional time and support to learn the strategy, perhaps by observing the strategy in action as used by a colleague or by having a coach available to provide structured support and feedback. In addition to individual teacher insights, leaders can look at patterns across the school. Are you getting similar feedback from most teams, or are they implementing a particular practice at different levels? The patterns will help leaders determine whether to take action on a large-scale or schoolwide basis or if teams require differentiated support.

Analyze Patterns and Priorities

Through the analysis of the data they gather from the tools in the previous section, leaders can answer the questions, What is the evidence telling us about the needs of teachers and teams as they relate to schoolwide quality instruction? What priorities for improvement in schoolwide instructional practices emerge from the data? School leaders can use data from any of the tools to examine strengths and identify potential areas targeted for improvement. Through the use of specific tools, leaders ensure that the inference is based on evidence, not on hunches. For example, if a leader sees that student academic discourse is taking place infrequently across the school, the inference may be that there is a need for more strategies to intentionally engage students in academic conversations. To further support this kind of analysis, we provide some additional guiding questions that leadership teams can consider.

- Is there a collective schoolwide vision of effective instructional practice? Has it been established with input from all members of the staff?

- Is the vision communicated and referenced on a regular basis?

- What areas of schoolwide instructional practice are considered highly effective? What areas might need improvement?

- Do teachers and teams need to build shared knowledge around quality instructional practices in the identified area of need? If there are multiple areas of need, which would be the highest priority for support or implementation? Why?

- What specific skills do teachers and teams need to enhance this area of instructional practice? How might those be developed?

- How are teams getting support while implementing practices targeted for improvement? How are teachers giving and getting feedback?

- Can leaders use some classrooms to showcase high-quality practices in an effort to provide a quality model that other teachers or teams can observe? How might you use these to empower teachers with effective models of instruction?

- Are there any implications for support from school leadership (for example, changes in structures, policies or practices, or resources)?

- How is implementation of new practices going to be monitored, supported, and celebrated?

By compiling the evidence of schoolwide instructional practice collected through the tools, leaders can create something similar to a photographic mosaic, in which a large picture actually comprises several smaller pictures. In addition, leaders can use the continuum of practice in figure 3.7, which provides a big-picture view of the implementation indicators.

Knowledge and Practice	Level of Use or Implementation			
	Limited	Emerging	Established	Strategic
Shared vision and collective commitment to deliver quality instruction	Teams are not yet focused on improving instruction across the school and may not be aware of areas of need.	Teams are aware of areas of need related to instructional practice and are committed to improving.	Teams are committed to and focused on improving specific instructional practices in order to achieve a schoolwide vision.	Teams continuously reflect on their school vision and suggest areas to further improve in order to provide students with high-quality instruction.
Alignment of content to essential standards	Teams don't question the alignment of their instruction to the standards.	Teams are beginning to make adjustments to ensure that instruction is aligned to the standards.	Teams routinely examine the alignment of their instruction as it relates to the standards and the expectations for proficiency, as well as the need to ensure that all students, including those who may be at risk of marginalization, are learning.	Teams formally adjust their curriculum maps, assessments, and practices to ensure alignment to the appropriate standards.

Shared knowledge around quality practices	Teams have not established conversations about and focus on quality instructional practices.	Some training around quality practices has taken place, but it may not be squarely focused on an identified need.	Teams have identified specific needs of the school and students, and this information leads to the design and delivery of targeted professional learning.	School staff continue to monitor the needs of students and adjust their focus for professional learning as needed.
Implementation of quality practices	Implementation varies widely from teacher to teacher, team to team.	Expectations for implementation have been made clear, and staff are beginning to implement new practices with support.	Teams embed new practices within their instructional planning so that they are intentional about their implementation.	There is a high level of quality instruction, and team members continuously seek new ideas.
Opportunities for practice, feedback, and support	No feedback takes place after professional development on new strategies.	Teams agree to move forward and practice the strategies identified for implementation, getting feedback from their colleagues and other support people.	Teams routinely seek feedback on their implementation of new practices and work interdependently to clarify and build confidence of their use across the team.	Teams value the opportunity to observe each other as they implement new practices.
Examination, reflection, and celebration of impact	No celebration of implementation nor impact of the practices takes place.	Teams are beginning to see the impact of their new practices on the learning of students, including those who are low-achieving.	Teams routinely examine the impact of their practices on student learning and celebrate large and small wins as well as learn from their failures. They also make adjustments based on their new learning.	There is an observable mindset of collective efficacy across teams, and members know that they can continue to improve student learning through their collective efforts and refinement of practice.

Figure 3.7: Continuum of practice for implementation of quality instruction.

*Visit **go.SolutionTree.com/PLCbooks** for a free reproducible version of this figure.*

As shared in previous chapters, leaders can use this continuum on multiple occasions to monitor growth and highlight areas needed for improvement. Next, let's examine some actions that leaders might take to improve schoolwide instructional practice.

Act on Evidence to Improve Practice

When considering how to act on their analysis of the evidence they gather from the tools in this chapter, the question leaders should focus on is, How do we move forward? We recommend that leaders engage others in a shared vision of quality instruction, embed safeguards to ensure alignment to the standards, build shared knowledge in targeted areas of instructional quality, get schoolwide commitment to use new practices, monitor and support implementation of new practices, and build in reflection and celebration opportunities.

A Shared Picture of Quality Instruction

One of the most powerful activities school leaders can use to activate conversations is to create a shared picture of quality instruction. Leaders can view this as an extension of the school's vision statement, and engage teams in deeper conversation about the instructional practices they would consistently see if their school became what they would want for their own children. For instance, many schools' vision statements make a reference to all students receiving high-quality instruction. However, unless a conversation takes place that defines a collective picture of what high-quality instruction looks like (and doesn't look like), it is unlikely there will be clarity or consistency. There are multiple ways to organize such an activity, but the goal remains the same: engage all members in identifying the type of practices they will work toward so that all students can learn at high levels. For example, a school's vision statement might read something like this: "Our school strives to provide students with academically rigorous, relevant, and engaging learning experiences in a supportive and safe environment that gets students ready for their future work and community."

In preparation for further clarification and consensus, leaders can use a staff meeting to engage school members in carousel conversation. In advance, the leadership team can create posters with headings taken from the key words in the vision statement. For example, they might create posters with the following headings: *academically rigorous*, *relevant and engaging opportunities*, *prepared for the future*, *safe environment*, and *supportive environment*. Members of the school can rotate among the posters and list or describe the practices that would support each element. They may also describe the practices that would be incompatible with each element. Once posters are completed, and all staff have the opportunity to provide input, the leadership team could draft the indicators of quality instructional practices toward which all teachers would strive. After everyone had the opportunity to review the draft and provide input, leadership would engage in reaching consensus among all staff.

For example, figure 3.8 shows what one poster might look like after participants have a chance to engage in dialogue and reflect.

Some schools have adopted a formal model of instructional delivery to ensure quality instruction. This helps to clarify the elements or components of quality lesson design and delivery. For example, the Sheltered Instruction Observation Protocol (SIOP; Vogt, Echevarria, & Short, 2016) was designed to ensure all students, including those learning English, have access to and achieve the core curriculum through effective practices. The SIOP model includes the integration of the following eight

Academically Rigorous, Relevant, and Engaging Learning Experiences
Looks like or sounds like: • Aligned to the standards   • Appropriate for various levels of complexity   • Fosters meaningful interaction with peers around learning   • Uses real-world, relevant problems and information that motivate and interest students   • Student is an active problem solver   • Embeds student choice   • Clear targets for learning   • Exemplars for quality work   • Supports to help dependent learners become more independent and achieve higher-order thinking
Doesn't look like or sound like: • Low-level questioning   • One-way instruction (sit and get)   • No opportunities for students to reflect on their learning   • Unclear targets for learning   • No guidelines for quality

Figure 3.8: What key elements of a vision statement look like and sound like.

components, all of which have specific features or indicators of implementation with key practices.

1. **Lesson preparation:** Includes identifying content and language objectives for English learner students, as well as selecting specific techniques and supplemental materials to be used

2. **Interaction:** Includes strategies that promote student-to-student interactions, including grouping of students and other techniques to support language development

3. **Building background:** Includes identifying techniques for connecting students' personal experiences and past learning to lesson concepts

4. **Practice and application:** Includes strategies for providing students with application and hands-on practice

5. **Comprehensible input:** Includes techniques for presenting content information in ways that students will understand, including modeling and framing academic tasks

6. **Lesson delivery:** Includes improving student time on task, the active use of learning objectives, and strategies for engagement

7. **Strategies:** Includes specific strategies such as higher-order questioning, scaffolding techniques, and other strategies to promote learning

8. **Review and assessment:** Includes strategies for reviewing key concepts, and building in checks for understanding and feedback to support student learning

Another example is the 5E model, first developed in 1987 and later summarized for the Office of Science Education, National Institutes of Health by the Biological Sciences Curriculum Study (Bybee et al., 2006). This model supports quality learning in science and embeds the following components into the design of learning activities.

1. **Engage:** Using phenomena, problems, or scenarios to capture students' attention, access their prior knowledge, and stimulate their thinking

2. **Explore:** Providing time and resources for students to explore their ideas and think, plan, and investigate

3. **Explain:** Having students make connections between their new and prior learning to make sense of a particular concept

4. **Elaborate:** Encouraging students to apply their new learning to real-world applications

5. **Evaluate:** Having students review and assess what they have learned, and reflect on how they learned it

While some districts and schools may adopt a specific instructional model, others may identify their own indicators of quality instruction, as was the case at Park Avenue Elementary School in Stuttgart, Arkansas. Under the leadership of Principal Pam Dean and PLC coach Matt Devan, staff at the school defined their vision for quality instruction. Titled Instructional Expectations, as shown in figure 3.9, the educators set specific agreements about how they would structure their lessons to increase the likelihood of achieving high levels of learning. The compilation of their work is posted in the team rooms, and they reference it while designing their units of instruction.

An example of a district-created resource specifying instructional expectations came in response to the COVID-19 pandemic in the spring of 2020. To ensure effective delivery of virtual instruction across all classrooms, instructional leaders in Kildeer Countryside School District 96 in Buffalo Grove, Illinois, provided teachers a daily instruction framework. This framework not only set the expectation that all teachers will provide students with the elements of effective instruction but provided them with a Google Slides template containing placeholder slides for:

- An engaging lesson opening
- A clear learning objective

Staff Agree Students Need to Know:

- What they are learning—visually and verbally, objective, learning target, point of the lesson

- Why it is important—various ways, how it is relevant, benefits of the lesson

- How the lesson will flow—how we will learn this as a class, routine, agenda, first, then, and so on

- If they learned it—checking for understanding, opportunities to demonstrate understanding, what happens when they struggle

Staff Agree Teachers Need to Know:

- How they will make the curriculum materials relevant, interesting, and engaging for their students

- How they will facilitate opportunities for discourse and engagement (teacher to student, student to student, and student to teacher)

Source: © 2020 Park Avenue Elementary School. Used with permission.

Figure 3.9: Park Avenue Elementary School instructional expectations.

- Intentional activities designed to model, practice, and build independence in learning (for example, *I do, we do, you do*, also known as the gradual release of responsibility)

- Providing students with feedback and extensions

In a time that could easily become chaotic and result in a lack of quality instruction, this template provided support for quality lesson design and delivery in a virtual or hybrid classroom, and guided teachers to easily embed their own content information while consistently addressing the elements (Spiller, 2020).

Safeguards to Ensure Alignment to the Standards

Earlier in the chapter, we discussed the need to support the alignment of instruction to the standards, with priority being placed on those identified as essential. Schools can formally adopt protocols for backward design of units in which they have identified essential standards. For example, embedded within the protocols are specific strategies for ensuring alignment, including the step of unwrapping standards and identifying the level of complexity for each learning target using a framework such as Depth of Knowledge (DOK; Webb, 1997).

- **Level 1: Recall and reproduction**—Includes tasks requiring recollection of facts or using simple skills and procedures. For example, it includes basic reading and text comprehension (explicitly stated ideas and details), writing or reciting simple facts, or recalling definitions and terms.

- **Level 2: Basic application of skills and concepts**—Includes tasks that require more than one mental step and go beyond basic recall and reproduction. Students process information such as comparing, classifying, organizing, summarizing, predicting, and estimating.

- **Level 3: Strategic thinking**—Involves short-term higher-order thinking processes. Students must use a plan to solve problems based on evidence and justify their thinking choices.

- **Level 4: Extended thinking**—Involves tasks in which students synthesize information from multiple sources, often over an extended period of time. Students may also need to transfer knowledge from one domain to solve problems in another.

Teachers may also create schoolwide commitments to post student-friendly learning targets in each classroom that align to essential standards.

Shared Knowledge in Targeted Areas of Instructional Quality

For schools and districts that are making systematic changes in the quality of instruction, Marzano (2017) recommends creating a system that ensures teacher development. To accomplish this, leaders should make sure that teachers are clear about why the school is embracing a particular strategy or innovation; have a plan for how teachers acquire new learning and how that learning will be supported; provide self-assessments to teachers and use the results to determine next steps; observe classrooms for evidence of implementation; and assess the results.

Virtually any change in practice requires new learning (Muhammad & Cruz, 2019). Leaders can't expect any practice to be implemented without first building shared knowledge. Schools can build shared knowledge in multiple ways, including teacher attendance at traditional professional development events, professional reading, and working with consultants. However, the premise of a PLC is that while leaders might initially plant seeds to gain initial knowledge of new practices, they use the power of job-embedded professional learning to ensure implementation of those practices while they study their effectiveness. In job-embedded professional learning, teams engage in collective learning and action research, applying newly learned practices within the context of their day-to-day teaching. As part of their processes, teachers reflect on and discuss the implementation and impact of the practices as they relate to their students.

Part of this learning can come from sharing the evidence gathered from the tools in the Assess the Current Reality section of this chapter (page 81): walkthroughs, teacher interviews, and so on. Sharing the information with the guiding coalition as well as with the staff may be the most important action to take with these data. Facts can be a powerful tool to open the eyes of those who are unaware of a current reality. Make sure to keep data aggregated so that teachers don't feel it's being used to evaluate them. It is especially important to celebrate the positives that these tools reveal so that teachers stay motivated.

Teacher interviews are an especially rich source of feedback about implementation of new practices. Some teams or teachers may express confidence and enthusiasm about the practices they are working to implement. However, feedback from teachers may reveal a need for continued support. For instance, evidence from the feedback may point to a lack of clarity about a particular practice or a reluctance to implement for fear of failure. Leaders can use this feedback to determine the level and type of support needed in order to make further progress toward implementation.

Schoolwide Commitment to Use New Practices

Once leaders have established shared knowledge around effective instruction, they can engage their teams in a discussion about next steps to ensure that teams actively implement new strategies. It helps to gather input from each team by asking the question, "What practice does your team want to focus on first, and how do you think it will impact learning?" Giving teams a choice in how they will move forward helps to build ownership and consensus without creating a one-sided edict. The process encourages growth in practices and minimizes the likelihood that teams will feel overwhelmed because they participate in planning the implementation of something they feel they can do. Having teams make a commitment to trying a particular practice in public (that is, in front of other teams) builds accountability, especially if there is a reasonable time frame for reporting back so that members share how their implementation worked. Having such a time frame established will not only embed accountability but will create momentum for putting a new practice in action in a more timely fashion.

Monitor and Support While Celebrating Teams' Success

As teams move forward and engage in new instructional practices, leaders can monitor the level of implementation using a variety of strategies. While observing teams, leaders can ask how the new practices might be embedded into an upcoming unit of study. During classroom observations, some teachers may emerge as bright spots. Leaders can use these bright spots to model practices in front of others during team meetings (we call this *pop-up PD*), or have teachers make targeted observations in their classrooms (we call this *pop-in PD*).

Some specific strategies for monitoring the progress of teams include targeted learning walks, lesson study, teacher self-assessment, and examining artifacts. All of these provide valuable information about how implementation is going as well as opportunities to highlight what's going well so that leaders can recognize and celebrate successes.

Targeted Learning Walks

A powerful strategy for monitoring the level of implementation is the use of learning walks. Prior to engaging in such an activity, leaders can describe the practice and intent, clarifying that it is intended to be used as a means to gather schoolwide evidence of particular practices they have been working to implement. As part of the overview, leaders can clarify that it's not meant to be evaluative toward any teacher, and that evidence participants gather will be anonymous, that is, they will not specify names or classrooms. Additionally, everyone will have the opportunity to engage in the process.

To begin this activity, leaders structure groups of teachers to walk through the school while instruction is taking place to observe evidence of an instructional element in place. For example, a school may be working to make targets clear for students and engage them in giving and getting feedback. Prior to the meeting, the school leader would discuss the process with the assembled teams, which can be grade alike, course alike, or mixed. On a shared document, all educators define the look-fors of clear targets and quality feedback practices. In the discussion, members describe what they would see happening on the part of the teacher, the student, or through artifacts in the classroom. They might also indicate anything that they shouldn't see happening, as appropriate. Then, the leader schedules teams for their learning walks at specific times, perhaps organized by common preparation periods. Before walking through the classrooms, the groups review evidence charts and leaders clarify the process for observing in class and recording information.

The group can brainstorm the evidence of the specific strategies members will be looking for in their observations. For instance, if they are looking for evidence of active student engagement, they might list indicators such as *students are clear on the task, students are actively working or collaborating with other students to complete the task, the task is relevant*, and so on. Then they can create in advance a simple checklist that participants might use, such as that in figure 3.10.

Strategy 1:	☐ Strategy was being used.
	☐ Strategy wasn't being used.
	☐ Strategy wasn't being used but it wouldn't be appropriate.
Strategy 2:	☐ Strategy was being used.
	☐ Strategy wasn't being used.
	☐ Strategy wasn't being used but it wouldn't be appropriate.

Figure 3.10: Learning walk template.

*Visit **go.SolutionTree.com/PLCbooks** for a free reproducible version of this figure.*

Learning walks help teachers identify for themselves evidence of the school's collective practice. The improvement process is not simply driven by the principal.

Teachers are actively engaged, using the snapshot evidence they collect on their learning walk to reflect on the areas to celebrate and identify incompatible evidence. Collectively during a post-walk debriefing session, members can assemble these snapshots to create a larger picture of school practice, which helps them see the big picture of implementation. See figure 3.11 for an example of what this might look like for a team that has collected evidence about student engagement. Note that the discussion around evidence can also lead to some probing questions, which are listed on the right side of the chart.

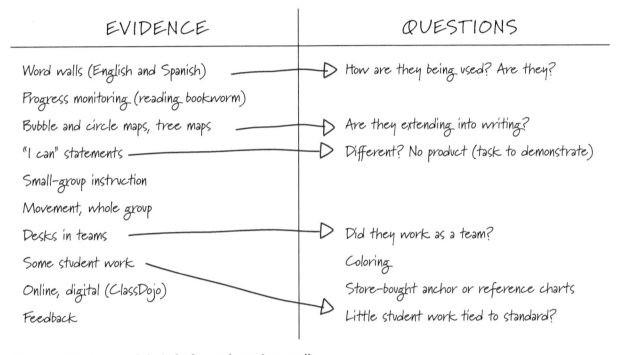

Figure 3.11: Group debrief after a learning walk.

Keep in mind that many instructional strategies may not be observable in every classroom every day. Take, for example, the idea of increased student dialogue in mathematics. It's not appropriate to use this strategy in every lesson. Therefore, the learning walk information should include an indicator of whether the strategy is appropriate to the learning target. The goal is to aggregate *all* of the information to determine whether teachers are using the strategy more frequently than in the past. As an example, one year in Chris's school, the leadership team wanted to know how much writing students were actually doing during class time and asked teachers and leaders to do frequent learning walks in all content areas. Through the process, they were able to gather evidence that gave them an accurate picture of how much writing students did during a typical school day.

When analyzing the classroom learning walk data, it is important to have a starting-point baseline. During early implementation, take note of how much teachers are using the strategy or innovation. These might be teachers who have used it in the past or the teachers who are getting on board quickly. Share the data regularly with the guiding coalition, taking care to use aggregate numbers rather than identifying individual teachers. Have the guiding coalition discuss what's happening from their perspectives on their teams.

Lesson Study

Many schools have embraced the idea of lesson study. This is a Japanese model in which teacher teams work together to plan and carry out lessons collaboratively (Ermeling & Graff-Ermeling, 2016). After the team collaboratively plans a lesson, one of the team members carries it out while the other team members are in the room observing the lesson as it's being taught and gathering data about what students are learning. After the session is complete, the team members get together to review the information they have collected and use it to improve the lesson based on what they learned. Another team member then teaches the lesson again while teammates observe for student learning. Depending on the size of the team, and amount of time available, the cycle may continue and allow other members the chance to teach. It should be noted that teams initially benefit from having a facilitator guide them in the process.

This method is a great way to develop highly effective collaborative teams. Leaders must ask themselves how teachers learn quality instruction in their schools. Is the focus on outside experts, or is the learning embedded into the work of collaborative teams? Moving from outside experts to teams learning together is an important step because it allows for the practice, feedback, and peer coaching support that are necessary to truly embed new practices.

Teacher Self-Assessment

Staff members can use the tool in figure 3.12 to reflect on their own current level of implementation. Teachers can use the results for private reflection on their practices, but ideally they will share their data with team members to obtain feedback and clarify specific needs for support.

The self-assessment can be converted to an electronic form that can quickly compile results; or leaders can provide it in print. When seeking general feedback and input on needs, leaders can keep the assessment anonymous.

Vertical Examination of Artifacts

In addition to leaders examining artifacts produced by teams, schools can use the power of vertical teams. For instance, each grade level can present or share artifacts related to some aspect of instruction. Perhaps a school has been working to build opportunities for students to engage in goal setting. Each team might bring some examples of how members are engaging students in the process, including specific

This self-assessment tool will help our school identify the level of implementation of _____.
We will use the information from this assessment to decide how to support you in order to deepen our implementation. Please complete the survey by placing a mark in the Yes or No column depending on your experience with this strategy or innovation. In the What Help Do I Need? column, please identify the support you need, such as resources, planning time, or direct support, as specifically as possible.

Implementation Statement	Yes	No	What Help Do I Need?
1. I don't know enough yet to try this in my classroom.			
2. I don't see how this strategy can be used in my situation.			
3. I haven't used the strategy in my classroom yet but am planning to do so soon.			
4. I understand why we are using this new strategy but haven't tried it yet.			
5. I have been given enough training to try out this new strategy.			
6. I have the resources (that is, materials) I need to try out this strategy.			
7. I have used this strategy in my classroom but don't yet feel confident that it works for me.			
8. I have used this strategy several times in my classroom and feel confident about its use.			
9. Using this strategy has made a difference for my students.			
10. I would be happy to help my team with this new strategy.			
11. My team and I have co-planned lessons with this strategy.			

Figure 3.12: Teacher self-assessment.

Visit **go.SolutionTree.com/PLCbooks** *for a free reproducible version of this figure.*

forms they use, or their plan to ensure that students intentionally reflect on their learning. Each grade-level or course-alike team would see how the others are building the strategies into their instruction, as well as the results through student work samples. Looking at relevant artifacts in a vertical fashion allows members of the school to compare strategies as well as expectations that build from grade to grade. We suggest that when engaging in such a process, schools use a clear protocol for giving and getting both warm and cool feedback. *Warm feedback* is considered positive in nature, something that is recognized as effective. *Cool feedback*, on the other hand, is constructive in nature and offers the recipients insights on possible ways to improve their work.

In figure 3.13, we provide an example of a protocol that leaders can use for course-alike or grade-level teams to swap and review lessons to ensure alignment of instruction and assessment. The context for this particular protocol would be partnering two teams who then take turns presenting a particular unit of study. The other team provides feedback on the protocol.

Timekeeper:	
Ten minutes	**Get ready to share:** All teams review their work in the unit. Prepare to share: • Unit focus • Essential standards and learning targets • Formative and end-of-unit assessments • Shared picture of proficiency
Four to five minutes	**Presentation:** The first team presents its unit overview, highlighting the previous bullets. During this time, the review team follows along and jots down any notes or questions it has during the presentation (no talking). The presenting team also poses a focusing question for the participants, which highlights an area in which they'd like feedback or input (for example, "We'd like everyone to look at our formative assessments to see if they make sense and align to the end-of-unit outcomes").
One minute	**Clarification:** The review team can ask logistical questions (if any), but these shouldn't focus on content. For instance, the review team may want to clarify the manner in which materials were presented to students.
Four minutes	**Gathering information:** Participants silently examine the unit, take notes, and come up with questions based on what they see in the unit. They reflect and provide warm and cool feedback based on: • Clarity of student outcomes • Alignment of instruction and assessment • Strategies for engagement and high-quality instruction
Four minutes	**Warm and cool feedback:** Participants engage in sharing their warm and cool feedback among themselves (aloud) while the presenting team listens. Possible prompts for this feedback include: *I noticed . . .* *I wondered . . .* *Something I'd like the team to consider is . . .*
Two minutes	**Presenting team reflection:** After listening to feedback, the presenting team members reflect on what they heard and share how they intend to integrate the feedback into their plan. (Note: At this point, the teams switch roles and re-engage in the protocol.)

Figure 3.13: Vertical unit review protocol.

*Visit **go.SolutionTree.com/PLCbooks** for a free reproducible version of this figure.*

As leaders monitor the implementation of instructional strategies, we suggest that they embed recognition and celebration of efforts and impact on a routine basis. If a school has determined that it will work on a schoolwide basis to improve a specific area of instruction, then small activities can be embedded throughout the year to ensure that this focus area stays in the forefront. When activities can do the double duty of celebrating and sharing the new impact of instructional practices, it increases not only efficiency, but strengthens the collective efficacy of teams.

When monitoring the implementation of instructional strategies or innovations, it's essential to be mindful of what's going well, not only to make sure that success continues but because recognition and celebration of successes are strong motivating factors. Leaders may see some indications that particular teachers are having a lot of success with this strategy or innovation. Think of how teachers provide extensions to students who have already mastered a learning target. When teachers have mastered a strategy, what might those teachers do to extend their own learning? Can they be recruited to provide model lessons to teachers who want to see the strategy in action? Could they submit an article about the strategy to their professional organization's journal? Can they do a workshop at a staff meeting or professional learning day? The intent of spotlighting highly effective teachers or teams is not to overwhelm but to multiply their impact and to ensure their continued professional learning. Leaders must clarify this intent with any teachers they approach to fulfill such roles, and get assurance of their willingness to participate.

Improving Instruction Is an Ongoing, Incremental Process

The overall quality of instruction can have significant influence on schoolwide achievement. By using tools to examine the major elements of instruction, leaders can identify strengths and take action to improve areas in a targeted fashion. The work of improving instruction is incremental and best achieved by building shared knowledge and consensus for moving forward among individual teachers who, of course, are also members of collaborative teams. It's not an overnight process and requires opportunities for practice and feedback, monitoring, and support. Finally, improving instruction requires recognition and celebration of efforts to implement new practices and the impact they make on student learning. In the next chapter, we will discuss strategies for assessing the quality of schoolwide systems of support.

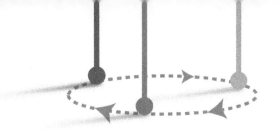

Chapter 4

SCHOOLWIDE SYSTEMS OF SUPPORT

As schools progress past the initial steps of the PLC process, new issues start to arise. Teams are starting to come together on instruction, but leaders may begin to see inconsistencies in how teams are handling interventions and extensions to support students, leaving gaps in student achievement and equity. A multitiered system of supports, such as response to intervention (RTI), is a schoolwide system that addresses this issue. The question leaders should ask themselves is, "How is our school providing support to our students?" As the following scenario illustrates, teams often find it difficult to navigate interventions and extensions without some guidance.

> At a high school in its second year of operating as a PLC, the leadership team spent its first year laying the foundation for its work, developing its collaborative teams, and working on the four critical questions. As they've read more widely about the RTI process, the leadership team members have grown concerned that they haven't really developed a schoolwide system of support but have instead left it to each team to respond to students who need more time and support. Today the leadership team is meeting to plan its next steps on implementing its support system. Members begin the meeting by making a list of all of the different ways teams have found to support students. It is readily apparent that there are many different ideas about how to do this throughout the building. Then they begin to list the problems teams are

facing. The science leader starts by saying his team is experiencing a problem because some students need help from a number of different teachers, who then end up competing for time with these students. The mathematics leader adds that in any intervention group, her team sees a wide diversity of learning issues, which makes it hard to find the best way to help. The ELA leader agrees and explains that he has students still struggling to read complex text, let alone learning how to analyze and write about ideas in the text. The social studies leader brings up the concern that her team really can't get time with its students who need support because the only time it has carved out is before and after school, and many students aren't available then.

The leadership team agrees that expecting each team to develop its own response system hasn't been effective and that, instead, team members need to develop a schoolwide program that allows students to receive high-quality initial instruction, to engage in opportunities for intervention to close the gaps they have in learning at high levels, and to access extensions when they've demonstrated mastery of essential standards.

What's happening in this high school is a situation we often encounter when we work with teams who are new to the PLC process. There are so many urgent decisions to make—laying the foundation, finding collaboration time, identifying essential standards—that developing a schoolwide system to respond to students' needs gets put to the side. Collaborative teams begin to individually develop ways to support their students as team members become more proficient at using data and working collaboratively.

However, when the teams lead the response process without a schoolwide system, issues such as lack of access and equity quickly emerge. Students often need help in more than one course or subject, so they might be taken from initial instruction in one subject for support in another, or they may not receive help at all in some situations. Couple this with the idea that students who have achieved mastery should have access to extensions and enrichment, and the individual pieces no longer support an effective system. Because of this need for a truly schoolwide system, leaders must understand systemic response and be mindful of how extensions are as important as interventions. In this chapter, we'll discuss both considerations and then highlight some tools leaders can use to assess, analyze, and act as they support teams.

Understand Systematic Response

In their book *Taking Action*, RTI experts Austin Buffum, Mike Mattos, and Janet Malone (2018) present what they call the RTI pyramid, which is a useful way to visualize how RTI works. The pyramid, as shown in figure 4.1, consists of three tiers that organize instruction. Tier 1 is the initial course- or grade-level instruction that all students receive. Tier 2 is additional time and support for students who need supplemental help with course- or grade-level instruction. Lastly, Tier 3 is for students who need intense remediation on universal skills that most likely should have been learned in previous years.

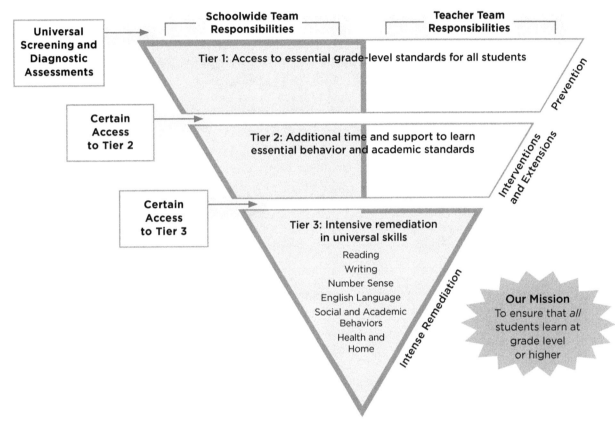

Source: Buffum et al., 2018, p. 18.

Figure 4.1: The RTI pyramid.

Buffum and his colleagues (2018) provide a detailed list of how different teams share responsibility for the many actions a school must take for an effective RTI plan. The bold line in figure 4.1 that separates the first two tiers of the pyramid into halves helps delineate these responsibilities. Buffum and his colleagues (2018) advise that schools should consider three types of teams that take the lead in different areas of responsibility. The first is the school leadership team, which should take the big-picture view and look after schoolwide responsibilities; the second are the collaborative teams that are responsible for the students they serve; and third is the school intervention team, which is responsible for the more technical responsibilities of ensuring that students who need intensive support are getting the help they need. This team may comprise subject-matter specialists, school psychologists, administrators, social workers, special educators, and behavior specialists. Buffum and his colleagues (2018) make the point that they use the term *lead responsibility* to show that they don't mean *sole* responsibility—there is some shared responsibility for each of the actions. To aid our discussion of how leaders can assess the overall success of their intervention system, we've listed the actions that Buffum and his colleagues (2018) delegate to the schools and teams in figure 4.2.

Tier	Schoolwide Responsibility Led by the Leadership Team	Collaborative Team Responsibility	School Intervention Team Responsibility
1	• Ensure access to grade-level essential standards for all students. • Eliminate below-grade-level tracks. • Identify essential academic and social behaviors. • Provide preventions (immediate response when students don't demonstrate proficiency on a common formative assessment) to support students.	• Identify essential standards. • Develop unit plans that allow time to teach, assess, and respond to essential standards. • Write and use common formative assessments. • Identify students who need Tier 2 support.	Not applicable
2	• Create a master schedule that provides time for support when no new Tier 1 instruction is occurring. • Identify students who have at-risk behaviors. • Plan and implement the teaching of academic and social behaviors. • Coordinate skill (how-to) and will (motivation) supports for students.	• Design and implement supplemental interventions for academic essential standards. • Develop preassessments for prerequisite skills as needed. • Monitor progress of Tier 2 students. • Extend student learning for students who have mastered grade-level content.	Not applicable
3	• Identify students who need intensive support. • Create a problem-solving team. • Prioritize resources available by greatest area of need. • Assess effectiveness of interventions.		• Diagnose and monitor Tier 3 interventions. • Ensure proper intervention intensity. • Determine if special education is needed and justifiable.

Source: Adapted from Buffum et al., 2018.

Figure 4.2: Responsibilities within the RTI system.

Leadership Team Responsibilities

Let's first consider what schoolwide actions the school leadership team should take. The most obvious task is to develop a master schedule that can support both collaborative team time for meetings and protected teaching time for supporting students. This intervention time must occur when there is no new Tier 1 instruction taking place; no student should have to sacrifice receiving essential instruction and risk falling further behind in order to get support.

In elementary schools, leaders often carve this time out of ELA and mathematics blocks that allow flexibility so that a teacher or specialist can provide the necessary support. All of the teams' teachers set aside the same time period so that every student is available and won't lose access to new content. To provide response based on student need, for example, the team may set up small groups for differentiated instruction geared toward the specific learning targets students haven't yet mastered. In some schools, the team moves students between teachers in order to provide the support they need at a given time. Specialists often take the responsibility for students who need intense intervention. These groups are flexible, and students can receive more or less support as their needs are identified.

For secondary schools, there are several different ways to designate intervention time, but it often is some sort of flex period that leaders add to ensure students aren't in their core or supplemental classes. This type of schedule allows students to be brought together in a flexible way. It also makes sure students aren't assigned to a particular session for an entire year or an entire quarter. To see many different ways secondary schools have found time for these interventions, see *It's About Time: Planning Interventions and Extensions in Secondary School* (Mattos & Buffum, 2015). Chapter 7, "The FLEX Schedule," shows how Jane Addams Junior High School in Schaumburg, Illinois, started with a traditional middle school master schedule and included flex time. In this chapter, then-principal Steve Pearce (2015) shares how he and his staff worked through several iterations as they learned what worked and didn't work for their school. Figure 4.3 (page 110) shows how the school was able to carve out time by slightly shortening each period from forty minutes to thirty-seven and briefly going over announcements instead of spending several minutes at the start and close of each school day.

Additionally, the leadership team has the primary responsibility for developing a continuum of academic and social behaviors to be taught and assessed. John Hannigan, Jessica Djabrayan Hannigan, Mike Mattos, and Austin Buffum (2021) list the following as academic behaviors: metacognition, self-concept, self-monitoring, motivation, strategy, and volition (grit). They list social behaviors as responsible verbal and physical interactions with peers and adults, appropriate language, respect for property and materials, independently staying on a required task, and regular attendance (Hannigan et al., 2021). In a traditional school, teachers set up the expectations for their own classrooms, and these often differ widely among

Announcements	Shortened
Period 1	7:38–8:17
FLEX	8:20–8:50
Period 2	8:53–9:30
Period 3	9:33–10:10
Period 4	10:13–10:51
Period 5	10:54–11:32
Period 6	11:35–12:13
Period 7	12:16–12:54
Period 8	12:57–1:34
Period 9	1:37–2:15
Announcements	Shortened

Source: Pearce, 2015, p. 153.

Figure 4.3: Sample schedule with built-in flex time for interventions.

team members. When the school leadership team takes responsibility for determining the expectations across the school building, as well as ensuring that a combination of classroom teachers and specialists teach and assess these expectations, it ensures equitable expectations no matter which teacher a student is assigned. A comprehensive guide to establishing a behavior system aligned to the RTI at Work™ process is available in *Behavior Solutions: Teaching Academic and Social Skills Through RTI at Work* (Hannigan et al., 2021).

The leadership team should also review course offerings to eliminate classes that are not on a grade-level track. When students enroll in a basic algebra course when others at the same grade level have progressed beyond algebra, they won't be taught the appropriate grade-level standards and will inevitably remain below grade level. Instead, the school should expect all students to take grade-level courses but provide the scaffolding and support the students need to learn the curriculum.

Because the leadership team is in charge of the big picture of supporting students, it is also responsible for examining and distributing the necessary resources for that support. In some cases, resources include teachers and specialists, and in other cases, they include materials. Along with this comes the need to consider priorities for time. If students need support in several different areas, the leadership team must consider how to balance these needs so that teams aren't competing for access to students. This is especially true when considering whether a student support need is about the *skill* or the *will* of learning. *Skill* interventions are provided around academic standards and *will* interventions for students who have or could have mastered the skill but lack the motivation to do so (Buffum et al., 2018). Some students need additional instruction to learn *skills*. Other students need help with motivation and work completion—the *will*. Some students need both. And, as we've heard many teachers comment, it's hard to distinguish between these two. Is the student unmotivated to learn or reluctant to admit that he or she needs extra help?

Collaborative Team Responsibilities

Collaborative teams are best suited to work with essential standards in the curriculum and, therefore, these teams are responsible for identifying these standards and creating pacing guides to allow time to teach, assess, and support students learning these standards. These teams write and administer common formative assessments, and analyze the results by examining students' responses to the items on the assessment. As they have the most professional knowledge about how to help students who struggle to learn their content, collaborative teams are responsible for developing strategies when students need more support to learn them. For Tier 1 support, collaborative teams use common formative assessments to diagnose where the learning stopped on essential learning targets as well as plan how best to provide additional instruction to move toward mastery. Tier 2 support is typically offered by collaborative teams when a student has already received Tier 1 instruction and support but still hasn't mastered essential learning targets for that grade level.

Collaborative teams, along with specialists, also have responsibility for teaching and assessing the essential behaviors identified by the leadership team. While the leadership team has primary responsibility for identifying the targeted schoolwide behaviors, it should survey the collaborative team members to make sure everyone has a voice in what these behaviors are. Regarding who teaches the behavior supports, Hannigan and his colleagues (2021) write:

> Similar to academic interventions, behavior interventions require the staff members best trained in this area to take lead responsibility in Tier 2. To this end, we highly recommend that the staff with the most expertise in intensive behavior intervention development—the school counselor, special education teacher, school psychologist, or social worker, for example—help develop, implement, and monitor the individualized plans. (p. 176)

School Intervention Team Responsibilities

Finally, the school intervention team is responsible for diagnosing and supporting students who need intensive support, otherwise known as Tier 3 support. These students have been identified as lacking important foundational skills that could prevent them from learning grade-level content. They provide and monitor these interventions to make sure they are effective and to ensure students aren't staying in an intervention for too long. If special education is needed, this team would refer and evaluate students. For example, the school intervention team might have identified a group of sixth-grade students as needing support to learn some essential fourth- and fifth-grade mathematics standards, so in addition to receiving instruction in sixth-grade standards in their regular mathematics class, they have a Tier 3 support group to learn the essential standards they've missed.

Extend the Learning for Beyond-Proficiency Students

Leaders must also be mindful of what systemwide support looks like for students who have mastered the essential standards and can benefit from enrichment and extension opportunities. Building on the RTI pyramid, we adopted a mirror image that adds three more tiers as shown in figure 4.4.

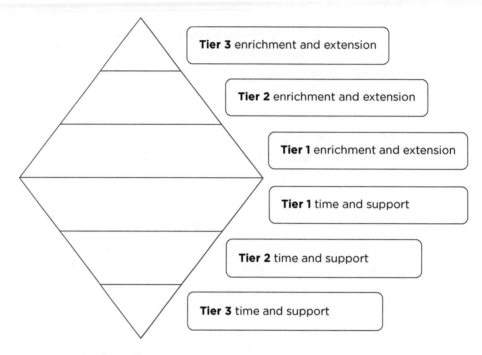

Tier 3 enrichment and extension

Tier 2 enrichment and extension

Tier 1 enrichment and extension

Tier 1 time and support

Tier 2 time and support

Tier 3 time and support

Source: Bailey & Jakicic, 2019, p. 179.

Figure 4.4: Extending the RTI pyramid.

As discussed previously, the upside-down pyramid represents the RTI process for supporting students who need extra help to achieve mastery. In the diagram in figure 4.4, this includes the bottom three rows. Additionally, in this diagram we add the top three rows to the diamond to represent the three tiers that schools will use to enrich and extend the learning of their proficient students (Bailey & Jakicic, 2019). In the same way that Tier 1 support in RTI considers what instruction *all* students have access to, Tier 1 support in the extended pyramid considers what extension opportunities *all* students have access to. Tier 2 support is offered to *some* students that are identified after common assessments as needing more than is offered to all students; Tier 2 extensions are offered to *some* students who have mastered the essential targets required for all students to learn. In the RTI pyramid, a *few* students need Tier 3 intensive support, and in the extended pyramid, a *few* students can benefit from more significant extensions.

What does this look like for the schoolwide system? How can leaders formatively assess the effectiveness of the instruction for these students? Starting with Tier 1 on the extension pyramid, leaders will want to make sure that students are engaged in work that is at a higher level of cognitive demand on the grade-level standards. That is, while some students are getting support to learn the grade-level essentials during Tier 1, students who have already mastered those standards should be engaging with activities that teachers develop at a higher DOK level—typically these are short-term instructional activities. In chapter 8 (page 205), we dig more deeply into how collaborative teams plan and execute these activities, including how to build scales to define them.

Since Tier 2 response happens for all students who need it during a time when no new instruction takes place, leaders must develop the master schedule to accommodate this requirement. Typically, the extension activities occur during the same time that students who need additional support are receiving interventions. Student groups for Tier 2 instruction may be together for a number of days or weeks at a time. Teams should plan lessons accordingly. One of the ways to do this is to consider lessons around the supporting standards that students didn't have as much time with during regular instruction. As we'll discuss thoroughly in the next chapter, teams identify *essential* standards, which all students must know, from their complete list of standards. They still teach the rest of the standards, called supporting standards, but don't have to assess and provide interventions on them. Extension can also include enrichment lessons on topics or standards not typically found in the general curriculum and lessons on topics students are interested to learn more about.

Tier 3 responses for already proficient students might come in the form of lessons delivered by a gifted and talented specialist or through an accelerated course or classroom, around topics identified by student choice, or working with a mentor teacher. In chapter 8 we provide additional detail about how a school identifies and plans these offerings.

In the following sections, we provide tools leaders can use to reflect on the current context of their school, gather information about the important steps of implementing a schoolwide system, and consider suggestions about making an action plan to build and sustain an effective system of support.

Assess the Current Reality

Take a few minutes to reflect on the idea of a schoolwide support system within the context of your school by answering the guiding questions in figure 4.5 (page 114).

Building a system that supports student learning requires shared leadership practices. That is, no one person can effectively be responsible for scheduling, assigning responsibility, delivering support, and monitoring student progress, though, as discussed earlier, different teams have different lead responsibilities. The same idea goes for a lone teacher trying to support a student with significant needs. The teacher needs a system of support for students with these needs so they will get the necessary

Guiding Questions	Reflection on Context
What evidence do we have that our staff take collective responsibility for all our students? Consider the current ways time and support are provided when students need more help.	
Have we identified the three teams we need for an effective response—leadership team, collaborative teams, and school intervention team? How well do they each understand their responsibilities in this process?	
Does the master schedule provide time for students who need Tier 2 and Tier 3 support to receive it without missing critical Tier 1 instruction? If not, what do we need to change in order for us to effectively serve our students?	
How are we currently tracking students who receive interventions and extensions? Are there ways to make this more effective?	
What is the current status of the extensions our staff provide to students who've reached proficiency? What next steps should we take in this area to meet all students' needs?	

Figure 4.5: Guiding questions to consider the context for a schoolwide system of support.

*Visit **go.SolutionTree.com/PLCbooks** for a free reproducible version of this figure.*

help. As such, the first thing leaders should consider about their context is whether there is a collective responsibility for student learning. As a principal, Chris can remember a time when she saw that shift in thinking from individual to collective responsibility with her own staff. The staff had started making the shift that had teachers working collaboratively to support students' academic learning. When they started building a schoolwide system for supporting students with academic and social behavior issues, however, the staff suddenly realized how much more effective they were than when teachers were responsible for the individual students on their class lists. Now individual teachers didn't have to find time at lunch or after school to work with students who hadn't completed their work; instead, the school had a plan for support during the school day. Since they had a variety of levels of support, if one response wasn't effective, they had another response to try. Creating this culture of collective responsibility often takes time, and leaders need to start building their response system even though not all teachers are championing collective responsibility at the start. Remember, some teachers need to see something work before they can make the needed change in practice.

The next matter to consider is whether you have the three teams in place needed to develop the overall system: (1) the leadership team, (2) collaborative teams where every teacher is a member of at least one, and (3) a school intervention team. If not, get these teams started as soon as possible, making sure all members are aware of the responsibilities for the team they're on (see Understand Systematic Response, page 106).

The final matter to think about is the status of the master schedule. Is there time allocated for all three tiers of support? Do teams realize that Tier 1 happens as a part of regular instruction but that Tiers 2 and 3 have to happen when there is no new Tier 1 instruction occurring? We also discuss this further in part 2 of this book (page 133).

When assessing their current system of support for students, leaders should keep in mind the question, What's our current reality? The biggest thing to look for is evidence that the school is developing a culture of collective responsibility. Because this is often a major shift for schools, leaders, including team leaders, coaches, and administrators, must monitor the actions that will show evidence that their staff members truly believe in collective responsibility. One piece of evidence they should see is teachers talking about *our kids* and *our responses* rather than *my kids* and *my responses*. When the team is building a list of its essential standards, members avoid talking about whether some standards might be too complex for some of their students to learn. Instead, they look for the standards that will be most important for student learning in their grade or content area. Another action leaders will see occurs at data meetings. Rather than focusing only on their assigned students, the team looks at the big picture of its results. Members examine actual student work, looking for clarity about student misconceptions or misunderstandings. They share their instructional strategies so that they can determine if one strategy was more effective for a group of students than others. They plan the response together. Interventions may be planned so that students are assigned to a particular teacher based on the learning target they need to have retaught rather than having the classroom teacher keep all of his or her students.

In this section we'll make sure leaders have the tools to gather information about these important steps as well as suggestions about making an action plan to build and sustain an effective system of support. To help them gather evidence, we suggest the following tools.

- Collective Responsibility Staff Survey
- Systems of Support Alignment Tool
- Master Schedule Checklist
- Effective Tracking Systems Tools
- Behavioral Supports Checklist

Collective Responsibility Staff Survey

The tool in figure 4.6 (page 116) is a staff survey intended to gather evidence about the current beliefs that staff members have about collective responsibility. The survey asks teachers to respond with *yes, no,* or *not applicable* to a series of questions related

Statement	Yes	No	Not Applicable	What Evidence Do You Have?
1. We believe all students can learn at high levels.				
2. We expect all students to be able to meet proficiency on all our essential standards.				
3. We value data for what they can tell us we should do next.				
4. We believe that we can collaboratively overcome outside challenges our students may have.				
5. Our team takes responsibility for all the students we are assigned.				
6. We chose essential standards that require high cognitive demand.				
7. We have reached consensus on what proficiency looks like for our essential standards.				
8. When students experience difficulty learning, we look to ourselves to put a plan in place to help.				
9. We collaboratively plan how to respond when students need support.				
10. We collaboratively plan how to respond when students need extensions.				
11. When assigning students extensions or support, we consider which teacher is most capable of effectively responding.				

Figure 4.6: Collective responsibility staff survey.

*Visit **go.SolutionTree.com/PLCbooks** for a free reproducible version of this figure.*

to this culture. However, we also ask them to identify evidence they have for their response, which requires more reflection than a simple response. The whole team can also work together to do this survey by brainstorming together what evidence they have to support their answers.

Systems of Support Alignment Tool

Earlier in this chapter we featured a chart (figure 4.2, page 108) laying out the responsibilities recommended by Buffum and his colleagues (2018). Putting all of the pieces in place for a robust intervention system takes time: members for each team need to be identified and must learn their responsibilities on their teams, frequently the master schedule needs to be revised to align with the time needs for interventions to occur, and the assessment system must be engineered to provide a continuum of assessments, from classroom formative to yearly summative. The tool in figure 4.7 (page 118) provides leaders with a checklist they can use to determine how well their school's system of support is aligned to best practice. This tool can help leaders keep track of the current reality and set specific next steps for the school to take.

This assessment might start with the leadership team discussing where responsibilities *are* and *are not yet* aligned. If some are not aligned, is that because, for their school, the best team to take the lead responsibility may not be the team identified by Buffum and colleagues (2018) to do that work? Leaders should ask themselves whether there are responsibilities on this checklist that haven't yet been assigned to a team in their school.

Master Schedule Checklist

When schools begin the PLC process, one of the initial tasks leaders must take on is developing a master schedule that will provide common meeting time for collaborative teams and common teaching time for teams providing interventions and extensions. To do this, the leadership team must first determine which teachers will be on which collaborative teams. In many cases, teams seem obvious. All first-grade teachers will plan together. All algebra I teachers will plan together. However, this becomes more complex when the leadership team looks more carefully at singletons, such as special education teachers who work with more than one grade level or content area, elementary art or music teachers, guidance counselors, or the high school ceramics teacher. And, if these teachers work electronically with someone in another school, both master schedules must allocate planning time in concert with the other school. Chapter 2 (page 39) lays out more specific details for developing collaborative teams for singletons.

The other major consideration is that leaders need to allocate time for Tier 2 and 3 support keeping the following things in mind.

- The support cannot happen at a time when collaborative teams are delivering new Tier 1 instruction.

Tier	Schoolwide Responsibility Led by the Leadership Team	Collaborative Team Responsibility	School Intervention Team Responsibility
1	☐ Ensure access to grade-level essential standards for all students. ☐ Eliminate below-grade-level tracks. ☐ Identify essential academic and social behaviors. ☐ Provide preventions (immediate response when students don't demonstrate proficiency on a common formative assessment) to support students.	☐ Identify essential standards. ☐ Develop unit plans to make time to teach, assess, and respond to essential standards. ☐ Write and use common formative assessments. ☐ Identify students who need Tier 2 support.	
2	☐ Create a master schedule that provides time for support when no new Tier 1 instruction is occurring. ☐ Identify students who have at-risk behaviors. ☐ Plan and implement the teaching of academic and social behaviors. ☐ Coordinate skill (how-to) and will (motivation) supports for students.	☐ Design and implement supplemental interventions for academic essential standards. ☐ Develop preassessments for prerequisite skills as needed. ☐ Monitor progress of Tier 2 students. ☐ Extend student learning for students who have mastered grade-level content.	
3	☐ Identify students who need intensive support. ☐ Create a problem-solving team. ☐ Prioritize resources available by greatest area of need. ☐ Assess effectiveness of interventions.		☐ Diagnose and monitor Tier 3 interventions. ☐ Ensure proper intervention intensity. ☐ Determine if special education is needed and justifiable.

Source: Buffum et al., 2018.

Figure 4.7: Systems of support alignment tool.

*Visit **go.SolutionTree.com/PLCbooks** for a free reproducible version of this figure.*

- The time must be flexible so that students can receive all tiers of support as soon as evidence suggests they need it and can be dismissed when they no longer need the support.

- The time must be embedded in the school day so that students can't opt out of attending intervention.

- The most appropriate professionals must be available to teach these interventions.

We offer the checklist in figure 4.8 for leaders to analyze the effectiveness of their master schedule after gathering information for all teachers.

Does our schedule provide time for collaborative teams to meet?	What modifications will we need to make to our master schedule to make it more effective?
☐ All teachers are assigned to at least one collaborative team. ☐ The schedule allows collaborative teams time to meet regularly for at least forty-five to fifty-five minutes per week. ☐ Collaborative team time is protected from agenda items not related to the four critical questions. ☐ Specialists and coaches can meet with the teams they work with. ☐ There is a plan in place for teams who need to work vertically.	
Does our schedule provide time to respond to student needs?	What modifications will we need to make to our master schedule to make it more effective?
☐ There is time in the schedule for students to receive Tier 2 support when no new Tier 1 instruction is occurring. ☐ Tier 2 time is flexible in a way that allows students to attend whenever they need help. ☐ Tier 3 time is allocated in a way that allows students to also access Tier 1 and 2 learning. ☐ Tier 3 time is flexible so that students can attend when they need help but can be dismissed when needs have been met. ☐ Collaborative teams have developed pacing guides and unit plans that allocate Tier 1 support time for students identified through common formative assessments.	

Figure 4.8: Master schedule checklist.

*Visit **go.SolutionTree.com/PLCbooks** for a free reproducible version of this figure.*

Effective Tracking Systems Tools

If systems of support are to be effective, it's vital that leaders track their data on which students are receiving which levels of support. If we learned anything during the sudden move to remote learning in 2020, it was that having specific and accessible data about student learning helped ensure students were receiving the level of support they needed. For example, a collaborative team might use a simple data table to assign students to Tier 2 groups after they have delivered the common formative assessment and provided an immediate response. The sample table in figure 4.9 (page 120) lists students who still need help when the class is ready to move on. As students demonstrate proficiency, teachers can delete their names from the table.

The school intervention team must also keep records for students receiving intensive support. Intervention team members regularly determine whether the level of support is appropriate for each of these students to make sure students don't become stuck in an intervention group after their needs are met. The chart in figure 4.10 (page 121) shows what this data tracking might include.

Standard: Quote accurately from a text when explaining what the text says explicitly and when drawing inferences from the text (R1.5.1a).

	Tier 2 Groups		
Learning Targets	**Classroom Teacher 1**	**Classroom Teacher 2**	**Classroom Teacher 3**
Quote accurately from the text when explaining what the text says explicitly.	Student 1 Student 2	Student 3	Student 4 Student 5 Student 6
Quote accurately from the text when drawing inferences from the text.	Student 1	Student 3	Student 4 Student 5
Annotate the text to show the explicit details the author provides as well as the places inferences might be made from the text.	(Teachers will add student names after they have given the common formative assessment on this target.)		
Use text features to answer text-dependent questions.	(Teachers will add student names after they have given the common formative assessment on this target.)		

Source for standard: National Governors Association Center for Best Practices (NGA) & Council of Chief State School Officers (CCSSO), 2010a.

Figure 4.9: Sample Tier 2 tracking tool.

Visit go.SolutionTree.com/PLCbooks for a free reproducible version of this figure.

Whatever tools that teams use to track their students, leaders need to determine whether their methods are working. The checklist in figure 4.11 can help determine if the tracking systems are effective.

Behavioral Supports Checklist

Equally as important as identifying essential academic standards as the foundation for academic supports is having systemwide expectations for student behavior. These expectations should include both academic behaviors (for example, motivation and self-monitoring) and social behaviors (for example, respect for property and materials, attendance, and responsible interactions with peers and adults). The school must have a proactive plan to teach these behaviors if it expects students to demonstrate them. In addition, teachers must implement these expectations equally across the school and should consider them non-negotiable. This means a teacher cannot opt out of expectations agreed on by the school. Figure 4.12 (page 122) demonstrates what such a behavioral supports assessment checklist looks like, with sample wording for implementation expectations.

Tier 3 Tracking				
Student Name	Standards Not Met	How Support Will Be Delivered and by Whom	Anticipated Retest Date	Outcome of Retest

Figure 4.10: Sample Tier 3 tracking tool.

*Visit **go.SolutionTree.com/PLCbooks** for a free reproducible version of this figure.*

Tier 2 Tracking	Yes or No	Ideas for Improvement
We have a Tier 2 data tracking system in place.		
Access is available for everyone who needs it.		
The collaborative team regularly updates the data.		
Teams use data to identify students who need Tier 2 support and on which targets they need help.		
The tracking system lists specific essential learning targets for each student identified.		
Tier 3 Tracking	**Yes or No**	**Ideas for Improvement**
We have a Tier 3 data tracking system in place.		
Access is available for everyone who needs it.		
The school intervention team or the teacher providing the support regularly updates the data.		
Teams use multiple data sources to identify students for Tier 3 support.		

Figure 4.11: Effective tracking systems tool.

*Visit **go.SolutionTree.com/PLCbooks** for a free reproducible version of this figure.*

Criteria	Consistently Implemented	In Progress	Not Yet
We have a schoolwide behavioral system, and both teachers and students are aware of the expectations we have established.			
All teachers consistently teach and monitor identified behaviors.			
Our system emphasizes positive relationships.			
Our plan includes both social and academic behaviors.			
Our plan includes a process in which students learn what expectations are and what they look like in practice.			
We recognize and reward positive behaviors.			
We have a process in place to identify students who need behavioral support.			
When students need additional support, our plan provides it without removing them from Tier 1 instruction.			

Figure 4.12: Behavioral supports checklist.

Visit go.SolutionTree.com/PLCbooks for a free reproducible version of this figure.

When schools don't establish systemwide expectations for behavior, students learn for themselves what's acceptable in each teacher's classroom. They recognize some of their teachers as *easy* and some as *hard*. With common expectations, students find it easier to understand and comply with expectations. At the same time, when teachers see that there is a schoolwide system to support students struggling with behavioral concerns, they know that they are not alone in trying to help them.

Analyze Patterns and Priorities

The scenario at the start of this chapter imagines a school that is just beginning to develop its system of support. We realize that some leaders will recognize this situation in their own schools. We also realize that others have a system in place and want to use formative assessments to determine ways to improve their system. To that end we suggest that schools that are relatively new to this process might initially want to focus on the first three tools: (1) the Collective Responsibility Staff Survey in figure 4.6 (page 116), (2) the Systems of Support Alignment Tool in figure 4.7 (page 118), and (3) the Master Schedule Checklist in figure 4.8 (page 119). They are the priorities that need to be in place first for an effective system—in other words, the big rocks, to use a metaphor borrowed from Stephen R. Covey, A. Roger Merrill, and Rebecca R. Merrill (1994). Covey and his cowriters (1994) tell the story of a man who puts large rocks in a jar and asks, "Is the jar filled?" When his audience replies in the affirmative, he then adds gravel to the jar. When asked again if the jar is filled, the group responds that yes, it is now. Then he takes out a bag of sand and adds it to the jar. This metaphor is helpful in illustrating that, to be most effective, it's always best to start with putting the big rocks in place and then move further into the details to fill up the remaining spaces.

Starting with the Collective Responsibility Staff Survey (figure 4.6, page 116) allows leaders to take stock of how effectively their school is building the right culture to be successful with the PLC process. As you analyze the responses from the staff, consider that the first four statements in the survey relate to the teacher's beliefs around collective responsibility and the last seven relate to actions the teams have or haven't yet taken. We know that the best way to change teachers' perceptions is to have them change their behaviors and witness the positive effects. Teams taking action will likely precede any change in attitude. This means that leaders should look first at statements 7 through 11 to determine whether there are necessary actions that need to happen before expecting statements 1 through 4 to reflect a shift in teachers' perceptions. At the end of this chapter, we have a tool leaders can use to lay out their priorities to determine what they need to do first, next, and so on. Leaders should keep the data they collected from the staff survey to help when completing that prioritization.

Figure 4.7, the Systems of Support Alignment Tool (page 118) is useful both for leaders in schools just getting started as a PLC and for those further along in the process. This tool can help leaders in schools in the first two years of implementation understand both the steps necessary to create an effective system of support and which team to assign this responsibility to. For leaders with more PLC experience, this checklist can help identify any gaps in their system. Also, this can help schools determine whether the right teams have been assigned each of the responsibilities. Once completed, leaders can use this tool with their leadership team, collaborative teams, and school intervention teams as a vehicle to discuss what improvements might be made no matter where they are in the process.

This leads us to the third tool, the Master Schedule Checklist in figure 4.8 (page 119). There is no doubt that it's difficult to develop a master schedule that will provide the criteria all stakeholders would like to see in a system of support. All staff members can use the checklist for input whenever the school is conceiving a new master schedule. Principals and other leaders who have to develop schedules know that they must start with the highest prioritized criteria and then work step by step to figure out how to make the other pieces fit. We suggest leaders stick to the most important priorities when designing the master schedule. The first is that student learning has to come first. While this seems obvious, practitioners know that schools sometimes make scheduling decisions around adult needs. For example, if two teachers are sharing a full-time position, they may request a specific schedule to fit their personal needs. Or, if schools are sharing staff, the schedule designer will try to cater to both schools. The reality is that neither of these considerations is more important than a schedule that allows interventions to occur smoothly across the system. The second priority for schedule designers is the ability to see options beyond the way the school has always done things. The Master Schedule Checklist includes space for staff to provide suggestions about making the schedule more effective, which can provide leaders with fresh perspectives. This outside-the-box thinking will make for a better schedule.

The Master Schedule Checklist can be useful for schools that are just getting started with a system of support. It can help schedule designers make sure they have included the most important components as they build the schedule. The space for recording ways to make the schedule more effective can serve as a bridge from the design of the current schedule to a more effective alternative.

Once the big rocks have been placed, the next two tools will help leaders add the gravel and sand—details they still need to put in place for an effective support system. The Effective Tracking Systems Tool in figure 4.11 (page 121) starts with a yes-or-no checklist but also asks for ideas for improvement. Leaders might use these areas of consideration as interview questions for various school stakeholders including, of course, teachers, but also specialists, school service personnel, and even tech support. If the sudden onset of remote learning in 2020 had a good side, it was in revealing to all staff members how important it is for all teams to have their documents in online folders available to all staff who need access. Many schools developed a system of folders that were organized by collaborative teams and shared with administrators, coaches, and support staff in addition to the members of the collaborative teams. The team folder might contain team norms, SMART goals, agendas and minutes, the essential standards, the pacing guides, unit plans, common formative assessments, common summative assessments, and data and data trackers. Collaborative teams make sure folders stay up to date by making any necessary changes during meetings.

The last tool, the Behavioral Supports Checklist in figure 4.12 (page 122), is intended to help leaders identify areas for continued improvement as they build support for students who aren't yet proficient on academic and social behaviors. Areas marked *not yet* should help initiate a planning process by the appropriate staff members, and areas marked *in progress* need to be regularly monitored until they are completed.

As leaders gather evidence and begin to analyze it, they should keep in mind the question, What patterns and priorities emerge in the evidence? Use the data from the previous tools to chart the progress of teams on the continuum provided in figure 4.13.

Knowledge and Practice	Level of Use or Implementation			
	Limited	Emerging	Established	Strategic
Teams have developed a culture of collective responsibility for student learning.	Individual teachers are responsible for the students assigned to them. They often refer to them as *my* students.	Teams are in the early stages of accepting responsibility for all students they are assigned. While they may develop plans for support together, they are sometimes reluctant to believe another team member can effectively support students on their class lists.	Teams accept responsibility for all students they are assigned. Teams believe that any one of its members can provide the support students need to learn. Members refer to students as *our* students.	Teams accept responsibility for all students they are assigned. Teams often strategically assign a team member to work with a group of students based on the success the team member has had with student learning with specific content or those students.
Teams have designed an effective system of support across the school.	Individual teams have created and implemented plans for supporting students.	The leadership team has begun developing a system of support for the school; however, some teams are worried that this will take away their ability to make decisions. Leaders have begun to discuss the system with teams so that they understand how each piece works together.	The leadership team has designed a system of support and assigned lead responsibility for the tasks that need to be completed. All teams have understood the system and use it effectively.	The system of support is working well for students and staff. When issues arise, they are quickly resolved in a way that best supports student learning. Teams knowledgeably discuss where students are in their learning and what support they are receiving.
The master schedule allows students to receive support without missing new Tier 1 instruction.	The leadership team hasn't started working on building a master schedule with parameters that allow students to receive support without missing some Tier 1 instruction.	The leadership team has built a master schedule that generally allows students to receive support in core instructional areas; however, there are some areas of conflict that the team hasn't yet worked through.	Teams are using a master schedule developed by the leadership team that provides time for students to get support without missing Tier 1 instruction.	The leadership team routinely analyzes the effectiveness of the master schedule in providing time for support for students. Each year the leadership team makes changes to eliminate emerging conflicts.

Figure 4.13: Continuum of practice for implementing a schoolwide system of support.

continued →

*Visit **go.SolutionTree.com/PLCbooks** for a free reproducible version of this figure.*

Knowledge and Practice	Level of Use or Implementation			
	Limited	Emerging	Established	Strategic
The school has an effective system to track student supports.	Teams are responsible for keeping track of which students have received extra support. Not all teams have found an effective way to do so.	The leadership team is gathering ideas for creating an effective tracking system. Collaborative teams have provided input to the leadership team about both ideas they've found effective and issues they've encountered in their work.	The leadership team has created a systematic way to keep track of students who are given extra time and support or enrichment. Tracking templates are easy to complete, and teams use them regularly. The tracking systems are available to all stakeholders on a shared drive.	In addition to having a systematic way to collect information about students receiving support or enrichment, the leadership team periodically goes through this information to look for any patterns that could lead to changes in scheduling, instruction, pacing, or resources.
The leadership team has developed and implemented an effective behavior system.	Some but not all teams have developed common expectations for student behavior.	The leadership team has begun to develop a positive behavior system including a plan for ensuring all teachers and students are aware of the expectations.	The leadership team has developed a schoolwide behavior system, and all teachers and students are aware of the established expectations. The system emphasizes positive relationships.	The leadership team regularly reviews the robust behavior system to make sure it's kept up to date. For example, it may add online behavioral expectations for remote instruction.

As always, schools should be open to continuous improvement. Systems of support change over time as teams learn more and confront more situations. Remote instruction brought on by the COVID-19 pandemic required schools to quickly change the way they offer interventions. The most successful schools are able to adapt quickly because they have the most important foundation pieces in place.

Act on Evidence to Improve Practice

When building a schoolwide system of support, leaders must expect that the system will evolve over time as teams become more effective with their assessments. However, it's critical to have a vision of what the ideal system looks like to make sure no one attempts to take shortcuts or detours. To this end, we suggest the activity in figure 4.14 for leadership teams.

The leadership team members discuss each of the five areas they are assessing to make sure they have a common understanding of what each includes. Team

Area Assessed	Current Reality			Current Priority for Action		
	Not Addressed	In Progress	Completed	1 Low	2 Medium	3 High
1. Culture of collective responsibility Teams are responsible for all students, not just the ones listed on teachers' individual class rosters. Teams share the responsibility for responding with time and support.						
2. Effectiveness of system of support A schoolwide system allows students access to all levels of support and flexibility to move between levels or away from support when the data indicate a change is necessary.						
3. Master schedule allocates time The master schedule provides time for teams to meet and allows teams to provide time and support in the three tiers of response.						
4. Effective tracking system Protocols are in place to help teams manage information on which students are getting additional time and support or extensions.						
5. Effective behavioral system A schoolwide system is in place to teach, assess, and support student behavior. The foundation of the system is strong positive relationships as well as positive rewards when students do well.						

Figure 4.14: Common vision tool to agree on what a schoolwide system of support looks like.

Visit go.SolutionTree.com/PLCbooks for a free reproducible version of this figure.

members individually determine what their current reality is for implementation (*not addressed*, *in progress*, or *completed*). Then they identify their priority for making this happen (*low*, *medium*, or *high*). After all team members have had a chance to complete the survey, they build a composite of information using one template to record the collective responses. Once they have collected these data, they look for items that have a high priority that the majority has marked as *not addressed* or *in progress*. Then they go back and look for items that are medium priority and marked either *not addressed* or *in progress*. Once leaders have collected data from the leadership team, they can create an action plan to complete those items that end up with the highest priority.

As discussed earlier in this chapter, developing quality support systems for students relies on three different types of teams: (1) the leadership team, (2) the collaborative teams, and (3) the school intervention team. First, let's focus on the actions the leadership team may take using the tools in this chapter. Using the data from the common vision tool in figure 4.14, the leadership team will be able to establish priorities for their next steps. For example, if it's the beginning of the school year and the master schedule doesn't support all of the actions necessary to have an effective system, it may not be possible to build a new master schedule at this time. The leadership team will likely want to keep a running list of issues that it needs to solve and plan for a new, more effective schedule for next year. On the other hand, if the team sees that the school doesn't have a culture of collective responsibility, it will likely want to make that a high priority and quickly begin to take action. Once they have established priorities, leaders will want to develop a coherent action plan for improvement.

Let's explore some actions leaders might take depending on what evidence they collect with their formative tools.

1. The school doesn't have a strong culture of collective responsibility.

    o   Build shared knowledge by providing opportunities to learn more about schools that have effectively built a culture of collective responsibility.

    o   Share research and best practices to further build shared knowledge.

    o   Rephrase statements that teachers make to show that they haven't yet bought in to collective responsibility (for example, change *my kids* to *our kids* or *I will do this* to *we will do this*).

2. The school has a team-centered support system and needs to move toward a schoolwide support system.

    o   Establish the parameters necessary for an effective system, such as making time in the master schedule to provide support, developing behavioral expectations, and keeping track of student needs.

- Establish an action plan with time lines for implementation.
- Make expectations explicit.
- Provide training for how to teach, assess, and respond to behaviors.
- Check in regularly with collaborative teams to gather feedback.

3. The master schedule needs to be refined.

- Share examples from schools that have successfully established a system of support.
- Provide time for gathering input from collaborative teams about their specific needs.
- Keep the focus on the school's mission that all students will learn at high levels and make all decisions with that in mind.

4. Tracking systems are inadequate.

- Have the leadership team identify what information needs to be available and who needs access to the information.
- Develop an effective system of organization for folders to ensure they're available to everyone who needs access.
- Train all users on the system.

5. The school lacks a schoolwide behavior system focused on positive relationships.

- Work with the leadership team to explore systems similar schools have found effective.
- Use data such as attendance, discipline referrals, and so on to drive decisions. During initial implementation, check in regularly to see how effectively student learning is happening.

Once leaders have identified areas of concern, the planner in figure 4.15 (page 130) can help those leaders and leadership team members develop the next steps they need to take.

The PLC Process Is a Winding Path

Becoming a high-performing PLC is not a linear process. Some schools start with a robust system of support, but others are more like the school in the chapter's opening scenario. Some schools have a system of support in place that hasn't proven effective, and so those schools need to make some decisions about how to change course. No matter where a school is in the work of establishing a system of support, remember to celebrate the small wins regularly so that staff remain encouraged about the future. Recognize creative and successful ideas that collaborative teams have used with the

Area of Concern	Leaders' Action Steps	Time Line	Teams' Action Steps	Time Line
We need to make changes for next school year in the master schedule in order to allow students to move in and out of interventions.	1. Solicit feedback and ideas using the Master Schedule Checklist. 2. Review sample master schedules from identified schools. 3. Have a tentative master schedule available for teachers to provide feedback.	January February–March March 31	1. Provide the leadership team with specific examples of where the master schedule isn't working effectively. 2. Make the leadership team aware of any scheduling ideas.	January January–February
We don't have an effective tracking system in place for Tier 2 and 3 students receiving support.	Create a schoolwide system of folders so that all teams are using the same process to keep track of students, and everyone who needs access to the information has privileges. Develop a template for all teams to use to record information.	ASAP	1. Make sure all team members know how to navigate the folders for their team. 2. Train all staff on how to use the agreed-on templates to keep track of students.	ASAP End of November
We need to shore up our behavior system to include issues with remote learning.	Determine the areas of concern about student behavior with remote learning, considering both academic and social behaviors. Develop a plan to teach students the expectations around these concerns.	November	1. Help brainstorm areas of concern to submit to the leadership team for consideration. 2. Make sure all members of the team are aware of and responsible for implementing this new plan. 3. Participate in any positive reinforcement ideas expected.	September October All year

Figure 4.15: Action planner for establishing a schoolwide system of support.

Visit **go.SolutionTree.com/PLCbooks** *for a free reproducible version of this figure.*

whole staff. Share stories of students overcoming gaps in learning so that all teachers see how the system works. Remember that celebrating short-term wins helps keep the staff focused and energized.

It's time now to turn from our schoolwide focus to the specific work of collaborative teams as they address and answer the four critical questions of a PLC. In part 2, we'll begin with the question of what students need to know and be able to do.

PART 2

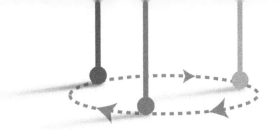

Chapter 5

A FOCUS ON GETTING CLEAR ABOUT WHAT STUDENTS SHOULD KNOW AND DO

In the PLC process, the work of collaborative teams is to answer the four critical questions (DuFour et al., 2016). In this chapter, we'll focus on critical question 1: What do students need to know and be able to do? How teams answer this question will drive all their other work. For leaders assessing the work of their teams, the question becomes, How are teams clarifying what students need to know and be able to do?

When teams are overwhelmed by the process, they struggle to fulfill their mandate to ensure that all students learn at high levels. The following scenario illustrates how a team might enact PLC elements but still lack clarity because it isn't answering critical question 1.

> *Instructional coach Jamie Anderson visits collaborative team meetings in her high school to get a sense of what professional learning the teams need. As she visits with the biology department, she begins to worry because team members seem to be all over the place in their work. While they say they are planning the next unit on heredity, it's apparent that they haven't really fleshed out their current unit on cells. Some teachers are emphasizing learning targets that other teachers aren't even mentioning. The team discussions during this meeting involve the question of how they can find time to reteach concepts students need help on. The team members believe they have so much content they need to teach because their students must pass an end-of-year*

test in biology. They also share their concern that three different middle schools feed into their high school, each of which emphasizes different content. As a result, they have to start from scratch to make sure students have the prerequisite knowledge needed to learn this year's content.

Jamie's concern is that she was an English teacher and knows little about the biology content. When she asks the team members about their unit plans, they admit that they've been teaching the course the way they've always taught it, which means they are using a district curriculum guide that was created before the new Next Generation Science Standards came out. They have written common end-of-unit assessments, but teachers use them when they've completed the unit in their individual classrooms, meaning that teachers may be using the assessments days or weeks apart from one another. They explain that they are all struggling because of how the new standards are written—they're very different from the previous standards. They wish there were a product that the school could purchase to make this transition easier. Jamie realizes that these teachers are not resisting the PLC process, they just can't see how it will work for them because they are so overwhelmed.

When collaborative teams fail to identify their essential standards before they engage in assessments and interventions, they often feel overwhelmed with having too much to teach, too much to assess, and too much to plan responses to. Therefore, choosing essential standards first is the best foundation to get this work started. This is even more important when the team, as in the scenario, is moving to a new set of standards.

Once essential standards are identified, the team focuses on these standards for their other products, such as pacing guides, unit plans, and unwrapped standards. They write common formative assessments for identified essential standards, and plan extra time and support for students who are identified as not yet proficient as well as extensions for those students who are already proficient. Since choosing essential standards is the foundation of the work of answering critical question 1, it's important for teams to spend time making sure they are doing this well so that all of these products are effective. Leaders must also be sure they understand and support the essential standards process and know what products to look for and assess. This chapter goes into depth on the process of designating what students need to know and be able to do, and then moves on to tools leaders can use to assess, analyze, and act to support teams in this critical work.

Understand the Essential Standards Process

One of the important products teams create when they answer critical question 1, then, is a set of essential standards for the course or grade level. These standards may also be called power standards, priority standards, or some other variation. Educational consultant and author Larry Ainsworth (2010) defines essential standards as

> a carefully selected subset of the total list of grade-specific and course-specific standards within each content area that students must know and be able to do by the end of the school year in order to be prepared to enter the next grade level or course. (p. 323)

Teams that have not yet identified essential standards should engage in the process described in this chapter. If teams have already identified them, members must become familiar with the identified essential standards, make sure they understand what each standard means, and agree about what proficiency will look like. As discussed in chapter 2 (page 39), teams begin the PDSA cycle by planning what they will teach and assess in each unit. Choosing essential standards begins this process. However, the set of standards is not the only product. After choosing the essential standards, teams must unwrap or break them down to discuss more specifically what the standards mean and what proficiency with them will look like: that is, teams are identifying learning targets.

Next, teams should develop a pacing guide to support them in teaching, assessing, and providing time and support to students who need it. Once they have paced the essential standards, teams then need to build unit plans with more detail about what they will teach in each unit. These plans should list the learning targets they will teach, ideas for suggested formative and summative assessments along with dates for administering those assessments, and a general list of the number of days that will be necessary to effectively teach this unit. We'll further discuss each of these steps in the following sections, starting with why it's important for teams to designate essential standards.

Once the essential standards have been identified, it's also important that teams communicate them to other stakeholders, including students, parents, and community members. When these standards are communicated to students it helps involve them in their own learning and the assessment process. Student involvement in learning and assessment is one of the most important things a team can do.

The Why Behind Essential Standards

In answering critical question 1, collaborative teams examine all their grade-level or content standards to determine which of these standards are essential for *all* students to learn. Prior to PLC implementation, most teachers probably worked in isolation to decide which standards to spend the most time on, to interpret what proficiency looks like for those standards, and to develop assessment items to test student learning on those standards. When teachers work in isolation, and therefore emphasize different content, students move through the school unevenly prepared for the next course or grade. For example, if one teacher emphasizes multiple types of writing in an ELA class and another focuses only on narrative writing, the teacher in the next grade will have students from both of these classrooms. Rather than being able to pick up where the prior grade's teachers left off, they have to scaffold in areas not emphasized the year before.

Based on Marzano's (2003; Eaker & Marzano, 2020) research, effective schools must identify what he calls the guaranteed and viable curriculum. Determining a guaranteed and viable curriculum is what collaborative teams do when they answer critical question 1. The curriculum is *guaranteed* when all teachers in a grade or course teach the same content, and it's *viable* when they have the time to teach it effectively. The reality in schools, though, is that standards are often written in a way that is open to individual interpretation. Unless teams work together to discuss what the standards mean and what proficiency on those standards will look like, the school can't claim to have a truly guaranteed curriculum. At the same time, most grade levels and content areas simply have too much to teach—there just isn't time in the school day and year to make sure *all* their students have learned *all* the standards. Some schools attempt to cover the curriculum superficially rather than teach it deeply and make sure all students have learned it. In order to provide a truly viable curriculum, schools and districts must, instead, work collaboratively to identify what all students must know in all courses and at all grade levels.

When teams answer critical question 1, they are ensuring equity for their students. DuFour and Marzano (2011) discuss the importance of equity for all students when they remind us, "In a professional learning community, educators are committed to helping students acquire the same essential knowledge and skills regardless of the teacher to whom they are assigned" (p. 90). This means that it no longer matters who the classroom teacher is—the rigor and content of the instruction that teacher provides will remain the same. What teams realize over time is that when students come to them commonly prepared from the grade or course before theirs, they will have more time to spend teaching new content rather than scaffolding content from the previous grade or course.

Determining what the essential standards are for a course or grade level should be the responsibility of teachers most familiar with that content—those who teach it. In some cases, a school district wants all its schools to have the same essential standards and, therefore, uses a team composed of representative teachers from each school to choose them. In other cases, each school chooses its own set of essential standards and every teacher in that school participates in the process. The advantage of having the same standards districtwide is that the district curriculum teams can create benchmark assessments to monitor implementation across schools, students can move easily between schools in a district, the curriculum teams can more effectively create curricula across the district, and transitions between elementary to middle school and middle to high school are smoother. The advantage of each school having its own essential standards is that *every* teacher is involved in the process, gains a common understanding of what the standard means and what proficiency looks like, and has ownership in the final product. We've even worked in districts who've had each school start the process so that all teachers are involved, and then, after a few years, have schools come back together and use representatives to choose a district set of essential standards. Because all the teachers had been using their essentials for a period of time, the process went very smoothly, and most were happy with the final set of standards.

Often the size of the district makes the decision of which of these processes to choose easier; for example, a small district with only one school at each grade span can easily have one set of essential standards districtwide. On the other hand, very large districts would likely find it too cumbersome to try and have the same set of essential standards districtwide. Another consideration is whether the schools have been using a set of standards for a number of years or whether there are brand new standards. For example, when the Common Core was adopted in almost every state, we found that having every teacher involved in the process of choosing essential standards was an excellent way to have all teachers learn more about the standards themselves.

Leaders must make the decision early in initial PLC implementation about whether to have a district set of essential standards or to have each school choose its own. When there is ambiguity about the decision, teams tend to bypass critical question 1 and move on to the other critical questions of learning. This leads to teams trying to assess and respond to everything they teach—an insurmountable expectation.

Choosing Essential Standards

Leaders must decide how to provide teams the time to complete the work of identifying essential standards. Many districts have a day early in the school year for professional development. If this is the case, choosing essential standards can happen on that day. If not, leaders may be able to provide teams with release time (typically one full day) for team members to complete this work without interruptions. The third option is for teams to use their collaborative time over several meetings at the beginning of the school year, or they can work unit by unit as they plan throughout the school year. We've worked with schools who used all of these options successfully. Often the decision is based on what curriculum materials currently exist for collaborative teams. Take, for example, a team that has already developed effective unit plans based on its standards. Before team members start each unit, they may do their planning (in the PDSA cycle) by examining all the standards they're teaching in the unit, deciding which are essential and which are supporting. They will likely also have to rework the number of days they will teach each of the essential standards to allow more time to assess and respond. On the other hand, if a team doesn't already have unit plans, members might find it more effective to choose all of their essential standards at once so that their planning (in the PDSA cycle) is building those unit plans.

It benefits teams to learn the history of the standards for a course or grade level at their schools. Almost all states adopted the Common Core standards in ELA and mathematics after they were released (NGA & CCSSO, 2010a, 2010b). Some states later adopted new standards in ELA and mathematics. In some cases, states totally revamped standards, but in others they only made slight changes by rewording or adding a few new standards. Many states have also adopted the Next Generation Science Standards (NGSS Lead States, 2013), some more recently than others. How deeply teachers understand the standards they are working with affects the time it will take to carefully answer this first question. The good news is that teams will have a much better understanding about their standards after doing the work of choosing them. Leaders will want to make sure that teams effectively answer critical question 1 as the foundation of the other questions. Whether they are coaches, team leaders, or administrators, the more leaders understand about the process and are able to see their teams engage in this work, the better they'll be able to support teams that might be stuck at some stage.

Whether this is done building by building or districtwide, the process itself is the same no matter what grade-level or curricular-area team is doing the work. It's critical to remember two things. The first is that essential standards are the guaranteed curriculum and represent about one-third of all the standards assigned to the course or grade (Ainsworth, 2010). Secondly, the leftover standards, which we call *supporting standards*, can't be left behind. Teachers must still teach supporting standards; however, they do not formatively assess them and students don't receive extra time and support if they don't learn these standards the first time.

Make sure that all participants are familiar with the criteria they will use to choose essential standards. The acronym REAL, created by educator Ted Horrell and his colleagues (Many & Horrell, 2014) and drawn from work by Ainsworth (2004), is a useful framework.

- **Readiness:** Standards that are a prerequisite for future learning

- **Endurance:** Standards that are important to know beyond the school year

- **Assessed:** Standards that appear on high-stakes tests

- **Leverage:** Standards that have application across multiple content areas

As a team works its way through the list of standards, members use these criteria to determine which standards they will put on their list of essential standards. A standard doesn't have to meet all four criteria to be essential but will likely meet more than one. Essential standards are those that are important enough for teams to use intervention time to make sure all of their students have learned them. When teams we work with get stuck deciding whether a standard is essential, we ask them, "Would you spend intervention time if a student hasn't mastered this one?" Often this makes the decision much easier.

Avoid Common Misunderstandings About Essential Standards

Having done the work of answering critical question 1 with many schools, we see some misunderstandings that some have about the process. These are our recommendations to help counter these misunderstandings.

1. **Teams must still teach both essential and supporting standards:** They spend more time on the essential standards, and assess and provide support if students aren't yet proficient on them.

2. **Teams must not choose the simplest or easiest of the standards:** *All* students must learn at high levels and will only do this when they have access to rigorous curricula.

3. **Keep the language of the standard intact:** Teams may lose the meaning of the standard if they simplify it too early in the process.

4. **Make sure that choosing essential standards impacts the work of the team:** Allow more time for teaching, assessing, and responding to these standards.

All participants should have a copy of the standards for their grade level or course to use during the process of identifying essential standards. Whoever is facilitating the process (team leader, coach, or administrator) should look at the total list of standards to determine how to put them into smaller chunks to make the process easier. For example, in ELA, rather than doing all of the seventy to ninety standards at one time, the facilitator might divide them into three chunks: (1) all reading and foundation standards, (2) all writing standards, and (3) speaking and listening and language standards. In mathematics, teams might choose to do a couple of domains together.

The protocol in figure 5.1 (page 142) explains the steps teams can take to choose essential standards. It is often helpful, if possible, to have a facilitator to guide the process. If this isn't possible, team leaders, coaches, or administrators should have a thorough understanding of how they can facilitate the work. For a more detailed explanation of how to facilitate or coach teams on this work, we recommend chapter 2 in our book *Make It Happen* (Bailey & Jakicic, 2019).

Step	Action	Anticipated Time Line
1.	The team discusses the criteria it will use to choose its essential standards: readiness, endurance, assessed on high-stakes tests, and leverage.	Five minutes
2.	The team considers how to chunk the standards, if necessary. For example, in ELA the first chunk can be the reading and reading foundations standards, the second chunk the writing standards, and the third chunk the language and speaking and listening standards.	Five minutes
3.	Each team member independently works through a chunk of standards and chooses those that he or she believes fit one or more of the criteria. The final list should include about one-third of the overall content.	Five to ten minutes per chunk of standards
4.	The team builds consensus on the standards one at a time, making sure all team members are involved in the process. Some standards will start with total agreement (everyone believes it *is* or *is not* essential), but most of them will involve discussion to reach consensus.	Thirty minutes per chunk
5.	The team examines data about student performance. Are there areas of particular strength or weakness? If so, the team ensures its essential standards reflect this by adding additional standards to shore up the weaknesses, if necessary.	Twenty minutes
6.	The team uses documents released by the district or state to ensure that the expectations the members have drafted align to the expectations for students. These might include test specifications, blueprints, or documents developed by the standards writers. For example, if assessment blueprints show an emphasis on text-dependent questions, it's important that the team incorporates this emphasis in its draft list.	Twenty minutes
7.	Team members work with the other teams in their school to vertically align their essential standards.	This occurs once all of the teams have developed a rough draft of their standards. The overall process will take about an hour.

Source: Adapted from Ainsworth, 2004; Bailey & Jakicic, 2020.

Figure 5.1: Protocol for choosing essential standards.

*Visit **go.SolutionTree.com/PLCbooks** for a free reproducible version of this figure.*

After they have identified their essential standards, teams still have work to do. It is important that all team leaders understand the steps it will take to completely answer critical question 1.

1. Identify essential standards from the current list of standards for the grade or course.

2. Unwrap these standards into learning targets by discussing what they mean and what proficiency looks like.

3. Develop a common pacing guide listing which essential standards the team will teach in each unit.

4. Write unit plans with both essential and supporting standards, listing the learning targets taught in that unit, planned common formative assessments and common summative assessment ideas, and days needed for each component.

The Unwrapping Process

Once teams have identified the essential standards, the next step is to unwrap or unpack them into learning targets. This requires the team to examine the standards themselves to identify all the skills and concepts, or learning targets, students must learn and teachers must teach. Many teachers tell us that they have done this work before, often to plan the curriculum and instruction by arranging all the learning targets into units of instruction. Our experience has been, however, that they don't always have access to the products they created because they haven't used the unwrapped standards in several years, or the teachers who did the work are no longer on the team. We know that teams don't want to redo work that's already been done. We also know how important it is for teams to have a clear understanding of the learning targets that come from their essential standards.

Therefore, in our trainings with teachers, we typically start with *why* the unwrapping process is so important and recommend that leaders do the same in their schools. When teams engage in this work, they are building consensus on what the standard means as well as on what it will look like for a student to be proficient. This will lead to better common formative assessments.

As teams engage in this work, it's important they have clarity and agreement on two important terms: (1) standards and (2) learning targets. We define a *standard* as the narrowest item listed by a state that describes what students should know and do. *Learning targets*, on the other hand, are the smaller skills, strategies, and pieces of content information a student needs in order to be able to master the standard. We know that some teams want to quickly put these targets into student-friendly language; however, we recommend they wait to do this until after they have developed pacing guides and unit plans. The reason for this is that sometimes teams lose the meaning of the actual standard, including its rigor, when they move to student-friendly language. Some learning targets are *explicitly* stated in the standard while others are *implicit,* meaning teams have to discuss the underlying expectations revealed in the unwrapping process. Consider, for example, the grades 11–12 reading standard in social studies: "Evaluate authors' differing points of view on the same historical event or issue by assessing the authors' claims, reasoning, and evidence" (NGA & CCSSO, 2010a). The two explicit learning targets are (1) evaluate authors' differing points of view on the same historical event or issue and (2) assess authors' claims, reasons, and evidence. But when the team unwraps this standard, members also discuss three additional implied learning targets: (3) analyze the text to determine its point of view, (4) understand the underlying conditions and circumstances around an event or topic that might influence a point of view, and (5) know the terms *claim*, *reasons*, and *evidence*.

There are many different ways to unwrap standards and many different templates. Some districts want teams to use a template the district provides, and we offer one in this chapter we've found easy to use (figure 5.2). What they all have in common is that the process asks teams to interpret what the standard means and what students will have to do to master that standard.

Finding the Learning Targets to Teach and Assess

1. Circle the verbs (skills).

2. Underline the nouns (concepts) to be taught.

3. Double underline any prepositional phrase (context). Not all standards have a context. Context clarifies the conditions a student might be expected to learn a target. For example, a reading target might have the context "in a story" or "in two pieces of text"; a mathematics target might include "with whole numbers."

4. Write separately each verb (skills) and noun (concepts) combination as a separate learning target.

5. If a prepositional phrase (the context) is included at the beginning or the end of the standard, include it in the target.

6. Discuss the possible implicit learning targets. These often are prerequisite skills (not taught in a prior year or course) that students must learn.

7. Discuss the order in which the targets will be taught. Are there some that cross into multiple units of instruction? Are there some that are developed over time?

8. For each learning target, build consensus on the DOK level for that target. Consider more than the verb!

9. Discuss a possible summative assessment.

10. Consider which targets will need a common formative assessment during the unit of instruction and what they might look like.

Figure 5.2: Protocol for unwrapping standards.

*Visit **go.SolutionTree.com/PLCbooks** for a free reproducible version of this figure.*

The process first asks the team to examine key words: the verbs and the nouns and noun phrases. Verbs identify what students need to be able to do and give some insight into the cognitive demand they are expected to use. Nouns and noun phrases represent the content students must know—what the teacher will need to deliver direct instruction about. In our work with schools, we ask teams to circle the verbs and underline the nouns or noun phrases.

As they do this work collaboratively, team members will discuss what they will need to teach (by identifying individual learning targets), as well as the targets' levels of complexity using a framework such as DOK, which we discussed in chapter 3 (page 73). The DOK taxonomy describes the cognitive demand (rigor) that is required to be able to know or do what a learning target is describing. This conversation includes a discussion about what proficiency will look like on that target. The team roughs out what the summative assessment will be at the end of the unit and identifies where in the unit teachers will need to stop for a common formative assessment. The team members may also sequence the learning targets in the order they will teach them.

Consider the third-grade reading standard in figure 5.3. Note that not all the cells on the template are completed—only those that are important to the standard being unwrapped. In this example, only those learning targets the team feels need to be on a common formative assessment have that cell filled in.

Standard: Describe the relationship between a series of historical events, scientific ideas, or steps in technical procedures in a text, using language that pertains to time, sequence and cause and effect (3.RI.3).				
What Will Students Do?	**With What Knowledge or Concept?**	**In What Context?**	**DOK Level**	**Common Formative Assessment**
Describe	The relationship between a series of historical events, scientific ideas, or steps in technical procedures	In an informational text	3	
Determine	The structure of the text being read—time sequence and cause and effect		2	Given a piece of text, the student can identify its structure.
Annotate or highlight	A text to show its structure		2	Given a piece of text, the student can highlight the parts of the text to show its structure.
Use	Language that pertains to time, sequence, and cause and effect		3	
Identify	Key terms that let the reader know two things are being compared (such as *but*, *however*, and *in contrast*)		1	
Summative Assessment: The student will be asked to read a third-grade scientific text and answer questions that require analysis of the relationships between ideas in the text.				

Source for standard: NGA & CCSSO, 2010a.

Figure 5.3: Sample unwrapped standard.

*Visit **go.SolutionTree.com/PLCbooks** for a free reproducible version of this figure.*

When Teams Unwrapped Previously

If teams have already unwrapped their standards, we suggest a modified process to help make sure they are prepared for developing effective common formative assessments. As we have learned in our work, teams are reluctant to redo work they've already engaged in, and rightly so! We've developed a modified process for teams who have previously unwrapped their standards but didn't take the next step into defining proficiency and discussing which targets should be commonly assessed.

Using the template in figure 5.4, the team completes columns 1 and 2 with the standard and the learning targets revealed in the unwrapping process. If team members did not identify the DOK of the standard and each of the learning targets when they first unwrapped the standards, they should do so now. They then move to column 4 and describe a likely summative assessment. Finally, they look at the learning targets and discuss which of those targets should be assessed using a common formative assessment during the learning process.

Developing Pacing Guides and Unit Plans

Many schools use the terms *pacing guide* and *unit plan* interchangeably. We see a difference, however, in the role of each in a PLC. Teams in a PLC must agree on common pacing. This means that they must teach the same standards and learning targets at the same time and must be prepared to give common formative and common summative assessments at the same time. We often see teams struggle with this. They say that different teachers have different students and must adjust instruction for their students. However, if educators truly believe all students can learn at high levels, this means they must provide all students the same opportunities. Going slower means some classes omit some content, which means those students won't have the same opportunities. When teams are able to use common formative assessments and provide extra time and support in Tiers 1 and 2, teachers better understand how they can use that time for their students who need more time to learn, rather than slowing down initial instruction for all of their students. To do this requires teams to work together to build consensus on the amount of time to teach the essential standards and the dates of the common formative and summative assessments. Any leader can facilitate this work, but team leaders who know the content the best are often most effective.

Pacing guides, then, are documents that lay out all the essential standards taught in the school year. Teams identify the units of instruction they will teach and which essential standards they will teach in which units. They develop a scheme for common assessments and plan when will they stop instruction to make sure students have learned something essential. Teams don't, however, have to develop the assessments at this time.

1. Standard	2. Learning Targets	3. Common Formative Assessments	4. Summative Assessment
(Develop) and (use) a model to describe the function of a cell as a whole and ways parts of cells contribute to the function (MS-LS1-2). DOK 3	Develop a model of a cell to describe the function of a cell as a whole and ways parts contribute to the function. DOK 3	Students will develop a model of a cell based on both the provided text and the notes they took while conducting investigations.	Students will rework their original cell models to include what they learned in their lab investigations.
	Use a model of a cell to describe the ways parts of cells contribute to the function. DOK 3		
	Know the names and functions of cell organelles. DOK 1	Students will demonstrate knowledge of the names and functions of cell organelles.	
	Describe how the cell membrane controls what enters and leaves the cell. DOK 2		
	Explain why plant cells have cell walls and animal cells don't. DOK 1		

Standard: (Develop) and (use) a model to describe the function of a cell as a whole and ways parts of cells contribute to the function (MS-LS1-2). DOK 3

Develop a model of a cell to describe the function of a cell as a whole and ways parts contribute to the function. DOK 3

Use a model of a cell to describe the ways parts of cells contribute to the function. DOK 3

Know the names and functions of cell organelles. DOK 1

Describe how the cell membrane controls what enters and leaves the cell. DOK 2

Explain why plant cells have cell walls and animal cells don't. DOK 1

Students will develop a model of a cell based on both the provided text and the notes they took while conducting investigations.

Students will demonstrate knowledge of the names and functions of cell organelles.

Students will rework their original cell models to include what they learned in their lab investigations.

Source for standard: NGSS Lead States, 2013.

Figure 5.4: A modified process to use unwrapped standards to determine common formative assessments.

*Visit **go.SolutionTree.com/PLCbooks** for a free reproducible version of this figure.*

Building unit plans, then, is the next step. *Unit plans* are more detailed than pacing guides and help teams determine more precisely which learning targets belong in each unit and how many days teachers will need to teach the unit. The unit plan lists the standards team members will teach (both essential and supporting) and the learning targets that come from those standards. To do this, teams must discuss each of their essential standards and whether to teach them all together in one unit or in several different units.

Take, for example, this first-grade foundational skill standard: "Know final -e and common vowel team conventions for representing long vowel sounds" (RF1.3c; NGA & CCSSO, 2010a). Team members will unwrap this standard into several different learning targets for teaching long vowels, which they will likely teach over several different units. In the pacing guide, then, the team should put these learning targets into its units rather than just listing the standard. Another nuance of the process we often encounter is when teachers choose an essential standard and list it throughout the year when in fact they're teaching it early in the year and then expecting students to apply it later. For example, elementary teachers sometimes choose the reading standard about asking and answering questions (R1.2.1; NGA & CCSSO, 2010a) as an essential standard and list it on unit plans throughout the year. The question we ask is, "Are you actually teaching it all year, or are you teaching it and expecting students to use it in subsequent units?" The answer to this question guides when teams will assess the standard. If they are expecting students to use it, they should assess it before they expect students to apply it.

Sample templates for pacing guides and unit plans are available as free reproducibles (**go.SolutionTree.com/PLCbooks**) from *Make It Happen* (Bailey & Jakicic, 2019).

How Leaders Support the Work of Answering Critical Question 1

Answering critical question 1 (What do students need to know and be able to do?) can be intimidating for teams just beginning to implement the PLC process. Often, teams want to look to experts to answer critical question 1 for them. It's critically important for leaders to communicate to teams that no one has more expertise to answer this question than they do. Teachers work every day with standards—*they* are the experts.

Leaders can also help teams answer critical question 1 by preparing resources for them. Make sure every team member has a clean copy of the standards that they can highlight and write on. It's also helpful to provide standards documents for each grade level to the grade-level teams one level above and below; a third-grade team, for example, would receive second- and fourth-grade standards documents in addition to third-grade standards. Take some time to research any documents from the state that will guide the work of choosing essential standards. For example, for the Common Core mathematics standards, there is a document that identifies major, supporting, and additional clusters, which indicates where a team should put its emphases (Achieve the Core, n.d.). This document represents the thinking of the original authors of the mathematics standards about their relative importance for each grade level. Many states have blueprints for their high-stakes tests showing how they emphasize different standards. Provide teams with current data about student performance in their curricular area so that they can use them to make sure they are emphasizing any weak areas for students.

Make sure that teams have an accessible place to keep the documents they create. We recommend that the school set up a series of online shared folders for teams to use. The leadership team should also have access to each of these folders.

Set realistic expectations for teams around doing this work. Once teams have their essential standards, they will need time to unwrap them, build a pacing guide, and develop unit plans. This work is part of the PDSA cycle described in chapter 2 (page 39). Teams may build their unit plans throughout the year as they prepare to teach each unit. Teams that have new standards should receive some additional release time. If they've never taught these standards before, it will take much longer to unwrap the essential standards, develop the pacing guide, and write unit plans.

Assess the Current Reality

While we've worked with schools who have total decision-making autonomy about what materials they use and how they plan their units of instruction, for most schools, district-level leaders determine the expectations about curriculum implementation. These schools receive materials and work under expectations about pacing from their district leaders, meaning that they have limited ability to make decisions about how they implement the curriculum. Which of these situations leaders experience in their schools will make a difference in how collaborative teams answer critical question 1. The best way to start is to reflect on the current context. Leaders can use the guiding questions in figure 5.5 (page 150) for that reflection.

The question that leaders should ask themselves as they consider how to assess their teams in answering critical question 1 is, "What's our current reality?" In this section we offer a number of tools to help leaders assess their teams and figure out how to offer support.

- Collaborative Team Checklist for Essential Standards
- Product-Monitoring Tool
- Observational Checklist for Essential Standards
- Effective Communication With Stakeholders Tool

Collaborative Team Checklist for Essential Standards

The tool in figure 5.6 (page 151) is designed to be a checklist for team members to complete to gather information about which products related to critical question 1 have been developed and which still need to be completed. This will help both

Guiding Questions	Reflection on Context
Will we choose essential standards as a school or will representatives from the district choose them?	
How long have teams been working with the current standards? Are they deeply rooted in the work of instructional design?	
How much autonomy do teams have with the curriculum? Is there a prescribed district curriculum that must be followed?	
How much time do collaborative teams have to consult vertically with other teams?	
Have the teams, as they are currently configured, unwrapped their standards? Has this work been done recently or at least with the most recent set of standards?	
What work needs to be done in order to have pacing guides and unit plans that provide the time needed to teach, assess, and respond to the essential standards?	

Figure 5.5: Guiding questions to consider how teams will answer critical question 1.

Visit go.SolutionTree.com/PLCbooks for a free reproducible version of this figure.

leaders and the team itself determine what next steps they need to take. Individual team members can use this checklist separately, or the leader can interview the team together to gather the data.

Consider what a leader might learn if he or she sat with a team and discussed each of these criteria. Leaders might use this immediately after teams have completed this initial work (progressing from choosing essential standards to finishing unit plans typically takes a year or so) or may use it in subsequent years to help the team focus on *adding to* or *refining* their products. For example, they may only write one common formative assessment in a unit during the first year, but they want to add another one the next year—teams can add notes about future plans like this in the final column.

Statement	Yes	No	Notes for Future Use
1. We have a list of the *essential standards* for our course or grade level that we chose with the REAL criteria in mind (readiness, endurance, assessed, and leverage).			
2. These essential standards come from our state's standards for our course or grade level.			
3. Our essential standards represent about one-third of our curriculum.			
4. We've unwrapped the essential standards to identify the learning targets that we need to teach for students to master these standards.			
5. We've listed both explicit and implicit learning targets from our essential standards.			
6. We've identified and discussed the cognitive demand (DOK) each learning target requires.			
7. We've discussed what the summative assessment will look like for each essential standard.			
8. We've planned where we will stop to administer a common formative assessment.			
9. We have a pacing guide that ensures we have enough time to teach, assess, and respond to our essential standards.			
10. Our pacing guides list the assessments we have developed or have a place to list them as they are written.			
11. We have unit plans that account for the expected number of days a unit will take to complete and determine when we will administer common formative assessments and the common summative assessment.			
12. Our unit plans list the learning targets we will teach and the order we will teach them. In some cases, we will list specific activities when we know they are important to teaching a specific learning target.			

Figure 5.6: Collaborative team checklist for essential standards.

*Visit **go.SolutionTree.com/PLCbooks** for a free reproducible version of this figure.*

Product-Monitoring Tool

Leadership team members should regularly monitor the products teams are generating. Leaders and teams *must* think of this scrutiny as a formative process during which teams receive useful feedback. Imagine a school in which each of the collaborative teams have been choosing essential standards. The leadership team dedicates one of its meetings to check in on this work. Teams report where they are in the process and what they've learned. One team might report it is experiencing problems with the process. The entire leadership team, then, takes time to learn about what's getting in the way for that team. Some leadership team members might share how they overcame similar obstacles. Others may provide an alternate way to approach the problem. Because the leadership team members have developed trust with each other and are willing to be vulnerable about their successes and problems, the team that is struggling is likely to receive this feedback without trepidation. The team leader who was experiencing difficulty leaves with several ideas about how to move forward.

The tool in figure 5.7 offers a framework for monitoring the work of teams. We suggest leaders monitor four products: (1) essential standards, (2) unwrapped standards, (3) pacing guides, and (4) unit plans. The middle column in the tool makes suggestions about what to look for, and the right-hand column provides space to note any teams that will need additional help.

Observational Checklist for Essential Standards

In addition to monitoring products teams generate when answering critical question 1, it is important for leaders to make sure that these products actually impact what happens in the classroom. To help with this, we offer the observational checklist in figure 5.8 (page 154) that leaders can use to gather information when visiting classrooms.

Effective Communication With Stakeholders Tool

Leaders should consider the stakeholders who should be aware of the essential standards that their school or district has chosen. The first, and most important, reason for this is that these identified standards should be easily accessible for all staff members in the school. Collaborative teams should know what standards are guaranteed by the course or grade level *before* them and what the course or grade level *after* them expects. Specialists and special educators who teach multiple grade levels need to have access to each of the essential standards chosen by the teams with which they work so that they are able to ensure the students they teach have access to a guaranteed and viable curriculum. Equally important is that students are aware of the essential standards they are expected to learn. Teachers should identify these during instruction as well as during assessment. Students should be able to answer the question, What must I learn as a result of this lesson? Finally, parents should

Product to Monitor	Expectations for Exemplary Work	Teams to Support
Essential standards	☐ Come from state standards ☐ Represent about one-third of the curriculum ☐ Chosen with REAL criteria (readiness, endurance, assessed, and leverage)	
Unwrapped standards	☐ Template completed for each essential standard ☐ Identify learning targets (both explicit and implicit) ☐ Identify DOK levels for both the standard and all learning targets ☐ Team has discussed a rough outline of the summative assessment ☐ Identifies the learning targets the team will assess using a common formative assessment	
Pacing guide	☐ Identifies units ☐ Represents all essential standards ☐ Identifies common formative and summative assessments	
Unit plans	☐ Identify unit time lines ☐ List both essential and supporting standards ☐ Allocate time for common formative assessments and response ☐ Use learning targets to define lessons ☐ Eliminate curricula or activities that are not aligned with standards	

Figure 5.7: Product-monitoring tool.

*Visit **go.SolutionTree.com/PLCbooks** for a free reproducible version of this figure.*

have knowledge about the purpose of essential standards as well as which essential standards their children are expected to learn. The tool in figure 5.9 (page 154) lists suggestions for how to communicate to these groups.

Analyze Patterns and Priorities

When teams prepare to answer the question, What do students need to know and be able to do?, leaders need to keep two things in mind. The first is that teachers may not understand the why of the work. When pressed, they admit they have too much to teach but they are afraid to leave anything out that might be on the high-stakes

Learning Targets	Yes	No	Not Observable
Teacher communicates learning targets to students during instruction and displays them in the classroom.			
Learning targets appear in student-friendly language.			
Learning targets appear on assessments.			
Teacher is using an instructional strategy that is appropriate to the learning target he or she is teaching.			
Opportunities for Time and Support	**Yes**	**No**	**Not Observable**
Teacher provides time for response after each common formative assessment and aligns the response with essential learning targets.			
The response is specific to the misunderstanding or misconception of the students who need support.			
Teacher reassesses students after the response.			
Student Involvement	**Yes**	**No**	**Not Observable**
Students keep track of their own learning.			
Students are aware of proficiency expectations for the current learning targets.			
Students know which learning targets the teacher is teaching and assessing.			
Student Work Samples	**Yes**	**No**	**Not Observable**
Student work samples align with the essential learning targets that the team identified.			
Work samples represent the rigor of the current learning targets.			

Figure 5.8: Observational checklist for essential standards.

*Visit **go.SolutionTree.com/PLCbooks** for a free reproducible version of this figure.*

Stakeholder	Ways to Communicate Essential Standards
Staff members	☐ Easily accessible in team folders ☐ Available during team meetings ☐ Appear on pacing guide and unit plans
Students	☐ Visible in classrooms during lessons as student-friendly learning targets ☐ Identified on assessments ☐ Student data notebooks or other documents available for student use
Parents and community	☐ Easily accessible on the school's website ☐ Distributed and discussed at open houses and parent-teacher conferences ☐ Used in the reporting system

Figure 5.9: Effective communication with stakeholders tool.

*Visit **go.SolutionTree.com/PLCbooks** for a free reproducible version of this figure.*

test. They worry about their own competence in choosing essential standards. They believe the authors of the standards know more than they do.

Evidence that a team needs more support understanding the why of the work will most likely come from classroom observation—there will be little evidence that the team has chosen essential standards and therefore little evidence that this work has had an impact in their classrooms. Simply asking how choosing essential standards has impacted what and how they teach their curriculum is likely to reveal an underlying concern about leaving anything out. When leaders uncover this worry, the best way to respond is to remind teams that they still find a place in their curriculum for supporting standards, but they spend less time teaching them and don't assess and respond if students haven't learned them. When asked to consider how they taught everything in the past, most teachers see how they have emphasized some standards over the others. Now leaders are asking them to do this collaboratively so that students are commonly prepared for the next grade or course.

The second thing to keep in mind is that many teachers won't know *how* to choose essential standards effectively without some training or support. If leaders leave this matter ambiguous, many teachers will be reluctant to dig in. Consider the feedback we often get from teams when they start to choose essential standards. We commonly hear statements like the following.

- "The state test covers *all* of the standards—how can I make choices?"

- "What if we make the wrong choices and our students do worse on the test?"

- "Everything I teach is important. Learning mathematics is linear. If I skip a step, they can't learn new concepts."

It's important that leaders acknowledge these concerns but also focus on what we, as educators, know. We know that research tells us that a guaranteed and viable curriculum is the top factor that research has identified in high-performing schools (Marzano, 2003; Eaker & Marzano, 2020). We know that hundreds of schools across the country, by using this process, have reported increases in student learning in their applications for model PLC school status (AllThingsPLC, n.d.).

As leaders monitor the work of answering critical question 1, they will likely see whether teams understand how to do so effectively. When teams are new to the PLC process, leaders should look at these products one at a time, starting with the essential standards. When this is the case, leaders should not wait for perfection but concentrate on helping teams learn as they go. The central resource for all things PLC is called ***Learning** by Doing* (DuFour et al., 2016), after all, and that applies to everyone in the organization, not just students. Are teams engaged in the right work? Will this work result in effective products? One strategy a leader might want to consider is to use the tools *with* the team. Have the team members themselves consider whether their products are effective. When teams feel that leaders' actions *support* rather than *evaluate* their work, they will be more open to improving what they're doing. Thus, when analyzing the evidence gathered from these four tools (figures 5.6, 5.7, 5.8, and 5.9), it is important to consider what the evidence reveals about whether teams have embraced the why and if they feel confident about the how.

Using the Collaborative Team Checklist for Essential Standards (figure 5.6, page 151) and the Product-Monitoring Tool (figure 5.7, page 153), leaders can first determine what products each of the collaborative teams have created and what they still need to complete. It's important to realize that not all teams proceed at the same speed with this work. Some ways this process might be impacted include newly adopted standards, newly formed (or reformed) teams, or new curriculum materials. Most of the time elementary teachers teach all subjects, so they must go through the process in an iterative fashion, working with one content area each time. Thus, the first way to analyze this evidence is to develop a working list of where each team currently is in developing products. The Collaborative Team Checklist for Essential Standards is set up so that the statements are aligned to the order a team will usually complete products. Statements 1 through 3 refer to essential standards, 4 through 8 refer to the unwrapping process, 9 through 10 to pacing guides, and 11 through 12 to unit plans. By looking for gaps in work products, leaders can see if teams are stuck at one step of the process.

The next way to analyze evidence from these two tools is to dig deeper into the quality of the products the team is creating. As described earlier in this chapter, the leadership team often uses the Product-Monitoring Tool as it shares products, experiences, suggestions about how to accomplish the work, and problems it has to overcome. The middle column recommends criteria that exemplary products should exhibit, and the right-hand column is a place to list specific collaborative teams that need support.

Once teams have developed the products, it's important for leaders to make sure these products are impacting the classroom and student achievement. Using the Observational Checklist for Essential Standards (figure 5.8, page 154) for classroom observations, the most obvious sign that teachers are working with essential learning targets is that they routinely display the lesson's learning targets for students to see and reflect on. These targets should represent the smaller bits of learning students must acquire to be proficient on the essential standards and should appear in student-friendly language. Teams can write them as "I can" statements so that students see what they will be able to do when they've mastered the target. Teams should be careful, however, to use academic and domain-specific terms that students need to learn in each unit. These learning targets should also align to any activities students are engaged in. Keep in mind that checking for visible learning targets shouldn't be a gotcha moment. There are reasons the teacher may not display a learning target right away, such as when asking students to construct new knowledge based on a variety of learning opportunities; the teacher may wait until those activities are completed to reveal the learning target. In many science lessons, for example, students explore a phenomenon, investigating how something works before understanding what the learning target is. Think about a science class studying Bernoulli's principle, which explains why airplanes can stay in the air: the air moving more quickly over the curve of the wing decreases the air pressure so that the pressure under the wing is greater and keeps the plane aloft. Students might do various experiments with air pressure to observe the phenomenon in several situations before the teacher reveals the scientific principle they're learning. The question leaders should ask themselves is, "Do students know why they are engaging in this work and what teachers expect them to be able to do as a result?"

There should also be evidence of how the teacher is responding to the results of common formative assessment data when observing a response day, or time set aside after a common formative assessment specifically to respond to student needs. Leaders might see small groups of students working with the teacher, various centers with differentiated activities, or even groups engaged in work at different levels based on their needs as identified in these assessments. The response should be specific to the learning target and should provide both support and extensions based on the evidence teachers have gathered. As leaders take stock of the response, they should be aware that similar responses should be occurring in the classrooms of teammates. If leaders see inconsistent responses, it's possible the team isn't planning the response together.

We know that involving students in learning and assessing has a tremendously positive impact—a 1.44 effect size (Hattie, 2012). As described in chapter 3 (page 73), Hattie's work uses a meta-analysis of education research to compare education practices to determine which have the greatest impact on student learning. Student involvement in learning and assessment has one of the highest effect sizes he reported. Consider what practices are in place for classroom teachers to involve their students. Do students get their assessment results back *by learning target*? Do students know where they are on the continuum for mastery of learning targets? Do they have some role in planning how they will build this mastery? These actions allow students to truly understand what they are expected to learn and what proficiency looks like, and allow them to keep track for themselves where they are in their learning.

The Effective Communication With Stakeholders Tool (figure 5.9, page 154) is useful for leaders to gather evidence that effective communication about essential standards is happening with the shared responsibility of both teachers and leaders. Publishing essential standards on the school's website is something a principal can do. Published documents that lay out essential standards grade by grade or course by course can be provided for teachers to use during conferences.

In addition, leaders can learn a lot about effective communication by listening to different stakeholders. For example, a survey after a school's open house might ask parents to respond to an item like, "I know what my child is expected to learn this year." Leaders might ask students when visiting classrooms what they were expected to learn during this lesson. Again, the purpose of gathering this information is to identify what might help collaborative teams communicate better.

When analyzing evidence gathered from assessments, leaders should focus on the question, What patterns and priorities emerge in the evidence? Use the evidence from the previous tools to identify where teams are on the continuum in figure 5.10.

Once leaders have identified where teams fall on this continuum, they can develop an action plan to provide whatever help and support they see that teams need. We'll explore the actions they should consider in the next section.

Act on Evidence to Improve Practice

The question leaders should ask themselves when considering how to act is, "How do we move forward?" Action is necessary when leaders identify an area of concern from the evidence they've collected. Let's say a school principal has collected evidence that leads her to believe a particular team's members don't understand why they're doing the work of choosing essential standards. They need more clarity. As we say to teachers, "You can't just say it again louder and slower!" Assuming that the team is aware of the research about a guaranteed and viable curriculum, the principal might want to share examples of schools who have done this work successfully. One source that offers many examples is available on the Evidence of Effectiveness tab on the allthingsplc.info website. Schools must complete a rigorous application process to appear on this website. Many of them have links to their work products, and all of them have email addresses for building leaders who are willing to share their work. Sometimes all that team members need is for someone to get them started in this work by providing time, putting together resources, and finding a facilitator.

But what should happen when a team has created products that aren't as effective as the leader hopes they will be? This can be disheartening to a team that is eager to move on to new work, so facilitating these discussions requires leaders to emphasize how high-performing teams are always seeking to get better. When we work with teams, they have often completed parts of the work before we visit. What we've discovered about this process, however, is that no matter how many years a team has been together, the work is never completely finished—standards change, assessments change, teams learn more, and the way they deliver instruction changes as research continues to emerge. We've worked with teams that unwrapped their standards in 2010 when the Common Core first came out. Some teachers have retired, and new teachers have come on board. We encourage teams to use the idea of continuous improvement by continually looking at their products to see if they are still being used effectively. We encourage teams to think of their list of essential standards, for the first year of use, as a draft. They may see that there are standards that shouldn't be on the list or some that need to be added as they apply them. After that, teams should be aware that all of the products that answer critical question 1 (essential

Knowledge and Practice	Level of Use or Implementation			
	Limited	Emerging	Established	Strategic
Teams have reached consensus on the essential standards to be learned by students in every grade or course.	There is little understanding about the purpose of choosing essential standards, and many teachers are doubtful that focusing on only some standards will help students do well on high-stakes tests.	Teams have been trained on the process of determining their essential standards and have a plan to complete this work.	Teams have built consensus around the essential standards in their curriculum by using the REAL criteria and having vertical conversations with the grade or course before and after theirs.	Teams have built consensus around their essential standards and continue to have discussions about whether they need to either add or delete standards to the list.
Teams have unwrapped the essential standards in order to have a list of learning targets to be commonly assessed.	Teams have not yet begun unwrapping their essential standards, or this work was done earlier but many of the current team members weren't involved in doing this work.	Teams understand the purpose of unwrapping standards but haven't yet begun the process.	Teams have unwrapped their essential standards to identify the learning targets to be assessed or used the modified process to update their work.	Teams have unwrapped the essential standards and are using that work to develop pacing guides, unit plans, and common formative assessments.
Teams have built a common understanding about what proficiency looks like for essential standards and learning targets.	Teams have not yet begun to reach agreement about what proficiency looks like for their essential standards and learning targets, and consequently have different levels of rigor on their assessments.	Teams recognize the importance of agreeing on what proficiency looks like and are in the process of working through a common understanding for each of their essential standards and learning targets.	Teams have come to a common understanding about what proficiency looks like for each of their essential standards and learning targets.	Teams have agreed on what proficiency looks like for each of their essential standards and learning targets and have found or developed assessment items to link to that proficiency level.
Teams have collaboratively written pacing guides and unit plans to ensure they have sufficient time to teach, assess, and respond to the essential standards for their curriculum.	Teams haven't yet changed their pacing guides or unit plans to distribute time for students to learn essential standards.	Teams are working through the process to reallocate instructional time to teach, assess, and respond to their essential standards.	Teams have developed pacing guides and unit plans so that they have additional time allocated for essential standards to be taught, assessed, and responded to.	Teams reflect on the effectiveness of their pacing guides and unit plans and make changes as necessary.
Teams have communicated the essential standards to all stakeholders.	The essential standards are not communicated outside teams.	Teams have a plan in place to make sure that they are communicating essential standards to their students.	Teams have communicated essential standards to other teams, parents, and students.	In addition to communicating the essential standards to all stakeholders, teams have made sure the stakeholders understand why they did this work and how they chose these standards.

Figure 5.10: Continuum of practice for essential standards.

*Visit **go.SolutionTree.com/PLCbooks** for a free reproducible version of this figure.*

standards, unwrapped standards, pacing guides, and unit plans) should be reviewed every few years to make sure they are effective in ensuring all students learn at high levels. When teams are open to reflecting on their products, they are often amazed at how their views change as they do this work. When they see things that need to be changed, it doesn't mean they start over, but they do engage in discussions about how they can make their products better. In figure 5.11, we provide some specific examples of issues that might come to light as teams scrutinize their products and what actions leaders can take to improve them.

Product	What to Look For	What Action to Take
Essential standards	The team has chosen too many or too few standards.	We often see teams choose just a few essential standards to get started in their work. In such cases, suggest that the team choose all essential standards at the same time so that members compare each standard to the others. If the team has too many essential standards, ask members to consider whether they would want to intervene on each if a student hasn't mastered it. This often helps them separate essential standards from supporting standards.
	The team has chosen standards that lack rigor.	Be careful when making this inference. Primary grades often have standards with a DOK rigor level of 1. However, if a team seems to have chosen the easiest standards, sharing some questions released from the state test can help members see the disconnect between what they have on their list and what students will need to know for the state test.
	The team has chosen skills like *compare and contrast* instead of standards.	Sometimes teams misunderstand the work of choosing essential standards and think about broad concepts and skills rather than standards. Of course, it's easier to fix this at the start by making sure all team members have copies of their standards. However, if they've already done the work incorrectly, provide feedback to the team about how important it is to know whether students have mastered the essential standards.
Unwrapping	The team has not yet unwrapped all essential standards.	We recommend that the team unwrap all of its essential standards before developing its pacing guides. The reason for this is that some standards have learning targets that belong in different units in the curriculum. If the team hasn't unwrapped the standards yet, this might not be readily apparent. Provide the team members some examples from their standards of where this happens, such as this sixth-grade mathematics standard: "Fluently add, subtract, multiply and divide multi-digit decimals using the standard algorithm for each operation" (6.NS.3; NGA & CCSSO, 2010b), which might appear in several different units.
	The team has only listed explicit learning targets.	Ask the team some scaffolding questions: "What other content would students need to know in order to do _____?" "What lessons do you teach around prerequisite skills?" "How do you teach this?"
	The DOK the team has listed on the unwrapping document seems inaccurate.	Sometimes teams don't spend enough time reflecting on this step of the work—especially those that aren't as familiar with DOK. This will become more apparent when team members begin writing assessment items to match the rigor. Teams can access information about how each content area views the four DOK levels with a quick internet search; Norman Webb (2002), the author of the original work, published one around the four major content areas. Sharing documents like this should prove helpful.

Product	What to Look For	What Action to Take
Unwrapping	The team didn't list general ideas for assessment.	Remind team members that they don't need to develop the assessment at this time but rather to think about where it will be important to stop to do a common formative assessment. This will be important as they develop pacing guides and unit plans.
Pacing guide	The team has listed some standards as being taught all year long.	Leaders often can see this more easily than teams because they are likely looking more at the big picture and the team is focused on the discrete details. Once teams start to fill in their common formative assessments, this problem tends to come to light. This becomes a time to coach the team with specific questions: When you list this standard in unit 2, do you teach the whole standard then or just some learning targets? When you list this standard as being taught in all units, do you actually teach it multiple times or are you asking them to use something they've already learned?
	The team has not added enough time to teach, assess, and respond.	Pacing guides don't have to be as detailed as the unit plans. The key, though, is that the team allocates time in a way that emphasizes its essential standards. Ask clarifying questions such as, "You have one essential standard in unit 2 and four in unit 3, yet they each have the same amount of time allocated to them. Will you have enough time to teach and assess the four standards in unit 4? Have you added extra days to assess and respond in your units?"
Unit plans	The team is focused on activities rather than learning targets.	Teams that have listed activities rather than targets may or may not actually be teaching a standards-based curriculum. Make sure the team has unwrapped its standards and listed the learning targets. Using an upcoming unit, help the team see how its activities do or do not link to the target members expect students to know.
	The team has not included details about time for assessments and response.	Some teams get stuck here because they haven't eliminated anything from their past unit plans. A good facilitator can help them here. Ask, "What lessons or activities are *not* connected to either an essential or supporting standard?" Teams can eliminate these lessons easily. Then ask, "Which of these lessons or activities are connected to supporting standards? How can we compact them to get more time to teach the essential standards?"

Figure 5.11: Action planning for critical question 1.

Here's a Word of Advice

We recommend that teams think of their first experience with choosing essential standards as a learning process. Keep the first list as a draft and use them for a year. Throughout the year, make notes about what the team is learning. Are there some standards that teams should remove from the list? Are there others that need to be added? Most of the time there is a need for some revision to the initial list as teams become more familiar with the process and as they use assessments and responses based on their essential standards.

In the next chapter, we move on to critical question 2 and address how teams can find out whether their students have learned.

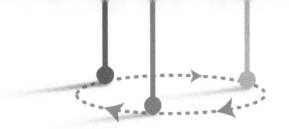

Chapter 6

A FOCUS ON MONITORING STUDENT LEARNING

One of the big ideas of PLCs is a focus on results of student learning. Members of PLCs don't use averages, hunches, or hope to determine whether each and every student is learning: they use *evidence*. Critical question 2, How will we know when they have learned it? (DuFour et al., 2016), requires teams to reach an agreement on the criteria and evidence that will tell members how *each* student is learning specific knowledge and skills. Answering critical question 2 also indicates the importance of designing or selecting assessments to gather evidence of student learning throughout the unit of study. Effective collaborative teams are hungry for this evidence. The evidence not only gives them feedback on their students' learning but on their instructional practices as well. Most importantly, however, it provides the team with knowledge of each and every student regarding the essential standards the team has prioritized. The teams in the following scenario have made a lot of progress with PLC implementation but haven't yet fully embraced the importance of focusing on results.

> *Principal Randall Johnson has been working with Lakeside Middle School teachers for the last two years to implement the elements of a PLC. He spent most of the first year engaging staff in revisiting the school's mission, vision, and collective commitments. In its second year of implementation, the school established a schedule that allowed collaborative teams to meet at least once weekly. During their collaborative time and with guidance from Randall and the other site leaders, teams focused on critical question 1. They identified their essential standards for each unit and*

unwrapped the standards to identify specific learning targets. This process helped the teams prioritize and agree on what students need to know and do, and the teams made strides in clarifying their collective expectations for student proficiency.

Some members of the teams, however, are now showing hesitancy in moving forward with critical question 2, which guides teams to design and use common formative assessments. During one team meeting, members express that they are uncomfortable making changes to assessments from their adopted curriculum because they aren't experts in assessment. They also assert that it would be a waste of time to recreate something different. When Randall asks teams how they are currently analyzing and using the results of student learning through these existing text-based assessments, the teams point out that students take the assessments online and are scored automatically. Because of this, teams are not really required to look closely at the results. They share that on average, approximately 80 percent of their students pass the assessments, and they feel that most students are doing well.

The teams at Lakeside have a mindset that is focused on averages and not *each* student—in other words; they do not have a true results orientation, which is the third big idea of a PLC (DuFour et al., 2016). Evidence of student learning is key to actualizing what Hattie and others describe as *collective teacher efficacy* (CTE): the collective belief of teachers that they can positively affect their students (Visible Learning, n.d.a). According to the meta-analyses conducted by Hattie and his colleagues, CTE has a 1.57 effect size, ranking it the most effective factor impacting student achievement (Visible Learning, n.d.b). However, leaders should note that CTE is not simply a mindset in which teams believe they can make a difference in student learning. While a positive mindset about impacting students has a beneficial effect, teams can only fully realize CTE when they have *evidence* of their impact from assessments that are aligned to what they want their students to know and do—put simply, there's a clear causal effect identified through their focused work. Effective teams identify specific skills that they want to establish in their students' learning, identify the specific evidence that will tell them whether they actually hit those learning targets, and collectively teach and gather evidence along the way. Once gathered, they use the evidence or results to make instructional decisions that will help their students learn more.

Teams that have not yet established common measures for gathering and analyzing evidence about what they desire their students to learn are missing the opportunity to closely examine the impact of their practice and use that knowledge to help students learn at higher levels.

Before developing assessments, teams must be absolutely clear on the different types of assessments and how they relate to the continuous improvement process. Schools and districts typically gather data on student learning through a variety of measures, each of which falls into one of three major categories and purposes. The chart in table 6.1 outlines these categories and provides examples of specific assessments that students may receive. The assessments that teams prioritize the most appear in bold. At times, teams may be overwhelmed knowing which assessments they should pay most attention to. By clarifying the purpose of each assessment type, leaders can help teams prioritize their focus on their current (unit-based) assessments, which provide immediate and actionable feedback on their students' learning.

Table 6.1: Examples of Assessment Types

Current (Unit-Based) Assessments	Progressive or Periodic Assessments	Cumulative or Annual Assessments
• Classroom formative assessment practices (individual teacher checks for understanding) • **Common formative assessments, including preassessments** • **Common end-of-unit (summative) assessments**	• Quarterly or trimester benchmarks or interim measures • Periodic progress monitoring of supports and interventions • Mid-course and cumulative assessments	• High-stakes annual state assessments • Language development assessments • Career and technical education certification exam

Note: Bold items indicate assessments that receive the most focus from teams.

Source: Adapted from Bailey & Jakicic, 2017.

While assessments in each of the three categories provide information, only current (unit-based) assessments are tied directly to what students are learning at any given time. Common assessments, both formative and end of unit (or summative), are the assessments that teams use to drive their inquiry and actions around student learning. They are directly tied to what teams want students to know and do based on the priorities for the unit. Unlike assessments found in the other two categories, common assessments serve to provide teams with timely and relevant evidence that they can act on to support students throughout the instructional process. As leaders support the work of teams with assessments, there are several practices to look for. In this chapter, we'll discuss these practices in detail and then provide tools leaders can use to assess, analyze, and act to help teams improve their assessment practices to ensure the highest level of learning for all students.

Understand Essential Practices for Effective Assessments

As leaders look at collaborative work centered on critical question 2, it helps to organize the skills and practices they will want to see into four major areas.

1. Collective purpose and mindset

2. Collaborative design of quality assessments

3. Analysis of results and taking action

4. Engagement of students in the process

Let's take a look at what leaders would hope to see in each of these areas, which serve as the fundamental elements of designing and using common assessments. Chapters 7 (page 187) and 8 (page 205) will continue to examine the practices that teams use to respond to the information from the assessments to answer critical questions 3 and 4.

Collective Purpose and Mindset

Teams move into the work of designing and using common assessments by first getting clear on their purpose. Frequently, teams are reluctant to move into the realm of common assessments because they may fear that either leadership or other members of the team might view data through evaluative eyes. It's important to clarify that the purpose of common assessments is not to compete but to collaborate for the benefit of all students. Common assessments have value in four major areas.

1. Teams can use the data coming from these assessments to learn whether their students have mastered specific skills and targets, and identify any trends (strengths and weaknesses) related to student learning.

2. Teams can use student evidence to identify the instructional practices that yield high levels of learning. Teams can in turn incorporate these practices into their plan for supporting students still struggling with the concept or skill.

3. Teams can use the information to document any curricular or instructional changes that need to take place in the future so that team members carry forward their learning the next time they teach the unit or lesson.

4. Teams can use the results of common assessments to provide students with feedback on their learning that activates a learner response.

As teams work to clarify the purpose of common assessments, many find it helpful to look back at their collective commitments and team norms to ensure their alignment with the school's mission and vision, as well as to address any qualms about sharing data. For example, a team might include the following statement in its norms: *We agree to use data from common assessments to collectively improve our practices and help students learn more.*

When teams are clear on their purpose for assessing student learning, they see the potential to answer powerful questions that can inform progress in student achievement, curricular alignment, and focused interventions. In our book *Simplifying Common Assessment: A Guide for Professional Learning Communities at Work* (Bailey & Jakicic, 2017), we highlight the types of questions that effective teams, through the use of common assessments, are continuously answering about their students' achievement in learning, the alignment of their instruction, and the assistance necessary to support student learning. Table 6.2 outlines the types of questions that teams consider when viewing common formative unit-based assessments; table 6.3 (page 168) presents questions for teams to consider regarding common summative unit-based assessments. Teams approach their inquiry around learning using protocols that guide teams to consider two question levels: (1) *wide-angle questions* are the big-picture questions teams pose as they look at their data from a distance and see general trends and patterns as a whole, and (2) *close-up questions* are those that guide teams to drill down and examine the learning of both specific groups of students and individual students to determine their particular strengths, weaknesses, and progress.

Table 6.2: Questions Teams Answer With Unit-Based Common Formative Assessments

	Wide-Angle Questions	Close-Up Questions
Achievement	What specific areas of learning did this assessment target? What was the standard for proficiency? In general, how did our students perform on this assessment? Were there common errors or misconceptions on the assessment?	How did specific students perform on this unit assessment? Were there students achieving above or below expectations?
Alignment	Did our instruction seem to align to the targeted learning? What potential gaps in our instruction might account for areas of weakness? What skill sets or standards did we design the assessment to measure?	Did we design our instruction to lead to proficiency on these targets? What implications for our instructional design come from these data?
Assistance	What students or groups demonstrate significant gaps in their achievement on this assessment?	Which specific students need additional assistance? How might we strengthen the areas we identified from the results of this assessment for specific students?

Source: Bailey & Jakicic, 2017, p. 10.

Table 6.3: Questions Teams Answer With Unit-Based Common Summative Assessments

	Wide-Angle Questions	Close-Up Questions
Achievement	What was the overall performance of students on this measure? Did our students meet the expected levels of proficiency?	Are there any concepts or skills we should carry forward in our instruction as we teach and assess in the next unit?
Alignment	Did we intentionally teach the skills and concepts we targeted in our original plan? Do the essential standards we selected align with those we prioritize in the assessment?	How might these results inform the design of our instruction the next time we teach this unit?
Assistance	How are student subgroups performing in relation to the majority of students? Are there clusters of students significantly above or below the targeted performance levels?	Are any students not consistently demonstrating progress toward mastering the foundational or essential skills we identified? Did we provide these students additional scaffolding or support as we taught the unit? What was the response to this support?

Source: Bailey & Jakicic, 2017, p. 9.

Each level of questioning serves a purpose in the continuous improvement cycle used by collaborative teams. Using these questions during the analysis of data helps ensure that teams are considering not only the results in learning of both individual students and groups but also examining the larger implications for adjustments in their curriculum, instruction, assessments, and differentiation efforts.

Collaborative Design of Quality Assessments

When teams begin the process of designing common assessments, they often dwell on whether items are rigorous enough or if they're well written. Examining artifacts related to common assessments can reveal a lot about the processes that teams use to create aligned assessments and their clarity around learning targets. Here are some specific indicators of quality assessments and practices that lead to their development that school leaders can look for as they examine these artifacts.

- Teams create a clear blueprint indicating the alignment between assessment items and learning targets.

  ○ Teams use an *assessment planning chart* (Bailey & Jakicic, 2017), which serves as a blueprint to align the assessment items to specific learning targets, such as the example in figure 6.1.

Learning Targets	Level of Cognitive Demand				What Proficiency Looks Like (on specific targets)
	Recalling DOK 1	Basic Reasoning DOK 2	Strategic Thinking and Complex Reasoning DOK 3	Extended Thinking DOK 4	
Compare two decimals with **like** *digits (for example, both hundredths).* **DOK 2**		Four multiple-choice items using like decimal pairs (hundredths and thousandths) and choice of >, <, or =			Students are proficient when they answer three out of four items correctly.
Solve real-world problems requiring a comparison of decimals to thousandths. **DOK 3**			Constructed-response item that provides an anonymous student solution to a problem that embeds the need to compare decimals to thousandths. Students must evaluate how a person solved a problem. Is the answer correct? Why or why not?		Students will provide the correct answer and provide support and reasons to justify their evaluation.

Source: Adapted from Bailey & Jakicic, 2017.

Figure 6.1: Sample common formative assessment planning chart for unit 4 in grade 5 mathematics.

*Visit **go.SolutionTree.com/PLCbooks** for a free reproducible version of this figure.*

- ○ Teams reference their assessment blueprint throughout the design and use of the assessments within the unit.

- Teams create assessment items to measure specific learning targets.

  - ○ Teams consider the type of item (constructed response, selected response, and so on) necessary to accurately measure the specific learning target when creating formative assessment items.

  - ○ There is a clear alignment between a learning target and the item or items that measure its achievement.

  - ○ Summative items may integrate multiple learning targets, but teams should be able to clarify which targets they are measuring.

- Teams align items with the content and rigor of the learning target.
  - Item types are appropriate for measuring the learning target with the appropriate level of rigor.
  - Teams examine existing items closely to ensure alignment with both the content and the rigor of the target.
  - Teams have included DOK references on the assessment planning chart or blueprint and unwrapping documents and have considered them when designing the items.
  - The text or passages used within the assessment items are at a level appropriate for the grade-level expectations, or teams have an intentional plan for scaffolding the complexity.
- There are sufficient items to reliably measure learning without consuming too much instructional time.
  - The teams design assessments with three to four selected-response items *or* one to two constructed-response items per learning target.
- Selected-response distractors consist of common errors.
  - Teams have brainstormed common or anticipated misconceptions prior to the design or selection of their items.
  - Members are intentional about using those as distractors on selected-response items or as nonexamples of quality work on their scoring guides or rubrics.
- There is a clear plan for consistent assessment, including the time frame and method.
  - The team takes the time in advance of giving the assessment to clarify the administration procedures and time frame for the assessment.
- Teams collectively define proficiency and establish scoring parameters, including the weighting of items, prior to administering assessments.
  - Teams have reached decisions on the weighting of each item on the assessment and considered the complexity of each learning target as part of the process.
  - Teams have established scoring rubrics or guides.
  - Teams have reached consensus about what they consider to be proficiency on the overall assessment or individual learning targets prior to administering the assessment.

○ If the task integrates multiple standards or learning targets, the scoring guide or rubric reflects specific feedback on each aspect.

Leaders can use these indicators to monitor the process teams use to create common assessments and the quality of their assessment design.

Analysis of Results and Taking Action

When schools first delve into the practices around team-developed common assessments, they face the risk that teams will perceive that simply giving the assessment is the end goal. Yet, as we have seen in our own experiences at schools and as is affirmed by the work on collective efficacy, the magic happens when teams examine the results of their assessments *and take action* to improve those results in the future (Donohoo, 2017; Hattie, 2012). In order to successfully and efficiently move through an analysis and engage in productive planning for next steps, however, teams need to use a protocol. A number of such protocols are available to help teams analyze their results, including those we provide in *Common Formative Assessment* and *Simplifying Common Assessment* (Bailey & Jakicic, 2012, 2017). In general, these protocols provide a structure that helps members of a team look strategically at the results coming from their assessments. Figure 6.2 (page 172) provides a basic protocol for analyzing assessment results that will guide teams through meaningful conversations and the creation of a game plan for their next steps. Note that the times indicated on the protocol are approximate. Teams can streamline some aspects of the protocol depending on the type of tools that teams use. For example, when using spreadsheets, teams can adjust the settings to conditionally format cells automatically to indicate student levels of proficiency.

A major function of the results analysis is to determine the status of student learning. Student by student and skill by skill, teams can analyze results to identify who needs additional time and support and in what specific skills or concepts. The actions stemming from this analysis are short term in nature. Teams use the information to help students in a timely fashion, using Tier 2 interventions. We further discuss how teams move through the process of taking action on intervention in chapter 7 (page 187).

In addition to the short-term goal of identifying students who need additional time and support and strategizing their interventions, team members consider long-term implications for their instruction and assessment. For example, they may realize that they need more time in their pacing guide to teach a particular skill or concept and will adjust it when they teach it next, increasing the likelihood that more students will attain the skill. Here are some key questions that teams can use as they analyze the implications for their curriculum.

- **Alignment:** Does the curriculum we teach and assess align with the standards? Do we accurately focus on supporting student learning of the skills and concepts that they need to be successful?

Protocol for Analyzing Assessment Results
1. Frame the meeting. (One minute) • Establish the purpose of the meeting. • Review norms (with a focus on norms that describe how the team will use data).
2. Review the focus of the assessment. (Three minutes) • Identify the essential standards and specific learning targets the team will assess and which items it designed to assess each of them. If appropriate, discuss prior instruction. • Review the expectations for proficiency (for example, two out of three correct on a multiple-choice assessment means a "Proficient" on the rubric). • Discuss any questions members have when they score student work.
3. Determine patterns and strengths in student responses and identify misconceptions that surface through common errors. (Seven to ten minutes) • For each learning target, examine the patterns based on student proficiency. • Evaluate which skills or concepts students seem to have learned at high levels. Determine reasons for those high levels (for example, what strategies led to that high level of learning). • Evaluate which skills or concepts require additional time or support on a large scale (that is, the whole class) versus those that require support through smaller groups.
4. Determine specific students who are not yet proficient on the learning targets measured in the assessment, as well as those who might need additional reinforcement *or* extension. (Five minutes) • Organize the information using a chart or spreadsheet that all members can access (each member can add his or her students to a specific group). • Once teams have identified the students who need help, regroup them by specific need (for example, students who made a calculation error versus students who chose the wrong solution pathway). {TABLE_BELOW}
5. Determine strategies for intervention, remediation, and extension. (Fifteen minutes) • Decide whether to develop small groups for reteaching or use a re-engagement lesson with the whole class. • Teams co-plan their strategies for supporting each learning target. • If necessary, go back to best practice information about how to teach the concept or about what strategies work best for struggling students. Consult instructional coaches or specialists if necessary.
6. Identify or develop the items teams will use to monitor whether students meet the learning target after teams have provided this response or support. (Three minutes) • The items identified by the team will provide information about which students still need help with this essential target after they receive interventions or support. In addition, discuss any implications for instructional strategies that teams should emphasize or curriculum adjustments they should make.
7. Discuss any learnings or insights related to the future work of the team. (Five minutes) • Examine any implications for the team's professional practice gained from the analysis, including adjustments or revisions to the curriculum or assessment (such as pacing or assessment items), identifying effective versus ineffective instructional strategies, or strategies to support or extend learning for students.

The table embedded in item 4:

Interventions	Reinforcement	Extensions

Figure 6.2: Protocol for analyzing assessment results.

- **Pacing:** Did we spend enough time teaching this skill or concept, or do we need to adjust the amount of time in our pacing guide to get better outcomes in our students' learning?

- **Assessment design and item clarification:** Do the items really measure what we want students to learn? Do any questions require revision so that they more accurately reflect student learning? Are we building student exposure to formats and tasks they will encounter on high-stakes assessments?

These questions guide teams to reflect on the implication for their instruction and assessment moving forward. By embedding this reflection, teams can document their own learning that took place during the assessment process and use that information to make specific adjustments the next time they teach that particular unit.

Engagement of Students in the Process

A final element of quality assessment practice is intentionally engaging students in the assessment process. Research strongly supports the practice of students giving and getting feedback on the skills that teachers target through instruction, and then identifying strategies to move forward to improve any gaps that exist (Hattie, 2012; Wiliam, 2018). As part of the assessment planning and implementation process, teams can strategize how they will share feedback with students as well as how students can record their progress, develop goals, and identify strategies for improving their learning. Teams can also adopt general routines that take place following the administration of their assessments that engage students with feedback on a timely basis. Such routines can include students analyzing the results of their assessments by learning target, making corrections based on new learning, tracking their progress, and re-engaging in similar tasks to solidify and practice new skills.

Assess the Current Reality

Prior to embarking on the process of assessing, analyzing, and taking action to support collaborative work around critical question 2, school leaders must have an awareness of their school's context as it relates to assessment. The guiding questions in figure 6.3 (page 174) facilitate leader reflection on any contextual insights that would lead to informed decisions.

To help leaders answer the question, What's your current reality?, we have provided several formative tools for gathering information about the work of teams on collaborative design of quality assessments. These tools can help leaders collect the evidence of particular teams or of overall implementation in a school.

- Examination of Artifacts Tool

- Teams' Analysis of Results and Taking Action Protocol

- Student-Involved Assessment Worksheet

Guiding Questions	Reflection on Context
What are the current assessments that the district supports and expects? Are teams clear on their purpose or potential value? How do teams currently use the information from those assessments?	
What is the current level of understanding related to the use of common assessments? Are there any misconceptions? What are the current practices in place around the design and use of common end-of-unit (summative) and formative assessments? What successes have teams experienced? What challenges have presented themselves?	
What team configurations might require adjustments in the design and use of collaborative assessment protocols? For example, does the school composition require that teams are vertical or multidisciplinary in nature? Are there teams made up of elective teachers who each teach unique subject matter? What opportunities do those members have to connect with job-alike teachers in other schools?	

Figure 6.3: Guiding questions to consider the context of assessment in the school.

Visit **go.SolutionTree.com/PLCbooks** *for a free reproducible version of this figure.*

Examination of Artifacts Tool

School leaders can monitor the quality of assessments by looking at the products teams create. Schools that employ shared electronic folders allow for easy access to these products, which ideally are organized by unit of study and essential standard. While looking at team-developed assessment products, leaders can look for evidence of the indicators represented in figure 6.4.

Teams' Analysis of Results and Taking Action Protocol

The tool in figure 6.5 combines the Protocol for Analyzing Assessment Results from figure 6.2 (page 172) with a set of observational questions leaders might look for as they observe a team analyzing its data. Using this tool as a guide for best practice during a team's analysis of formative or end-of-unit assessments, leaders can reflect on which aspects of the process appear strong and which aspects might need additional support.

Student-Involved Assessment Worksheet

In our book *Common Formative Assessment* (Bailey & Jakicic, 2012), we include a team worksheet, reproduced in figure 6.6 (page 178), that teams can use to reflect on the various elements of student-involved assessment practice. We created it because research overwhelmingly supports a strong correlation between engaging students in

Indicator	Evidence of the Practice and Observation Notes
Team has a clear assessment planning chart that outlines learning targets and provides information regarding alignment of items.	
Team has created or selected items to accurately measure specific learning targets.	
Team has aligned items with the content and rigor of the learning targets.	
There are sufficient items to reliably measure learning.	
Selected response distractors consist of common errors.	
There is a clear plan for giving assessment consistently, including the time frame and method.	
Team has collectively defined proficiency and scoring prior to administering the assessment, including the weighting of items.	

Figure 6.4: Indicators to examine team assessment artifacts.

Visit go.SolutionTree.com/PLCbooks for a free reproducible version of this figure.

Protocol for Analyzing Assessment Results	Observational Questions
1. **Frame the meeting. (One minute)** • Establish the purpose of the meeting. • Review norms (with a focus on norms that describe how the team will use data).	Did members come with their assessment results? Are they easily accessible? Did the team review norms?
2. **Review the focus of the assessment. (Three minutes)** • Identify the essential standards and specific learning targets the team will assess and which items it designed to assess each of them. If appropriate, discuss prior instruction. • Review the expectations for proficiency (for example, two out of three correct on a multiple-choice assessment means a level 3 on the rubric). • Discuss any questions members have when they score student work.	Was there a plan for the assessment (that is, an assessment planning chart)? Did the team have a clear connection between items and its learning targets? Did the team determine proficiency levels before giving the assessment?

Figure 6.5: Assessment results protocol with observational questions for leaders.

continued →

Visit go.SolutionTree.com/PLCbooks for a free reproducible version of this figure.

Protocol for Analyzing Assessment Results	Observational Questions
3. Determine patterns and strengths in student responses and identify misconceptions that surface through common errors. (Seven to ten minutes) • For each learning target, examine the patterns based on student proficiency. • Evaluate which skills or concepts students seem to have learned at high levels. Determine reasons for those high levels. • Evaluate which skills or concepts require additional time or support on a large scale (that is, the whole class) versus those that require support through smaller groups.	Was the team able to examine the data and identify patterns (big-picture view) and specific students who need assistance?
4. Determine specific students who are not yet proficient on the learning targets measured in the assessment, as well as those who might need additional reinforcement *or* extension. (Five minutes) • Organize the information using a chart or spreadsheet that all members can access (each member can add his or her students to a specific group). • Once teams have identified the students who need help, regroup them by specific need (for example, students who made a calculation error versus students who chose the wrong solution pathway). 	Interventions	Reinforcement	Extensions
---	---	---
				How did the team identify and flag the students who need additional time and support? Is there sufficient information that tells the team the specific skill interventions that students need?
5. Determine strategies for intervention, remediation, and extension. (Fifteen minutes) • Decide whether to develop small groups for reteaching or use a re-engagement lesson with the whole class. • Teams co-plan their strategies for supporting each learning target. • If necessary, go back to best practice information about how to teach the concept or about what strategies work best for struggling students. Consult instructional coaches or specialists if necessary.	Did the team identify effective instructional strategies through the conversation? Did the team develop a game plan for supporting students who are not yet proficient that incorporates those strategies? Is the game plan specific, and is follow-through clear? (That is, when, where, and who?)
6. Identify or develop the items teams will use to monitor whether students meet the learning target after teams have provided this response or support. (Three minutes) • The items identified by the team will provide information about which students still need help with this essential target after they receive interventions or support. In addition, discuss any implications for instructional strategies that teams should emphasize or curriculum adjustments they should make.	Did the team discuss the evidence it will collect following interventions to ensure that it has current information on student learning?
7. Discuss any learnings or insights related to the future work of the team. (Five minutes) • Examine any implications for the team's professional practice gained from the analysis, including adjustments or revisions to the curriculum or assessment (such as pacing or assessment items), identifying effective versus ineffective instructional strategies, or strategies to support or extend learning for students.	Has the team gained instructional or curriculum insights from its assessment results? Has it made or noted its adjustments for the next time members teach the unit?

the assessment process and their learning outcomes (Saphier, 2017; Wiliam, 2018). Knowing that this is a powerful practice, leaders can provide this tool to teams to help them reflect on their current practices related to student engagement and empowerment with meaningful assessment.

After having each team examine the evidence of its practices, leaders have teams report out the elements that they are celebrating, and share particular elements that they prioritized for improvement. Following the team shares, leaders can use the scores to identify common areas of strength and needs for improvement and guide next steps.

Analyze Patterns and Priorities

Based on the evidence they gather through the formative tools provided in this chapter, leaders can start to determine what the current level of use is among teams of each aspect of common assessments. Following are some guiding questions that a leadership team can consider as they examine their evidence of implementation.

- Do teams need to build shared knowledge around the *why* of common assessments and how they fit into the ongoing work of collaborative teams?

- Do teams need to build the skills and processes needed to *design* aligned assessment items that help gauge student learning of essential learning targets?

- Do teams need to build knowledge about best practices for *scoring and analyzing* the results?

- Are teams still learning the process of designing and using common assessments? *What support do teams need* as they apply their newly learned knowledge related to common assessments?

- Is there *collective agreement on expectations for scoring* proficiency on common assessments?

- Are some teams more advanced in the use of common assessments than others? How might you use the power of *example and peer mentorships*?

- What is the level of *student engagement* in the process?

Additionally, leaders can use the continuum in figure 6.7 (page 179) to summarize the level of implementation in the indicators related to assessment and help identify strengths and potential areas for improvement.

Directions: Using the following scale, rate your team's practice around the elements of student-involved assessment in the left-hand column. In the center column, put a check by the evidence of practice and add other pieces of evidence if present. Share your findings of strengths and priorities for improvement with your team and discuss possible strategies for increasing your practices in an element selected for improvement in the right-hand column.

1—We see no evidence of practice in this area.

2—We are in the process of learning and developing strategies in this area.

3—We demonstrate partial implementation of these practices and strategies across our team.

4—This is consistently implemented across our team.

Elements of Student-Involved Assessment	Evidence of Practice	Processes and Strategies to Increase Student-Involved Assessment
Students are clear on the learning targets. 1 2 3 4	☐ Team develops student-friendly targets and "I can" statements.	
Students actively engage in the identification of quality indicators. 1 2 3 4	☐ Students are involved in development of rubrics. ☐ Students generate assessments. ☐ The teacher provides exemplars and anchor papers to ensure student awareness of quality. These exemplars may be pre-annotated to highlight quality characteristics, or students may identify the characteristics and annotate themselves (individually or as part of a group).	
Students engage in guided self-assessment. 1 2 3 4	☐ Students self-monitor their understanding. ☐ Teacher models self-assessment.	
Students engage in guided peer assessment and collaboration. 1 2 3 4	☐ Students use assessments they have generated. ☐ Students use peer feedback circles (that is, providing feedback on each other's work).	
Students engage in self-monitoring and goal setting. 1 2 3 4	☐ Students engage in student-led conferences and goal setting, and they track their own progress.	

Total: _____ /20 points

Source: Adapted from Bailey & Jakicic, 2012.

Figure 6.6: Student-involved assessment worksheet.

*Visit **go.SolutionTree.com/PLCbooks** for a free reproducible version of this figure.*

Knowledge and Practice	Level of Use or Implementation			
	Limited	Emerging	Established	Strategic
Collective purpose and mindset	Teams are unclear on the real purpose of common assessments. They may perceive that they will be used to evaluate them and will simply result in busywork or comparisons between teachers.	Teams are building knowledge about the purpose and power of common assessment. While they may still have questions or concerns, they have a general sense that they are used to help students learn more and are not intended to be used for the purpose of comparing or evaluating team members.	Teams are working with a clear purpose as they design and use their assessments. While they may still have questions about the process, their focus is clearly on learning. The teams have moved from compliance to commitment to the process.	Teams have a high level of confidence and ongoing commitment in the use of common assessments. They continue to focus on improvement in both the assessment process itself as well as the use of results.
Collaborative design of quality assessments	Teams have not created an assessment plan to guide their assessment work. Teams haven't yet started to look at issues connected with writing quality questions or clarifying their expectations for proficiency.	Teams are learning the process for planning their assessments prior to each unit using a backward planning process. Learning targets drive the design. Teams are learning about writing quality questions and are applying it to their work.	Teams have a clear assessment plan outlining the learning targets and assessment items to be used. Considerations for rigor and alignment with high-stakes items are integrated within the design. Distractors in selected-response or multiple-choice items are common error answers. Teams are in consensus about the evidence members consider for proficiency in student learning and engage in conversations to reach that consensus.	Teams are confident in their planning process. They naturally evaluate the effectiveness of each assessment plan after the assessment is given to determine if the right targets were assessed and the best item type was chosen. Products are exemplary. After each assessment, teams reflect on the questions they used to determine if those questions were effectively written.

Figure 6.7: Continuum of practice for common assessment.

continued →

*Visit **go.SolutionTree.com/PLCbooks** for a free reproducible version of this figure.*

Knowledge and Practice	Level of Use or Implementation			
	Limited	Emerging	Established	Strategic
Use of results to examine practices and take action	Teams do not analyze results. They may look at averages for whole classes but are not using a protocol to dig more deeply and use the results to take action.	Teams are learning to move through the analysis of results by using a common protocol but need support or facilitation as they examine the results by learning target.	Teams use a protocol to analyze the results of their assessment and identify students who need additional time and support. Teams also reflect on the quality of their assessment items and note areas to change for the next time the unit is taught. Their analysis drives actions to further support students and reflect on their instructional practices.	Teams are taking both the short-term and long-term view of assessment results, making instructional changes to impact this year's students but also making the investment for future students by using results to refine their instructional strategies, pacing, and assessments.
Student engagement with the assessment process	Students are not actively part of the assessment process.	Students are clear on learning targets, but teams have not yet implemented intentional actions to tie evidence of learning to those targets.	Teams make intentional efforts to tie student evidence of learning and feedback to the learning goals. Students engage in the process of analyzing their strengths and weaknesses.	Students are continuously gauging their progress along their learning targets within the unit. They give and get feedback from various formative efforts and are empowered with strategies to close the gap in areas where they are not yet proficient.

Leaders can use this continuum on an ongoing basis, updating the picture of assessment practice across teams and using the level of implementation to guide next steps.

Act on Evidence to Improve Practice

What next steps are going to help teams move forward in the design and use of assessments? Using the continuum in figure 6.7 as a guide, school leaders can get a sense of the needs of their teams. If the majority of implementation levels falls into the Limited area of the continuum, leaders should first emphasize building shared knowledge about common assessments. We have outlined specific actions in the following sections that may be appropriate based on your analysis.

- Build shared knowledge about common assessment.
- Equip teams with processes to align common assessments with essential standards.
- Train teams in protocols for analyzing results and taking action.
- Establish clear expectations.
- Monitor and support teams.
- Celebrate the work.

Shared Knowledge About Common Assessment

Teams will be most effective when they truly understand the purposes and power of common assessment. Leaders can use a number of resources to guide teams in learning about the why of common assessments and the characteristics of quality assessment practices, including our own books on common assessments, *Common Formative Assessment* and *Simplifying Common Assessment* (Bailey & Jakicic, 2012, 2017). Here, we highlight the most crucial concepts for building shared knowledge with teams.

The first concept is to help teachers make the connection between what they want to see in student learning (that is, critical question 1) and the school's mission to ensure that all students are learning at high levels. It's not possible to know whether students are reaching high levels unless teams are intentional about gathering evidence. By answering critical question 2, teams get specific information about what students are learning right now—what team members are teaching. In addition, common assessments provide opportunities to learn how team members' teaching strategies impact that learning.

By agreeing with colleagues who teach the same course or grade level about the evidence that proves students have learned a skill, members can create more valid assessments. That means that team members analyze data together; they don't use data to evaluate each other but rather to determine how to take action to help students learn. These actions include developing interventions as well as improving teams' own practices through examining effective versus ineffective strategies.

When designing assessments, a team's goal should be to ensure *content* and *face validity*—in other words, assessments that are intentionally designed and appear to measure what teachers target for their students to learn. It's likely that many teachers are overwhelmed by the number of assessments they may be giving their students, and the perception of giving more might be daunting to some. Additionally, if teachers aren't involved or confident in analyzing the data from the assessments they are giving, they may not understand the differences among the different assessment types and how they can use the information to support student learning. When leaders first engage teachers with the notion of using common assessments, it's helpful to review the three main assessment types and clarify for teams that common assessments are those that are closely linked to what they are teaching, and are used by teams to improve learning, not as a means to hold teachers accountable. In addition, it helps to share with teams clear examples of common assessments at both the formative and end-of-unit levels. Table 6.1 (page 165) in this chapter can be used to communicate assessment types with teams.

Team Processes to Align Common Assessments With Essential Standards

Collaborative teams benefit from having a step-by-step process for designing formative and end-of-unit assessments that align with essential standards. Figure 6.8 shows a protocol we created to guide teams in the backward planning process of designing an assessment. Providing teams with a clear protocol will empower them to move forward with assessment design and increase the likelihood that they will produce aligned assessments. This is a simplified version of the process that we share with teams. More detailed processes can be found in *Common Formative Assessment* and *Simplifying Common Assessment* (Bailey & Jakicic, 2012, 2017).

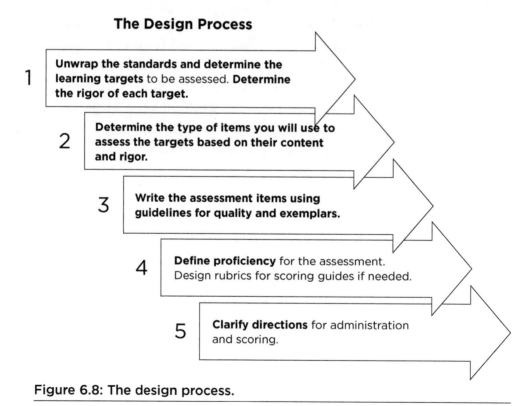

The Design Process

1. **Unwrap the standards and determine the learning targets** to be assessed. **Determine the rigor of each target.**

2. Determine the type of items you will use to assess the targets based on their content and rigor.

3. Write the assessment items using guidelines for quality and exemplars.

4. **Define proficiency** for the assessment. Design rubrics for scoring guides if needed.

5. **Clarify directions** for administration and scoring.

Figure 6.8: The design process.

The following list of indicators, simplified from a version earlier in this chapter in the Collaborative Design of Quality Assessments section (page 168), helps teams build knowledge about the qualities of well-designed assessments; they can also use these indicators as a check for quality.

- Teams create items to measure specific learning targets (skills and concepts identified from unwrapping the essential standards).

- Teams develop a clear blueprint indicating which items align to which learning targets (assessment items can also be labeled based on the learning targets they are measuring for students).

- Teams align items with the rigor of the learning target.

- Teams ensure a sufficient number of items to reliably measure learning (three to four selected-response items per learning target *or* one to two constructed-response items per learning target).

- Teams write selected-response distractors as common errors.

- Teams have a clear plan for giving the assessment consistently, including the specific time frame and method.

- Teams collectively define proficiency and scoring prior to administering the assessment, including weighting of items.

These indicators are valuable for leaders and collaborative teams to help them ensure quality as they implement common assessments.

Team Protocols for Analyzing Results and Taking Action

Earlier in the chapter, we shared a protocol in figure 6.2 (page 172) that teams can use to analyze the results of their assessments and formulate an actionable plan. Leaders can support teams in using such a protocol by creating opportunities to walk through the process with guidance. One strategy for doing so is to have teams come to a collaborative meeting with data from a common assessment with the leader in attendance. The leader initially introduces the analysis protocol, and then the session proceeds using an *I do, you do* or accordion approach, in which each step is discussed in whole-group fashion, and then "accordions" back to teams so they practice the step with their team's real data. Within each step of this guided process, leaders can build familiarity with the protocol, allow for clarification of the steps, and give teams an actual experience of going through the process. At the end of the session, we like to have teams share out a reflection or something they will do with the information they gained through their analysis. By providing this supported process, leaders can help teams proceed more independently in the work of implementing common assessments, having gained clarity and confidence.

Clear Expectations

Once teams have shared knowledge about the why and the how of common assessments and their design, leaders can establish clear expectations for how teams will put that knowledge to use. It's important to build consensus across the school about these expectations. To do so, leaders can ask questions such as, "Now that we are clear about the power and process of common assessments to help students learn more, what might be our first step for ensuring that we implement them on a schoolwide basis?" Through a collective conversation, schools can establish clear expectations and a commitment to move forward in the design and use of common assessments. Schools can incrementally embed the use of common assessments so that teams aren't overwhelmed. We suggest that teams first practice their new knowledge of common assessments by implementing them with a focus on one standard or learning target in an upcoming unit of study and engage in a reflection process following its completion. For example, a secondary school may establish the following expectation:

> *All core instruction teams will create and give at least one common formative assessment during one unit in the first semester and engage in a protocol to examine the results. During the second semester, teams will give at least one common formative assessment and analyze the results during each unit taught.*

An elementary school in which all classes are self-contained might begin by having a similar expectation, but clarify that teams only focus their common assessments in one content area, such as literacy. Again, leaders should build in opportunities for reflection and discussion of next steps following the time frame that they establish.

By having the conversation around expectations, leaders also provide teams an opportunity to clarify misconceptions and address any concerns that might still exist. As part of the process, teams also benefit from reviewing their norms and collective commitments, which will set the stage for more successful implementation of common assessments.

Monitoring and Support of Teams

We want to stress that leaders need to be intentional about monitoring how their teams are doing in the assessment process. Potential strategies for monitoring include sitting in on collaborative meetings in which teams are designing or analyzing assessments, looking at artifacts or products related to assessment, interviewing teachers about the work, or asking leadership team members for feedback or insights related to their teams' progress and sharing data.

Occasionally, it may be necessary to provide additional time and support to jump-start or strengthen skills within a particular team. In this chapter's Assess the Current Reality section, we provided tools for observing teams and interviewing teachers about the practices (see figures 6.4, 6.5, and 6.6, pages 175–178). Leaders can use these tools to determine specific areas in which teams need support and in turn use that information to decide how best to support the team. For instance, in response to observations that a team is struggling to identify assessment items in reading comprehension, an instructional coach (if available) or administrator may be most helpful to support the team's design of aligned items.

Monitoring teams in the work on assessment also provides leaders with insights about exemplary practices and bright spots across the school. Leaders can use these exemplary models to support other teams, such as by creating opportunities for effective teams to showcase products on a regular basis. In this way, teams share their processes and gain insights from each other. Teams can hear from those actually doing the work around assessment and learn from their triumphs as well as areas of struggle. They also benefit from seeing the tools used by effective teams. For instance, one highly effective team might share its Google spreadsheet that automatically color-codes students when they are considered proficient, and other teams can adopt similar tools without having to reinvent the wheel. Over time, all teams can highlight their products and the learning they experience in their processes—so it's not just about the bright spots but about everyone moving forward.

Celebration of the Work

The assessment process can be challenging work, and leaders will want to ensure that they are recognizing teams for their efforts as well as their impact. Leaders can create quick opportunities to celebrate growth in both areas. For example, to celebrate efforts around the process of common assessments, the leader can recognize a team for its first completion of a full instructional cycle in which it designed, administered, analyzed, and acted on the results of its common assessment. Leaders could also recognize teams for the impact they make by empowering students to monitor their own learning and set goals, resulting in more students achieving proficiency than in prior years. Leaders can structure these opportunities as announcements in an online newsletter or embed them in whole-staff gatherings. The goal of these celebrations is to ensure that teams reflect and recognize growth and impact in their practices, increasing their collective teacher efficacy.

Lead Assessment Practices to Improve Student Learning

When teams become confident and accurate in the design of their common assessments, and commit to a process of intentionally gathering information about whether their students are actually learning what they want them to learn, an important shift takes place. The focus is no longer on teaching; it's on student learning. In our view, the investment that leaders make to support common assessment practices will reap huge benefits, not only in the students' learning, but also in the empowerment and efficacy of collaborative teams. In the next chapter, we'll examine how school leaders can look more specifically at the actions that teams take to support students when they are struggling to learn.

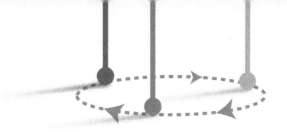

Chapter 7

A FOCUS ON SUPPORTING STUDENTS WHO NEED ADDITIONAL TIME AND SUPPORT

Teams that see the impact of their effort build collective teacher efficacy (Donohoo, 2017). They can see actual impact on student learning as the fruit of their labor. However, this can only happen when teams take action, using the information they gather from their common assessments to design and use powerful interventions. The English team in the following scenario hasn't yet reached the place where members are using their common assessments to inform their next steps for instruction.

> *As a routine process during the Weston Middle School leadership team meetings, members check in to share their teams' recent efforts, highlighting both celebrations and challenges. When it's the English chair's turn, she reluctantly shares, "We've been giving our common assessments and looking at the results after they're done, but I don't feel we're really using the information to help kids. It seems like we're doing this just to comply, and frankly, it's taking a lot of time. Several members of our team are wondering why we're even required to use them."*

Critical question 3 exists to prompt action on this very problem: What do we do when they haven't learned it? (DuFour et al., 2016). That is, how do we *respond* when students aren't learning? Simply delivering assessments and admiring the data won't help students close gaps, nor will it help teachers experience the sense of empowerment in supporting more students in their learning.

This chapter digs into the practices that teams use to effectively respond, not just react, to information about student learning in order to provide targeted support.

Likewise, the tools to assess, analyze, and act in this chapter are designed to provide leaders with insight into the level of implementation of these practices so that they too can respond by providing targeted support to their teams as needed.

Understand Essential Practices to Respond When Students Aren't Learning

Several key elements lead to teams building effective responses to students who need additional time and support within a schoolwide system of support such as RTI. There are many resources that provide a much more detailed overview of the RTI process, chief among them *Taking Action* (Buffum et al., 2018), but here we attempt to highlight those elements that will focus leaders' assessment of the school's implementation and help gauge the needs of teams. These elements include a collective purpose and mindset, structures and processes to ensure a timely response, interventions that target specific skills and concepts, effective and co-planned strategies based on results, and monitored impact. We discuss each in the following sections.

Collective Purpose and Mindset

We have observed the critical role that team clarity plays when moving into the intervention process. Members must understand the connection to the continuous improvement process (that is, the PDSA cycle—see chapter 2, page 39), with particular focus on the *study* and *act* portion of the process.

When first implementing the work of PLCs, there is significant focus around identifying what teams want students to learn and gathering evidence of that learning—in other words, actions that address critical questions 1 and 2. Once teams begin to click with these first two questions, the natural next step is to actually use the information to support student learning. However, teams need to build clarity about the nature of interventions and how, in a PLC, they differ from more traditional interventions or remediation. In a traditional intervention model, a classroom teacher may be the sole source of support for a wide range of student needs. Alternatively, those teaching in a more traditional setting may have the mindset that students who struggle should receive support from an expert outside of the classroom, relinquishing responsibility from the teacher. In a PLC, however, providing support to students who are struggling with their current learning is the collective responsibility of all teachers on a collaborative team. In a traditional model, the intervention itself may be loosely connected to the specific skills or concepts a student is to be learning in their classroom, while interventions in a PLC are directly tied to what students are currently learning.

As shared in chapter 4 (page 105), schools that embrace the PLC process work from the mindset that the entire staff, rather than individual teachers, takes collective responsibility for the design and delivery of support for students. It's important that team members understand the structures and purpose of a schoolwide tiered system of support and the role that collaborative teams play in the overall system. While the leadership team ensures that structures and procedures exist to allow all levels of support to take place, the responsibility for Tier 1 (instruction that all students receive) and Tier 2 interventions (additional time and support for students who need supplemental help) falls into the realm of team responsibility (Buffum et al., 2018). We've discussed in more specificity the role of the team in providing Tier 1 support around essential standards using common formative assessments in chapters 5 (page 135) and 6 (page 163).

Specific collaborative team actions that take place in Tier 2 include the following.

- Teams provide systematic interventions to students on a timely basis based on the results of common end-of-unit assessments.

- Teams collect data throughout the interventions to monitor their effectiveness.

- Interventions reflect best instructional practices and use research-based programs whenever appropriate.

- Support that students receive is directive, not invitational. Students receive additional time and support within their instructional program (rather than being required to attend before and after school).

- Teachers do not exclude students from core (Tier 1) instruction in order to provide intervention and support.

Although schools might have general discussions about the need to support the learning of all students, it's important to clarify assumptions and revisit collective commitments related to providing additional time and support that some students need. For instance, a collective commitment might be, "We are willing to do whatever it takes to ensure that our students learn." As part of the process of intervention, teams recommit to the notion that if they want to ensure learning for all, then their purpose as a collaborative team is to ensure that learning by providing targeted support. Teams make the connection between more effectively targeting essential standards in their assessments and their greater ability to impact student learning through targeted interventions, as shown in figure 7.1 (page 190), which depicts the use of formative assessments to measure specific learning targets throughout a unit of instruction.

As illustrated in figure 7.1, a response to formative assessments is embedded in a timely fashion during the journey of learning, not simply when the unit is finished or as measured by an end-of-unit or summative assessment. By responding to small pieces of learning, teams can take corrective action so that students can move forward within gaps in concepts or skills.

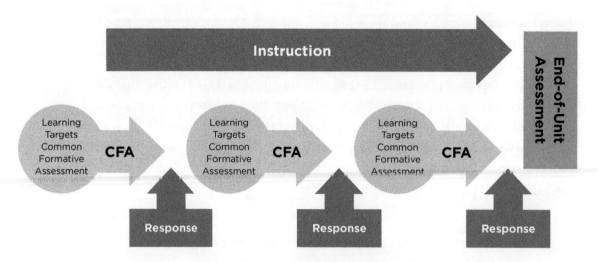

Figure 7.1: Connecting targeted assessments to targeted interventions.

Structures and Processes to Ensure Timely Response

Tier 2 responses or interventions are tied to what students need to know and do to learn their current content. The intent of those responses is to intervene intentionally and strategically so that students' misconceptions or lack of skills don't interfere with future learning. Effective teams don't wait too long before acting. Teams provide initial responses and support based on formative assessments. Ideally, these responses further propel student learning by correcting misconceptions or skill gaps. Toward the end of an instructional unit or time frame, teams can use data from end-of-unit (summative) assessments to determine whether students have integrated their skills along the way or if specific gaps remain for some students. Using these data, teams can continue to support the skill for those students during Tier 2, while still moving forward in instruction. For instance, if there are sixth-grade mathematics students who still demonstrate gaps in the essential skill of interpreting and computing quotients of fractions, the team can infuse ongoing support and monitor their mastery even after the unit of study is complete.

To ensure the timely delivery of Tier 2 instruction, teams must not only follow a cycle of continuous improvement (the PDSA cycle) but also find specific time to provide students with additional time and support. Some schools have created a schedule with time embedded for Tier 2; however, if this is not established, teams can identify time in their schedule to provide Tier 2 support two to three times weekly. Some strategies for weaving in time for Tier 2 include the following.

- Regroup students during specific days of the week, distributing them across a grade-level or course-alike team to provide student support, reinforcement, or extensions on targeted skills and concepts.

- Move an end-of-unit or summative assessment earlier in the pacing guide and use the data to identify students for differentiated support taking place on the remaining days. In essence, the team is using the end-of-unit assessment formatively by continuing to use the data to increase student learning.

- Introduce "push in" support from specialists during designated times to allow for small-group interventions.

- Designate the first fifteen minutes of class the day following the formative assessment for engaging students in corrective instruction (whole class or small group).

- Choose specific days in the pacing guide for response following an assessment.

- Establish priority days for specific content areas in order to accommodate students with needs in multiple subjects or courses (for example, Mondays might hold first priority for students needing support in mathematics, Tuesday in literacy, and so on).

No two schools are alike in how they structure or deliver systematic support to their students. Yet, despite differences among effective PLCs in how they structure their Tier 2 interventions, the big ideas surrounding interventions remain the same: interventions are timely and embedded, they are tied directly to the essential skills that students are learning, and they are the collective responsibility of collaborative teams.

Interventions That Target Specific Skills and Concepts

Common assessments of the skills that students are currently learning guide the content and focus of interventions. Figure 7.2 (page 192) describes these relationships between assessment and interventions.

Through the analysis of common assessments, teams organize results by student and by target, and use the information to identify those students requiring additional time and support. They examine results for each learning target to determine strengths, common errors, or patterns in responses. Teams can devise their own methods to organize data, such as color coding, but regardless of the format, the teams see who is not yet proficient, who is close to mastery but needs reinforcement, and who is considered advanced in a particular learning target or essential standard. Teams can group nonproficient students according to common needs identified in the analysis.

The delivery mode of an intervention response will vary based on what the evidence reveals. For example, if most students are proficient on a particular learning target, the response may consist of the classroom teacher providing corrective instruction to a small group of students. However, if the data show that most students are struggling with a skill or concept, an appropriate response may be to reteach or re-engage the whole class during core instruction.

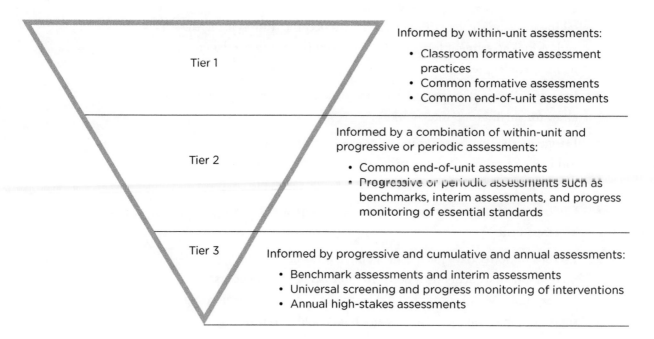

Tier 1

Informed by within-unit assessments:

- Classroom formative assessment practices
- Common formative assessments
- Common end-of-unit assessments

Tier 2

Informed by a combination of within-unit and progressive or periodic assessments:

- Common end-of-unit assessments
- Progressive or periodic assessments such as benchmarks, interim assessments, and progress monitoring of essential standards

Tier 3

Informed by progressive and cumulative and annual assessments:

- Benchmark assessments and interim assessments
- Universal screening and progress monitoring of interventions
- Annual high-stakes assessments

Source: Bailey & Jakicic, 2019, p. 140.

Figure 7.2: Connections between assessment and RTI tiers.

Effective and Co-Planned Strategies Based on Results

As part of their protocol, teams discuss the strategies found to be most effective in stimulating high levels of learning. These strategies may have been used by one teacher on the team or used by the group. Using this knowledge as well as the information regarding student groups and their needs, teams work to co-plan specific actions that employ those strategies so that more students move forward in their level of proficiency. This action plan outlines the specific strategies for intervention or reteaching those students who are not yet proficient and clarifies who will provide the interventions.

Some teams may swap students for their interventions while other teams may embed the interventions within their own set of students. Regardless, members of the team co-plan the response so that best practices are employed in an effort to close the gap for students not yet proficient. The plan may also address reinforcement or extended learning activities for student groups who already reached proficiency. Additionally, the intervention plan includes an intentional method to provide students feedback on their learning and engage them in making corrections. For example, if students are to construct an argument, a proficient response will likely need to include a clear position statement, as well as sufficient evidence and reasoning to support the position. Teams can employ rubrics to ensure that students get feedback that aligns with the elements of proficiency, and use that feedback to improve on their constructed argument.

Monitored Impact

Part of the process of continuous improvement is that schools monitor the impact of teams' work on student learning. This applies to the process of designing and delivering interventions at all levels. It's crucial to determine whether the support students receive is actually closing the gap. To that end, leaders should ensure that teams are monitoring the learning of individual students. Teams should know where each student is in his or her journey of achieving mastery, and acquiring that knowledge includes revisiting students' status after they receive support. In the case of program-specific interventions, schools should seek evidence of impact. The essential questions are, Have we closed gaps for students because of this intervention? What practices seem most effective in closing the gaps? These questions lead to an examination of what works and reinforce the notion of collective teacher efficacy—namely, building on the mindset that by providing focused support and using effective strategies, teams can make a difference in student learning.

Assess the Current Reality

As in every area emphasized in this book, we suggest that leaders take a big-picture view of their system of intervention. This includes examining the current context of the school's past practices around interventions and specific areas of learning that leaders must address.

Figure 7.3 (page 194) provides some guiding questions that leaders can use to reflect on their school as it relates to interventions.

The question leaders should be asking themselves when assessing the work of teams on interventions is, "What's our current reality?" Use the following tools to gather evidence.

- Protocol Observation
- Team Self-Assessment
- Intervention Impact Data Dig

Protocol Observation

When teams collect evidence of student learning, they typically need support to productively engage in its analysis and ultimately create an actionable plan to support improvement. Leaders can use the tool in figure 7.4 (page 194) while observing teams during their analysis of common assessment data and action planning for interventions to get a sense of their knowledge and implementation of the process, and identify any areas needing support.

Guiding Questions	Reflection on Context
What is the greatest area of need for our students' learning? What gaps in achievement exist?	
What interventions have been used in the past? How were they structured? Were they invitational or required for any student who didn't demonstrate mastery of skills? What was the focus? Who delivered the interventions? What was the level of impact from these interventions?	
What is the history of team-driven interventions? What did they look like? Were they program-driven (one size fits all), or were they targeted to support specific areas of need?	
Are there singleton teachers? How are students supported in their classes?	
Are there teachers who have routinely provided students with corrective instructional support? How have those bright spots been highlighted across the school?	

Figure 7.3: Guiding questions to consider school context around interventions.

*Visit **go.SolutionTree.com/PLCbooks** for a free reproducible version of this figure.*

Process Step	Comments
Teams come prepared to the meeting with data or student work from their common assessments.	
Teams organize their data by student and by learning target (electronically).	
Teams analyze each learning target addressed in the assessment to determine proficiency for each student.	
When examining and scoring student work, teams refer back to their criteria for proficiency (by learning target).	
Teams identify categories of misconceptions or errors demonstrated by students who are not yet proficient. Students are grouped based on common needs.	
Teams co-plan their response for students requiring intervention. Their responses employ specific instructional strategies they found effective based on the analysis of results in the team. If needed, the teams explore new strategies to use or seek support from others.	

Teams affirm the specific intervention plan including when the interventions will take place and who will deliver them (if the team shares students).	
Teams discuss how they will gather new evidence following student interventions.	

Figure 7.4: Team intervention planning protocol observation.

*Visit **go.SolutionTree.com/PLCbooks** for a free reproducible version of this figure.*

Team Self-Assessment

The Big Book of Tools for Collaborative Teams in a PLC at Work, written by our colleague William M. Ferriter (2020a), includes many useful tools. One of them, a checklist that teams can use to rate their effectiveness in the area of interventions, is reproduced in figure 7.5 (page 196). We love how Bill has organized this tool and the positive language it incorporates, making it accessible and approachable for use by collaborative teams. School leaders can facilitate the use of this checklist to engage teams in reflection on their collaborative processes around critical question 3.

In using this checklist, we suggest having the team of teachers first reflect on their practice on an individual basis and then compare their evaluations as well as any ideas they identified as possible next steps. Teachers can discuss areas of strength as well as those areas they feel the need to bump up, and strategize potential next steps to strengthen areas for improvement. Each team can share out the areas members would like to strengthen in order to identify common needs across the school, and suggest next steps.

Intervention Impact Data Dig

As a means of gathering information about the impact of interventions, leaders can engage others in a deeper analysis of the data—what we like to call a *data dig*. Using guiding questions to focus the dig into data, grade-level or course-alike teams can embark on unearthing specific information about the impact of their interventions. Following are questions for leaders to consider during the dig while monitoring the impact of interventions.

- How many students are receiving Tier 3 support? How many students typically require Tier 2 support? What percentage of our students (total team) do these numbers represent?

- What is the effectiveness of our interventions? What changes have we seen in student learning as a result of our efforts?

- Is there a difference in achievement among student groups (for example, gender, English learners, special education, or ethnicity)?

Checklist: Rating Your Team's Intervention Practices

Instructions: Using the following key, circle your rating for each indicator. Then record your next steps in the last column.

Rating Key

1 = We haven't tackled this yet.
2 = We are developing or refining our work in this area.
3 = This is an established practice for our team.

Your Rating			Key Indicator	Next Steps
1	2	3	Our team has identified the prerequisite knowledge necessary to master each of our grade-level essentials.	
1	2	3	Our team has developed a list of common misconceptions or mistakes for each of our grade-level essentials.	
1	2	3	Our team has developed lessons that include opportunities for intervention, extra practice, and extension.	
1	2	3	*Individual teachers* have well-established systems of collecting information about the intervention needs of students that are sorted by name and by need.	
1	2	3	*Our team* keeps updated lists, sorted by name and by need, of students who require additional time or support.	
1	2	3	Our team has strategies for supporting students who haven't yet mastered essential work behaviors.	
1	2	3	Our team has a system for reporting on the specific intervention needs of individual students to parents and other professionals working beyond the classroom.	
1	2	3	Our team has identified a set of intervention strategies or practices that we believe in and that we know have a positive impact on student learning.	
1	2	3	Our team collects data on the intervention needs of our students and uses those data to identify strengths and weaknesses in our teaching practice.	
1	2	3	Our team has developed opportunities for students to track their own progress and to plan their next learning actions.	

Source: Ferriter, 2020a, p. 185.

Figure 7.5: Checklist for rating a team's intervention practices.

*Visit **go.SolutionTree.com/PLCbooks** for a free reproducible version of this figure.*

- Who is progressing and to what factors do we attribute that progress?

- Who is not yet progressing, and what might we do to create a greater impact on their learning?

Teams can create posters and use graphic representations, such as bar graphs, histograms, or pictorial representations to communicate a summary of their findings and share their data with others. For example, one team might examine the behavior referrals taking place at its school and note a 10:1 proportion between male and female students being referred. The team might depict this information using a pictograph that shows ten emojis for boys and one for girls to vividly depict its data.

They can then use the information to formulate SMART goals and specific actions to support their attainment. The activity not only engages teams in examining their impact but gives them a big-picture look at the school, particularly if all teams report on their trends. Later in the year, teams can come back with updated information, including progress toward meeting their SMART goals.

Analyze Patterns and Priorities

Leaders can examine the trends and patterns emerging from the evidence they gather to identify potential gaps or areas of need. Following are questions leaders can reference while examining the evidence.

- What does the evidence reveal about teams' understanding of the connection between the school's mission and the role of intervention in the improvement process? What mindsets do team members have about providing support to struggling students? Are there any underlying incompatible beliefs about interventions that need to come to light so we can address them?

- Do the teams take collective responsibility for student learning?

- Are there structures (such as pacing of response days or specified times during the week) that will ensure that teams provide students with timely support?

- Do teams engage in protocols to examine results from assessments and respond in a timely fashion? Are all teams comfortable with how to analyze data from each assessment? How are they managing their data?

- Are Tier 2 interventions designed to target specific skills identified through team-based assessments?

- Do teams co-plan and work interdependently to identify intervention strategies?

- How are teams monitoring whether their interventions are helping students learn more? Do teams use data to reflect on their instruction? Are they seeing more students increase their proficiency on essential standards?

In addition, leaders can use the continuum in figure 7.6 to document the level of implementation for teams and provide a big-picture view of strengths and areas for improvement. This continuum can serve as an ongoing tool to measure the effectiveness of team-driven interventions for students. Leaders can use it to identify areas of strength and growth as well as highlight specific needs for improvement, guiding further actions.

Act on Evidence to Improve Practice

Following the analysis of the evidence and determining continuum placement (using figure 7.6) around team interventions, leaders can focus on the action areas that seem most appropriate to move forward and support higher levels of implementation, including one or more of the following: collective purpose and mindset around interventions, structures and processes to ensure timely response, and monitored impact of interventions.

Collective Purpose and Mindset Around Interventions

Before answering PLC critical question 3, teams need to build shared knowledge about the nature of interventions and how they connect to the vision established for the school. Teams can review the school's mission and vision as well as reflect on the collective responsibility teachers have to support student learning. The following are some basic questions to guide the conversation.

- What would we like to see happen to help students who struggle in their learning?

- What evidence would tell us that the systematic support for all learners is working?

Additionally, teams benefit from understanding the levels or tiers of intervention (described earlier in this chapter and in chapter 4, page 105) and the roles that collaborative teams play in a school's system of support. To ensure that all staff members are empowered with knowledge about what effective interventions can and should look like, leaders must clarify the following big ideas (Buffum et al., 2018).

- Interventions to support grade-level or course-essential standards are the collective responsibility of the collaborative team. It's not possible for all individual teachers to figure out how to address all the needs of their students; teachers need to work collaboratively and interdependently to do so.

- If learning is not optional, then interventions must be directive. Students not yet proficient in essential skills must receive additional time and support embedded in the school day.

Knowledge and Practice	Level of Use or Implementation			
	Limited	Emerging	Established	Strategic
Collective purpose and mindset	Conversations about the role of collaborative teams in the intervention process have not yet begun.	Teams have a general sense that they have a role in the intervention process, but they are uncertain about their ability to impact student learning.	Teams are clear on the why of their interventions, and the notion of students having access to additional time and support in order to ensure learning of essentials. They maintain a growth mindset about their students and their own teaching practices.	Teams have continued to examine and clarify the alignment of their schoolwide and team-based interventions to continuously improve their impact. Teams have a clear sense of collective efficacy around their ability to impact student learning.
Structures and processes to ensure timely response	No formal system exists to ensure access to additional time and support. Individual teachers determine this support.	Teams are working to identify a specific time in their pacing of lessons or schedule to ensure a response based on information from their assessments.	Teams make interventions accessible to all students. Interventions are required (not invitational) and support instructional learning targets.	Teams have an ongoing commitment to provide students with additional time and support, and teams continuously refine the processes for interventions.
Co-planned interventions targeting specific skills and concepts based on assessments	Interventions tend to be random or universal in nature and not targeted to specific learning targets (that is, skills or concepts).	Teams are beginning to apply and connect their work in common assessment of essential skills with the focus of their interventions.	Common assessments provide the data to inform the intervention. Teams co-plan the interventions that make the most of powerful instructional practices and specifically target misconceptions or skill gaps.	Teams not only implement Tier 2 supports on a routine basis but also embed instructional practices that engage students in giving and getting feedback. Their unit plans proactively embed additional support and differentiation in anticipation of the needs of their students.
Monitoring of impact	While individual teachers may monitor growth in student learning, teams do not monitor interventions.	Teams are beginning to explore the impact of their interventions.	Teams examine data following student interventions and reassessment to determine their effectiveness.	As part of the schoolwide process, teams actively and routinely seek feedback on the impact of their interventions.

Figure 7.6: Continuum of practice for team-based interventions.

*Visit **go.SolutionTree.com/PLCbooks** for a free reproducible version of this figure.*

- Interventions must be targeted to specific needs identified through assessments, not delivered in a one-size-fits-all manner.

- The best intervention is prevention. Leaders and teams must ensure that all students have certain access to high-quality Tier 1 (core) instruction focused on essential standards.

- Tier 2 interventions focus on the learning of essential standards for the current grade level or course. They are designed to target specific skills students have not yet mastered through the current year's core instruction.

- Tier 2 interventions are delivered by grade-level or course-alike teams, as they are most qualified to deliver support about what they are teaching.

- Tier 2 interventions are typically delivered two to three times per week.

- Tier 3 interventions focus on remediating skills not yet mastered in previous years. Tier 3 interventions are more intensive, requiring that students receive support four to five days per week.

- Neither interventions nor remediation should remove students from receiving core instruction or additional support.

Structures and Processes to Ensure Timely Response

As part of the process to ensure response time for students, leaders can guide teams to identify specific days or times within their schedule that would allow them to systematically provide additional time and support. While individual teachers may support students in their own classes, we advocate that teams still co-plan those interventions based on their analysis of student proficiency and identified skill gaps. Elementary school teams may need to begin their Tier 2 supports in one area only (for example, literacy) particularly if teachers are teaching multiple content areas. We suggest starting with the high-priority areas or greatest area of need. As an additional resource for structures that provide a system of support, leaders can look to AllThingsPLC (http://allthingsplc.info), which provides information on model PLC schools; users can sort the information there by similar characteristics.

If teams do not yet have clear protocols for analyzing and making sense of the data, and then acting on their findings, leaders can spend time walking them through the Protocol for Analyzing Assessment Results (provided in chapter 6: figure 6.2, page 172). Initially, leaders may need to provide support or facilitate the earlier portion of the protocol, such as ensuring that the data are organized by learning target and by student.

In addition to identifying effective practices as part of the protocol, teams benefit from having some general strategies for deciding how to design interventions. Two approaches that help teachers align their interventions to the identified needs of their students are (1) pile and plan and (2) learning progressions.

Pile and Plan

The pile and plan approach (Bailey & Jakicic, 2019) gives teams a framework to design interventions that target what students need instead of simply providing the same approach for all students. Here are the steps in the process.

1. Teams separate student work samples into piles of those who are proficient (or beyond) and those who are not yet proficient.

2. For students who are not yet proficient, teams consider the evidence to create hypotheses about what the students misunderstood or where the learning stopped. Create separate piles for each hypothesis. For example, a mathematics team may find a group of students that demonstrate simple mistakes on a task but demonstrate conceptual understanding of the process or concept. Team members may discover that another group of students lacked conceptual understanding of the process to accomplish the task, and still another group arrived at the correct answer but didn't elaborate on or explain its thinking. During the sorting, teams can reference rubrics to help them determine the quality or absence of elements and the skills that need to be strengthened.

3. For each pile, the team can collaboratively plan what the corrective instruction or intervention looks like based on the specific error types or missing skills. In this step, teams also reference the instructional strategies found to be highly effective during their initial teaching. For instance, using the example provided in step 2, the team members might provide the group that demonstrated a simple mistake some anonymous items and ask them to "catch" the errors. Students might also review strategies for checking the accuracy or reasonableness of their answers. The group demonstrating a lack of conceptual understanding might receive more concrete models to manipulate and build deeper understanding of the concept. Finally, the group that lacked elaboration would engage in developing justifications or explanations for why to take a certain mathematical step.

Learning Progressions

Another strategy that helps teams design targeted interventions is the use of learning progressions. When teams first unwrap standards, they identify smaller learning targets—in other words, the smaller steps of learning that lead to attainment of the standard. They can arrange these targets from simple to complex based on their rigor, and even organize the targets by DOK levels based on the identified rigor. In essence, teams are then empowered with a staircase or ladder of learning they can use to provide students with specific targeted interventions based on the evidence from their assessments. For example, a student may demonstrate that he or she has mastered the simple skills in the progression but may not yet have more complex skills. By identifying the level of proficiency in the progression, teams are directed to the next steps for support.

Monitored Impact of Interventions

In addition to the data dig highlighted earlier in this chapter (page 195), many schools create data walls to provide a visual record of where students fall in their proficiency. For example, schools may use different colored pocket charts representing each level of proficiency and an index card with each student's name placed in the appropriate level. As students demonstrate growth to a new level, they can see their growth reflected on the wall.

We also suggest that schools have an electronic version of standards mastery information. This can be created in a number of ways. Figure 7.7 is a sample spreadsheet layout that teachers can use to indicate where each student is on a proficiency scale for each essential standard. Teams can conditionally format the spreadsheet so that when a team member selects a certain level of proficiency from a pulldown menu, the cell changes color. As students receive interventions, teams can update their status as appropriate. This gives teams a tool not only to track specific student learning but to see in big-picture fashion the priorities for their focused interventions and curricular adjustments.

All Means All

Timely interventions play a critical role in a school's mission of ensuring that all students learn at high levels. Since collaborative teams are the primary source of curriculum-based interventions, empowering them with knowledge, skills, and support in their processes will build and strengthen the systematic responses needed to achieve that mission. Using evidence from the observation of team intervention practices as well as the examination of data and products related to student learning, leaders can continuously monitor the impact of those responses to ensure that they are effectively closing the gap for students.

In the next chapter, we discuss strategies to support teams in expanding their work to address the unique needs of students who are already proficient and need extensions for their learning.

Teacher	Student Name (last, first)	I can ask and answer questions (RL/RI.3.1).	I can recount stories, determine a central message, and explain with evidence (RL.3.2).	I can determine a main idea, recount key details, and explain with evidence (RI.3.2).	I can compare main idea and key details of two texts on the same topic (RI.3.9).	I can compare and contrast themes, settings, and plots of stories written by the same author about the same or similar characters (RL.3.9).	I can describe characters in a story (e.g., their traits, motivations, or feelings) and explain how their actions contribute to the sequence of events (RL.3.3).
Baker	Anderson, A.	2	2	1	2	1	1
Baker	Bailey, B.	3	2	3	2	2	2
Baker	Chen, C.	3	3	3	3	3	2
Baker	Davis, D.	3	2	3	3	2	2
Baker	Eller, E.	2	2	3	2	2	1
Baker	Frasier, F.	3	3	3	3	3	3
Baker	Graham, G.	3	3	3	3	2	3
Baker	Hernandez, H.	2	2	2	2	2	2
Baker	Irwin, I.	3	3	3	3	2	3
Baker	Jackson, J.	3	3	3	3	2	3

Source for standards: NGA & CCSSO, 2010a.

Figure 7.7: Sample essential standards tracking sheet.

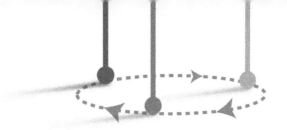

Chapter 8

A FOCUS ON RESPONDING WHEN STUDENTS HAVE ALREADY LEARNED

Some of the schools we've worked with will admit that critical question 4, What will we do when they already know it? (DuFour et al., 2016), is the one that they put aside most frequently because teachers assume it's far more important to help their struggling students, and they feel they don't have time to support both struggling and beyond-proficient students. The following scenario illustrates a typical situation.

> *Oakwood Middle School's guiding coalition has been taking time during each meeting to discuss the products of collaboration from each of its teams. At the start of the PLC process, team leaders would occasionally become defensive when given feedback about their products, which led to some reluctance to share by each of them. At a recent meeting, they spent some time learning about Brené Brown's (2018) definition of vulnerability: "the emotion we experience during times of uncertainty, risk, and emotional exposure" (p. 19). At the end of the discussion, they agreed to accept feedback from each other without being defensive or making excuses.*
>
> *At the first meeting in which team leaders are looking at products together since the vulnerability discussion, the guiding coalition wants to know how individual teams are answering critical question 4—What will we do when they already know it? Typically, during these meetings, they share products in Google Docs using a projector or SMART board so that everyone can see the actual products. The leader for the ELA team volunteers to go first at*

this meeting, sharing that students who are already proficient on essential learning targets are allowed to read books of their choosing. The science team leader goes next and says he doesn't have anything to offer since his team is just moving to new science standards and doesn't have time to plan extensions. His team will get to that next year. The mathematics team leader admits that her team hasn't done much planning for these students, but she shares that they use complex problems during lessons and on common formative assessments. She asks, "That's extending the learning, right?"

The instructional coach, recognizing that the sharing session hasn't been very productive, jumps in and asks whether this would be a good time to strategize about what it really could look like when systematic extensions are done well. The members of the coalition readily agree, saying they need training, models, and resources to effectively answer this question.

In fact, we've heard more than once that teams use the students identified as proficient to help struggling students during response time. Most teachers admit it really doesn't work because achieving proficiency doesn't make students highly effective teachers, and beyond-proficient students receive little benefit in terms of additional learning when they are working with not-yet-proficient students. But it's possible (and important) to support both groups of students.

Our goal for this chapter is to help leaders know what practices are in place for each of their teams; we then consider how leaders can help all teams move forward with effective practices to extend student learning.

In chapter 4 (page 105), we examine how schools effectively develop a systematic response for their students to make sure all students are learning at high levels. In this chapter, we focus on the work of individual teams so that leaders can diagnose what support teams need to more effectively answer critical question 4. Just as all students who aren't proficient on a standard don't benefit from the same intervention, not all teams benefit from the same support from their leaders. We'll begin with discussing what a quality response plan looks like and then move on to the tools to assess, analyze, and act.

Understand What a Quality Response Plan Looks Like

Schools have adopted many different plans to find time to give students who can learn beyond the designated proficient level opportunities to do so. They are often coupled with times set aside to deliver interventions for students who aren't yet proficient, since there can be no new Tier 1 instruction during these times. There are several important ideas that all extension plans must consider.

First, students can't be pulled from Tier 1 instruction for the response. The exception to this would be if a student is in an accelerated course; for example, a seventh grader taking eighth-grade mathematics. Lessons and activities must engage students at a higher level—that is, proficient students should not just get more problems to do in mathematics but problems that are more complex or interesting.

The group must have a qualified teacher to ensure students are getting the support they need to learn the additional content. We recognize that when using differentiated instruction in classes, there are times when each group is working more independently. Of course, this will be true for students receiving extensions. However, the lessons must be planned by qualified instructors, and students must have access to those teachers for direct instruction and support. What this really means is that having a paraprofessional assigned to these students for large periods of time is unfair to them.

Finally, the identification process must allow for flexibility and fluidity. This means that teams must avoid tracking students into groups for responses. Just as it's evident that a student won't *always* need interventions to succeed, a student won't *always* benefit from extensions. Whenever the needs change for students, so must the grouping during response time.

Leaders should keep a number of considerations in mind as they reflect on these ideas. These considerations include being mindful of the differences between acceleration, enrichment, and extensions to provide appropriate response, cultivating a growth versus a fixed mindset, knowing what proficiency looks like, using evidence in the form of data to make decisions, and choosing topics for extensions, enrichment, or acceleration.

Development of the Appropriate Response

The first consideration for leaders who are interested in learning more about teams' responses to critical question 4 is to look at the history of practices the school has in place for enrichment and extension. In our book *Make It Happen* (Bailey & Jakicic, 2019), we explore terms commonly related to this work. The first is *acceleration*. This means that students move more quickly through the regular curriculum and then receive instruction on the curriculum from the next course or grade level. For example, sixth graders might be taught the seventh-grade mathematics curriculum.

The second term is *enrichment*. In this case students are exposed to topics and content not covered in the curriculum all students receive. Teachers may offer instruction on supporting standards that aren't emphasized for all students and provide more opportunities to dig deeply into these standards, topics students might be interested in learning about, or topics related to, but not taught, in the regular curriculum.

The third term is *extensions*. Students receive access to curricula aligned to the grade level or content standards but scaled to a more rigorous level. When teams develop scales around their essential standards and learning targets, they consider what that standard might look like at a higher DOK level. Using this scale, the team can then develop instructional activities as well as assessment items to accommodate students' learning needs. Consider the following scenario about how an eighth-grade team determined the extension of one of its essential learning targets.

> The team begins its meeting by discussing what proficiency will look like on the following target: predict the physical properties of elements based on their positions on the periodic table. During this discussion, members talk about what kinds of direct instruction students will need and what they will need to know to be able to accomplish this target. For example, the team discusses the fact that students will have to understand how the periodic table was put together before they will be able to learn this target. Consequently, the team members list this as a simpler target in their scale. Then they discuss what it would look like if a student could go beyond the cognitive demand of the target. As they discuss this, one team member suggests having students develop generalizations about how the periodic table was constructed around the idea that certain elements have similar properties. This leads, then, to the idea that students who could benefit from extensions can create a checklist based on these similarities. The team develops the scale shown in figure 8.1 to guide its work.

4.0 Extended standard	Develop a checklist to easily predict the physical properties of elements based on their position on the periodic table.
3.0 Agreed-on proficiency	Predict the physical properties of elements based on their positions on the periodic table.
2.0 Simpler standard	Understand how the periodic table is put together.

Figure 8.1: Sample scale with extension.

While proficiency scales actually have five levels: 4.0 (extended standard), 3.0 (agreed-upon proficiency), 2.0 (simpler standard), 1.0 (partial understanding), and 0.0 (no understanding), only three of these levels include explicitly stated content (Hoegh, 2020). This is because levels 4.0, 3.0, and 2.0 express the content the student will learn about specific standards, and the 1.0 and 0.0 levels are the same for every scale, describing that the student is not yet able to learn the content.

Another term that is often used when discussing critical question 4 is differentiated instruction. We know that changes in demographics (such as the number of students speaking a second language and the number of students from diverse cultures) and the way we treat students with disabilities have increased the need for teachers to be able to provide a more differentiated classroom if all students are to reach high levels of learning (Subban, 2006). Educator and author Carol Ann Tomlinson (2017), probably the name most commonly associated with the term *differentiated instruction*, defines it as instruction that "provides different avenues to acquiring content, to processing or making sense of ideas, and to developing products so that each student can learn effectively" (p. 1).

Many schools added an additional dimension of differentiated instruction when they began remote learning in March 2020. Teams needed to consider the circumstances that surrounded the home situation during this time. Was a parent available to support and supervise students at home? Did students have an individual device to use throughout the day and access to the internet? What extenuating circumstances did students encounter, such as having to accompany parents to their job location? (Ferriter, 2020b).

The zone of proximal development helps teams consider what differentiated activities and lessons look like. The term *zone of proximal development* comes from the work of psychologist Lev Vygotsky (1978), who suggests that teachers consider three levels of instruction. The first level includes what students can do without support; the second, the zone of proximal development, is what they can do with teacher support; and the third is what they would not be able to do even with support. Author and education consultant Michael Roberts (2019) suggests that students already proficient should receive extensions developed around *their* zone of proximal development, which will be higher than other students. Teams, then, need to consider how to meet students where they are.

Growth Mindset

The terms fixed mindset and growth mindset come from the research and work of Carol Dweck (2016), a professor of psychology at Stanford University. She explains that those of us who have a fixed mindset think differently than those of us with a growth mindset. A *fixed mindset* leads one to believe that people are born with a certain amount of intelligence and that level can't be increased. Fixed-mindset folks may be afraid to engage in challenging activities because they fear they may fail. Those with a *growth mindset*, on the other hand, are energized by challenging activities and believe they can grow their intelligence by working hard and engaging in opportunities that make them think at a higher level. Therefore, they look at challenges as opportunities to learn more.

Leaders can apply the idea of mindsets in a number of different ways: Which mindset do teachers have about students? Which mindset do students have about themselves? Which mindset do teachers have about themselves? Let's first consider the question of what mindset teachers have about students. We know that when teacher expectations are low, students will not learn as much as when teacher expectations are high. In an update to his original research into the factors that influence student achievement, Hattie's research shows that the third highest influence is the effect size of teacher estimates of achievement at 1.29 (Visible Learning, n.d.b). When teachers have a growth mindset about their students, they will provide rich opportunities for students' learning. If, on the other hand, teachers have a fixed mindset about students, they will only offer the most challenging activities to students they believe have a high level of intelligence. For leaders, then, it's important to make sure teachers have experiences and information to embrace and use a growth mindset in their work with students. Some worthwhile resources for schools to use in helping teams develop their understanding of mindset and how to work with students to develop a growth mindset can be found in *Mindset* by Dweck (2016), Sarah McKibben's (2019) interview of Dweck for *Educational Leadership*, and the book *Developing Growth Mindsets* by psychologists Donna Wilson and Marcus Conyers (2020).

The second question asks what students believe about their own ability to learn. In schools where students are themselves engaged in understanding their own learning, one of the key concepts is their understanding of the concept of mindset. Students with a fixed mindset may be afraid to take on challenges. Leaders should strive to create schools where students welcome challenges and see them as a way to increase their intelligence. This chapter is about what we do with students who are already proficient. If they are afraid of challenges, we must turn that around before we can get them interested in increased rigor.

The third question is about teachers themselves. When teachers have a fixed mindset they, too, shy away from challenges. They are reluctant to embrace new learning and new ideas because they fear they might fail. These teachers may appear as resisters because they want to stick with what used to work and avoid trying out new strategies. The general observer knows, however, that our students are rapidly changing. They see the demographics of most schools are more diverse, technology has changed the need for learning facts and details, expectations for analyzing and drawing conclusions based on data have exploded, and communication is no longer done through paper and pencil. In other words, if we teach the same way we've always taught, we can't expect different results.

While understanding the concept of mindset is important to all students and teachers, it is an especially appropriate idea to include in this chapter about students who can and will learn more than the guaranteed and viable curriculum. Leaders have an obligation to make sure teachers are aware of and understand Dweck's (2016) important research and how their behaviors directly impact student learning. Leaders should pay attention when they see teacher behaviors that aren't aligned to practices that foster a growth mindset. These might include not allowing test retakes, setting different expectations for students identified as "smart" as opposed to students with disabilities or students for whom English is a second language, grouping students by perceived ability, allowing participation in sports only to the most able athletes, and so on.

What Proficiency Looks Like

The key to developing high-quality responses for students who can benefit from extensions is to have a clear understanding of what constitutes proficiency in each of the assessed learning targets. We discussed in chapter 6 (page 163) how responding to common formative assessment data needs to happen student by student, target by target. This fundamental understanding about effectively supporting students so that everyone learns at high levels can also be applied to how teams provide extensions. This means that teams should be able to look at data from each student around each learning target to see who is already proficient.

The team members agree to what proficiency on essential learning targets looks like when they unwrap their standards (see chapter 5, page 135). Teams can use the language of DOK levels in this work. After they've identified the learning targets that come from an essential standard, they discuss the expectations for thinking around each learning target and consider whether that thinking is DOK 1, 2, 3, or 4. This level of complexity guides the type of items they use to assess the target as well as the agreed-on expectations for accurate answers. For example, if they identify proficiency on a DOK 2 learning target, they know that to better understand how to extend that target, they must consider what that target looks like if it appears at a DOK 3 level. Consider this learning target identified by a fifth-grade ELA team: "Demonstrate understanding of nuance in word meanings." The team identified this target as having a DOK 2 expectation for proficiency. Team members might ask students who can achieve that target to reach for a similar target written at a DOK 3 level: "Use understanding of word meanings to more precisely explain ideas in writing." The extension might be for students to take a piece of their own writing and edit it by replacing generic words with more nuanced words.

To best identify students who are already at the proficiency level on an essential learning target, teams use constructed-response questions, which require students to answer thoroughly and explain their reasoning. Student answers to such questions can provide insight into their thinking about that learning target. In some situations, students may answer in a way that shows proficiency while other students might be able to demonstrate even more complex thinking if the question allows it. For example, if a middle school class is asked to evaluate an argument in a text, some students might correctly identify the argument and claims and may accurately analyze the support the author provides—an answer that would identify those students as proficient. Other students might include, along with the analysis the first group provided, insights into weaknesses they've identified in the supporting evidence provided by the author. These students have already gone beyond the proficient answer expected by the team. Along with identifying proficiency, constructed-response questions allow teachers to provide effective feedback to help proficient students think more deeply about a target. Feedback is regularly used in assessments to help students reach proficiency but can be equally effective when encouraging students to go beyond proficiency. Teachers use feedback to respond to students' ideas with descriptions about how they might improve or think differently about their ideas to exceed proficiency. For example, if a teacher asks a student to use evidence to explain what President Harry Truman knew when he made the decision to drop the atomic bomb on Hiroshima at the close of World War II, using a particular set of primary source documents (such as speeches, letters, or official documents), and that student provides an answer that is proficient by the teacher's rubric, the teacher might use feedback to encourage the student to dig deeper. Perhaps the teacher then asks the student whether this information changed before the United States dropped the second bomb on Nagasaki or from what eyewitnesses reported after the Hiroshima bomb.

Data-Based Decisions

In chapter 4 we shared a graphic (figure 4.4, page 112) that shows how the three tiers of extensions are a mirror for the three tiers of interventions. For each of the three tiers in the RTI pyramid, identification of students who can benefit from extensions is based on data. When collaborative teams begin to identify students for Tier 1 extensions, they start by examining the common formative assessments they plan to use for essential learning targets. They check to see if their questions are written in a way that allows students to show their thinking and thus provide evidence that they have either mastered or gone beyond mastery. Again, this likely means some kind of constructed-response question. They might be short-response questions, thinking maps, diagrams, picture models, or others. The team can then use the information they gather from student responses to plan an engaging lesson for these students.

There are a few different ways a student might be identified for Tier 2 extensions. If students have mastered all essential learning targets in a unit based on their common formative assessments and have shown proficiency on their end-of-unit assessments, they should receive Tier 2 extensions. Many teams couple this information with their benchmarking or interim assessments to identify beyond-proficient students.

When schools have an accelerated curriculum for Tier 3 extensions in certain content areas or a gifted and talented program, there is usually an identification process already in place. Identification for these programs usually includes standardized test information, teacher recommendations, and other checklists. These identification processes often use multiple data points to ensure students are ready to take accelerated classes.

Topics for Extensions, Enrichment, and Acceleration

Teams who are planning activities for extensions need to consider the length of time a student will be engaged in the activities. For example, Tier 1 extensions typically immediately follow a common formative assessment, and teams plan the lessons based on the student work and data from that assessment. Most commonly, these response lessons are relatively short, maybe one class period. The extension activities, then, must be planned to take students one class period to complete. These will be designed by scaling the learning targets assessed on the common formative assessment and planning activities that require more cognitive demand than was required of students in the initial classwork prior to the common formative assessment. For example, team members might ask students to rewrite an ending to a story in an ELA class, to explain what would happen if they changed a variable in an experiment in a science class, to investigate some primary source documents in a social studies class, or to solve a more complex problem in a mathematics class.

A student who is working in a Tier 2 group typically stays in that group for multiple lessons and even several weeks. Thus, teams can consider both those extensions already suggested in this section and enrichment opportunities. Teams might build extension opportunities around supporting standards that they didn't teach in depth during regular class time. Consider, for example, two eighth-grade ELA standards (NGA & CCSSO, 2010a).

1. Delineate and evaluate the argument and specific claims in a text, assessing whether the reasoning is sound and the evidence is relevant and sufficient; recognize when irrelevant evidence is introduced.

2. Evaluate the advantages and disadvantages of using different mediums (e.g., print or digital text, video, multimedia) to present a particular topic or idea.

If the team considers the first standard *essential*, members will spend more time teaching it. They will also teach the second supporting standard by including several examples about how authors use different media to provide evidence about a claim being made. However, team members may ask students who have reached proficiency on the essential standard to investigate further about how other media can be effective in presenting a particular idea. They may watch commercials aired during the Super Bowl to analyze how advertisers market products, evaluate a variety of websites to see how effective devices are included, or even compare print and video materials about a topic to see what information each portrays.

Enrichment might also consist of topics students identify that they'd like to explore or even an established list of topics and activities the team has put together to provide options for students. Interest activities or minicourses could include analyzing sports statistics, investigating science phenomena, creating visual art products, understanding the stock market, studying anthropology, studying extreme weather, and using a telescope to investigate space, to name just a few.

As explained in chapter 4 (page 105), the leadership team typically takes responsibility for Tier 3; however, collaborative teams may work with leaders to determine appropriate content-specific courses or activities. With this in mind, we planned the tools in this chapter for use by the collaborative teams, and they don't necessarily apply to Tier 3 planning.

Assess the Current Reality

As we discussed in chapter 1 (page 15), each school enters the PLC process with a story behind it—its context. Leaders should take a few minutes to reflect on the context in which they are going to be using formative tools to identify teams that need support. We recommend these guiding questions (figure 8.2) as a place to begin that reflection.

Guiding Questions	Reflection on Context
What are the current practices for enrichment, acceleration, and extensions for students in your school?	
Currently, what are the common expectations for teams regarding students who have reached mastery on essential learning targets and standards?	
How are students identified for any enrichment, extensions, or acceleration in your school?	
Who determines which teachers will work with these students?	
What expectations are set for providing engaging and diverse opportunities for students who have reached mastery?	

Figure 8.2: Guiding questions for leaders to consider the context of extensions at their school.

*Visit **go.SolutionTree.com/PLCbooks** for a free reproducible version of this figure.*

We offer several tools leaders can use to gather information and insights about how school teams are providing extension activities. These tools are intended to help leaders monitor the important expectations they should have for teams as they answer critical question 4 and answer the question, What's your current reality? These tools appear in the order that a school would likely use as it begins to develop a system or extensions; however, leaders might choose to start with any tool that they believe will help them answer a particular identified need. Consider the criteria in figure 8.3 as leadership teams use the tools in this section.

1.	Meet the expectations set by the leadership team around building time into unit plans for responses, developing and using effective assessments to identify and plan for responses, and developing quality instruction to extend the learning for proficient students.
2.	Effectively identify students for Tier 1 and 2 responses using evidence from assessments.
3.	Work collaboratively to provide a myriad of opportunities for students based on need, interest, and effective grouping practices.
4.	Develop engaging lessons and activities for students.
5.	Involve students in the process to ensure they understand the expectations from the team and to increase their interest and engagement.

Figure 8.3: Criteria for leaders to consider as they assess the work of teams around extensions.

Leaders can use the following tools singly to assess one particular aspect of the response program or in tandem to assess multiple aspects of the program.

- Common Expectations Tool
- Student Identification Tool
- Diversity of Opportunities Tool
- Student Engagement Look-Fors Checklist
- Student Perception Survey

Common Expectations Tool

The first tool, in figure 8.4 (page 216), is a checklist that leaders can complete themselves or ask teams to complete collaboratively to determine whether the team has met their school's common expectations for providing extensions and enrichment. This tool provides an overview of the important components that leaders should consider as a school begins the process of developing this response system to enrich student learning.

Student Identification Tool

It's critical that when teams identify students for Tier 1 and 2 extensions, they have a process based on relevant data rather than teacher opinion to ensure equity for all students. Additionally, when students are grouped based on specific criteria, planning the activities and strategies will be easier and more effective. Thus, the data should reveal specific information about student learning to allow teams to plan activities that will meet the needs of the identified students. Leaders can use a series of questions to guide team thinking about their identification process. The tool in figure 8.5 (page 216) lists these questions in order so that once a team reaches a point in the steps where they can no longer answer yes, they have a place to start planning. Leaders can use the tool to look more closely at how effectively each team's identification process is being implemented for students in Tiers 1 and 2.

Expectation	Yes	No	What Evidence Do You Have?
1. Teams have embedded time into their unit plans after each common formative assessment for support and extensions.			
2. Teams have designed common formative assessments to identify proficient students.			
3. Data from common formative assessments provide insights into students' thinking and learning.			
4. Groups of identified students are flexible and allow students to access extensions when appropriate.			
5. Enrichment groups have access to a trained teacher.			
6. Teams work collaboratively to plan extension and enrichment lessons.			

Figure 8.4: Common expectations of collaborative teams around extensions and enrichment.

Visit go.SolutionTree.com/PLCbooks for a free reproducible version of this figure.

Step 1: Getting Ready for Response	Yes	No
Are the essential standards identified and unwrapped?		
Are the essential standards assigned to specific units of instruction?		
Does the team have quality common formative assessments linked to learning targets from essential standards?		
Can the team analyze data from common formative assessments student by student and learning target by learning target?		
Step 2: Identifying Students for Tier 1 Extensions	**Yes**	**No**
Can the team identify students who are proficient on essential learning targets from a common formative assessment?		
Does the team know how to use student responses to plan extensions?		
Step 3: Identifying Students for Tier 2 Extensions	**Yes**	**No**
Does the team keep track of which students have been given extensions during Tier 2?		
Does the team have end-of-unit tests that could be used as a second data point in identifying students who can benefit from Tier 2 extensions?		
Can the team use benchmarking data as a second or third data point for identifying students who can benefit from Tier 2 extensions?		

Figure 8.5: Student identification for extensions.

Visit go.SolutionTree.com/PLCbooks for a free reproducible version of this figure.

Using this tool allows the leadership team to see where it will need to create or revise any processes it needs to shore up its identification of students who can benefit from extensions.

Diversity of Opportunities Tool

Leaders will find it useful to assess the current reality of how well teams are providing their students with instruction in multiple skills, lessons aligned to student interests, and opportunities to work with other students who have also reached proficiency and are learning at higher levels. The tool in figure 8.6 can help them keep track of the different ways they currently support their already proficient students. Additionally, teams might use the tool to explore additional opportunities they can create for their students. For example, if they find that they have no enrichment offerings based on topics of student interest, they might prioritize this as a next step.

	Extension	Enrichment	Acceleration
Increased rigor and supporting standards			
Topics based on student interest			
Opportunities to work with others			

Figure 8.6: Tool to assess diversity of opportunities.

Visit go.SolutionTree.com/PLCbooks for a free reproducible version of this figure.

The team then fills in each blank box in the tool to list all of their current practices in answering critical question 4. The example in figure 8.7 (page 218) lists some ideas that might come as teams brainstorm using this tool.

Not all boxes have to have a practice, but the discussion that a team has while completing this matrix is likely to spark new ideas. The team can then add these possibilities (maybe in a different color to set them off) as goals for the future.

We've found this tool is also useful when working with collaborative teams to help them think through different ways to think about how they can extend the learning. We usually recommend they start (in the first column and the first row) by thinking about the learning targets that were recently assessed on a common formative assessment. What would that target look like at a higher level of cognitive demand? What activities might students engage in to learn that higher level? Then we move on to the next row. We ask them to think about what they might do to learn more about specific interests students might have. What activities might students engage in that align with those interests? And then in row three, teams can consider whether they can create student groups that are more homogenous that might increase student engagement.

	Extension	Enrichment	Acceleration
Increased rigor and supporting standards	Engage at a higher level of cognitive demand with learning targets (for example, a student proficient on a learning target about what taxes are used for might describe what would happen if a country didn't collect taxes).	Read text with more complexity during Tier 1 or 2 and analyze using the same learning target as was on the common formative assessment.	Explore additional topics taught in later courses or grades.
Topics based on student interest	Research a topic not explored in class that is of personal interest.	Design a personal website.	Proficient mathematics students may work with sports statistics to create a fantasy team.
Opportunities to work with others	Small groups with beyond-proficient students work together on an activity.	Work on a longer-term project with students who have similar interests.	Participate in different groups of students when learning accelerated material.

Figure 8.7: Sample activities for the diversity of opportunities tool.

Student Engagement Look-Fors Checklist

In Marzano's (2017) *The New Art and Science of Teaching*, one of the areas he explores for quality instruction is engagement from students. He identifies the four components of engagement as (1) paying attention, (2) being energized, (3) being intrigued, and (4) being inspired (Marzano, 2017). While it's important for all students to be engaged in lessons, we suggest leaders pay careful attention to what beyond-proficient students are asked to do. Doing *more* work instead of doing *different* work can lead to students who tune out. To this end, let's explore a list of look-fors that leaders can use to know whether the lessons and activities will likely engage these beyond proficient students (see figure 8.8). Leaders can check for these ideas in actual classroom observations, in team planning sessions, or in student work products. Leaders may also want to add specific look-fors they want to see in their schools.

There is no cut score with this tool for how many items should be checked off to make an extension program effective, but both collaborative teams and leaders can use it to assess their current reality as well as to look for ways to grow the program over time.

Student Perception Survey

The final area we want leaders to explore related to this topic is whether or not students perceive they have access to quality activities to extend their own learning. As with any perception tool, the data reveal what students think about a topic or idea, which may or may not actually be reality. In this situation, leaders should make sure

Consideration	What Teams Are Doing	What Students Are Doing
Student voice and choice	☐ Teams have provided opportunities for student choice in projects, groupings, or specific activities.	☐ Students frequently engage in dialogue with their peers.
	☐ Teams plan lessons and activities that require students to support their opinions with facts.	☐ Students engage in debates and argumentation.
	☐ Teams develop questions asking students to take a side on an issue.	☐ Students study historical and scientific ideas that have been debated and argued.
	☐ Teams provide activities that are different than what's offered to the rest of the class.	☐ Students are enthusiastic about the work they're engaged in and are interested in sharing with others.
	☐ Teams provide opportunities for students to work both individually and in groups.	☐ Students can choose activities and lessons based on personal interest.
Rigor of lessons and activities	☐ Teams develop academic games for students requiring deeper thought or strategy.	☐ Students are motivated by increased rigor and see this as energizing their learning.
	☐ Teams include activities requiring research, conducting investigations, critiquing ideas of others, and making connections between ideas.	☐ Students see longer-term projects as ways to express their own individuality and will revise their work as they need to.
	☐ Teams provide opportunities for students to reflect on what they're learning.	☐ Students can develop a "thinking map" to explain a concept, article, or solve a problem.
	☐ Teams develop lessons that require students to transfer learning from one activity or lesson to a new situation.	☐ Students consider and pursue new ideas and questions while working on an activity or project.
		☐ Students have inquiry experiences that allow them to choose a question and find the answer.
Gratitude and mindfulness	☐ Teams help students self-assess their learning style or profile.	☐ Students learn about growth mindset and apply it to their own learning.
	☐ Teams provide opportunities for students to contribute to their community.	☐ Students develop surveys and draw conclusions about a topic of interest.
	☐ Teams use short videos, anecdotes, newspaper headlines, or similar media to motivate students.	☐ Students keep a gratitude journal, which provides specific topics and questions they can respond to as they reflect on their positive experiences.
		☐ Students get involved in altruistic activities.

Figure 8.8: Student engagement look-fors checklist.

Visit go.SolutionTree.com/PLCbooks for a free reproducible version of this figure.

they are effectively communicating the right information to students to avoid misconceptions. To do this we offer the questionnaire in figure 8.9 for leaders to gather information from students.

To students: please read the following statements about *academic extensions time* and mark this survey with the answer that best fits your experiences and understanding. A = Always, U = Usually, S = Sometimes, N = Not at all				
Question	**A**	**U**	**S**	**N**
Part I: Student Access				
1. I understand how students are chosen for different lessons during this time.				
2. I have been able to join several different groups during academic extensions time.				
3. Sometimes I work by myself and sometimes I work with a group during this time.				
4. I understand what I'm supposed to be learning during this time.				
Part II: Quality of Activities or Lessons				
5. I enjoy academic extensions time.				
6. I'm challenged during this time.				
7. I am interested in the topics taught during this time.				
8. I am learning new ideas during this time.				
9. I can choose what I want to work on during this time.				
Part III: Opportunities for Teacher Support				
10. The teacher helps me when I get stuck or am not sure what to do.				
11. The teacher gives me feedback about my work so that I can make it better.				
12. The teacher makes me show my thinking when I'm working.				
13. My teacher listens to students about what we want to explore during this time.				

Figure 8.9: Secondary student perception survey.

Visit go.SolutionTree.com/PLCbooks for a free reproducible version of this figure.

Survey questions are purposely divided into three areas: access, activity or lesson quality, and teacher support. Leaders can use this survey as a stand-alone data collector if they are investigating student perceptions or pair it with another tool from this chapter. For example, if leaders used the Diversity of Opportunities Tool to determine what teams are offering, the Student Perception Survey could add to their knowledge about those opportunities by adding the dimension of student perception.

Or, if leaders use the Student Engagement Look-Fors Checklist, the results from this survey can take their analysis one step further by seeing if their observations are borne out by what students think about their experiences.

Should all students take the survey or should leaders collect data only from students already engaged in enrichment activities? When we developed this survey, we intended it to be applicable to all students no matter which groups they've been assigned to. Consider, for example, the statement about enjoying this time. If students receiving support say *yes*, and students receiving extensions say *no*, that says a lot about the activities and lessons teams are providing.

Leaders can use a similar version of the survey for elementary students. See figure 8.10 for an example for elementary students who have a time set aside for interventions.

Question	Yes	No
Directions: Answer the following questions about your extra learning time.		
Part I: Student Access		
1. My teacher tells me what I am working on during this time and how it should help me.		
2. I get to work with a lot of different students during this time.		
3. I sometimes get to work by myself and sometimes work with different students during this time.		
4. I understand what I'm supposed to be learning during this time.		
Part II: Quality of Activities or Lessons		
5. I like this extra learning time.		
6. I like trying new things that are hard for me during this time.		
7. I am interested in the new things I'm learning.		
8. I am learning new things that I didn't already know.		
9. I have some choices in what I do during this time.		
Part III: Opportunities for Teacher Support		
10. The teacher helps me when I get stuck or have a question.		
11. The teacher always gives me ideas to make my work better.		
12. The teacher makes me show my thinking when I'm working.		
13. My teacher listens to students about what they like to learn during this time.		

Figure 8.10: Elementary student perception survey.

*Visit **go.SolutionTree.com/PLCbooks** for a free reproducible version of this figure.*

Analyze Patterns and Priorities

The common expectations tool (figure 8.4, page 216) and the student identification tool (figure 8.5, page 216) are likely going to provide information for schools that are relatively new to the PLC process about the technical aspects of developing a collaborative team's system of response. Leaders can use these tools to look at whether there are gaps in how teams are establishing their practices around finding time, instructional planning for the response, and identifying students. These tools will help leaders see if teams need support about how to do this work. Just as teams want formative assessments for students to focus on specific learning targets, these tools are designed to drill down into *specific, important* aspects of the team's plan, which include flexible access, data that support quality decisions and student identification, access to a qualified teacher, and collaboration among team members to design effective instruction. Because leaders are looking at whether these aspects are in place, both tools ask for a yes-or-no response. However, with the Common Expectations Tool, we also added a column for listing evidence that a team might use to support a yes answer. The purpose of this column is to connect the yes answer to specific artifacts that teams create.

As leaders focus more closely on the diversity of opportunities tool (figure 8.6, page 217), they may notice that it digs much deeper into the details of the types of responses teams have planned. We know that the members of each collaborative team represent the teachers who are *most* knowledgeable about the content they are teaching, and therefore they will be the most *qualified* to design lessons and units for already proficient students. When teams are just beginning to build their systematic response for extensions, they are likely to have only a few of the boxes completed and often they are limited to the row for increased rigor and supporting standards because these ideas flow easily from the curriculum this team offers. However, when the goal is for teams to develop rich opportunities for proficient students, teams need to look more closely at the other rows in this matrix.

In his book *Enriching the Learning*, Roberts (2019) suggests that collaborative teams consider three areas for extensions: (1) skills, (2) interests, and (3) social groups. We know that many teams do much of their planning for beyond-proficient students around skills, either more rigorous skills than in the general education curriculum or related skills that come from supporting standards that aren't emphasized during Tier 1 instruction. However, a robust program must also consider whether students are able to access learning about topics of interest to them, which is the second area suggested by Roberts (2019). While this is likely to be more difficult to put in place as interests can change by which students are identified, accommodating students' interests can have an enormous impact in engaging them. As we discussed in chapter 3 (page 73), giving students choices will increase their learning as well as their motivation. Giving students choices could be an opportunity for students to develop their own investigation of a topic, to try out new interests in music or art, to dig deeper into a problem they want to explore, and so on. Teams may start off with just a few choices but be able to add more each year.

The third area suggested for enrichment is to allow students opportunities to work in groups with other students who have similar interests or are ready to move beyond the regular curriculum. We know that tracking students doesn't work, but we also know that our already proficient students should be able to work with similar students in a flexible way. Of course, they won't all have the same interests, but they often benefit from collaborating with other students who think the way they do.

Using the Student Engagement Look-Fors Checklist (figure 8.8, page 219), leaders might first look at the total picture of how engaging the activities and assignments are for beyond-proficient students. While we already mentioned there is no cut score for the number of checkmarks to look for, the more areas that are checked, the more likely it is that the collaborative team has wrestled with multiple ways to ensure student engagement. Another way leaders can look at the data is to determine whether at least one area is checked off in each of the three categories. This provides evidence that the team is focused on instruction that is likely to be better than if they focused on only one of those categories.

The student perception survey (figure 8.9, page 220) shifts the focus of the evidence directly to students. As we discussed in chapter 5 (page 135), having students connected and involved in their own learning leads to significantly higher levels of achievement. As leaders or teams analyze the responses, they should intentionally look at each of the categories separately so that their responses can be as specific as possible.

Because this is a perception survey, the final data may or may not represent the actuality of what's happening for beyond-proficient students, but rather what they believe is happening. In some cases, teams may need to respond with changes in practice, but in other cases, they may need to respond with more communication about what's happening.

Use the evidence from the tools to identify where your teams are on the continuum in figure 8.11 (page 224). This is the first step in answering the question, What patterns and priorities emerge from the evidence?

As with the other continua included in this book, leaders can use it to identify the current reality of their collaborative teams as well as to guide them in planning next steps to support those teams that they identified as needing additional help in building or using extensions.

Act on Evidence to Improve Practice

As we've discussed throughout this book, evidence must lead to action. In table 8.1 (page 225), we've laid out the most common needs we've seen identified when teams and leaders want to consider their current reality about their response plan for beyond-proficient students.

Knowledge and Practice	Level of Use or Implementation		
	Limited	Emerging	Established	Strategic
Teams have used the clear, common expectations established by the leadership team to plan and implement their extensions and enrichment.	Teams have not yet begun to respond to the expectations laid out and are not yet providing extension and enrichment lessons for their students.	Teams understand the expectations that have been established and have begun designing effective identification practices as well as aligned lessons for extensions and enrichment.	Teams have aligned their work to meet the expectations established by the leadership team.	Teams regularly assess their current reality around these expectations and respond to any information they have to improve on their practices.
Teams are able to effectively identify students who have mastered the essential outcomes and can benefit from extensions and enrichment opportunities to learn more.	Teams are not yet able to use their current assessments to identify students who can learn at levels beyond proficiency.	Teams are using assessment data to identify students who can benefit from extensions and enrichment but haven't yet been able to use those data for effective planning.	Teams are using assessment data to identify students who can benefit from extensions and enrichment and are using this information to design lessons and units of instruction.	Teams are effectively identifying students who can benefit from extensions and enrichment and are working with these students to design lessons and units that are effective, engaging, and differentiated for interest, group dynamics, and identified needs.
There is a diversity of opportunities for extended learning for all students.	Teams offer a limited number of activities for extensions.	Teams have begun developing an assortment of activities for extensions with the intention of allowing students to choose from those options.	Teams assign students some activities (typically Tier 1 based on the learning target) but have choice for others (typically Tier 2). Students are often allowed to choose their group members when working cooperatively.	Teams survey students for areas of interest and develop personalized activities for them. Students are allowed to either choose whom they work with or work alone if that's their preference.
Students are highly engaged in extended learning and enrichment opportunities.	Teams are aware that this can be an issue for students, and know they need to take some steps to make sure all of their extension lessons are engaging but have not yet started to plan this way.	Teams have spent collaborative time gathering evidence from students about how engaging their extension lessons are and have plans to use this feedback in their lesson design.	Teams are collaboratively reviewing their instructional materials for extending the learning to add or rework them to be more engaging.	Teams have studied the research on engaged learning and are incorporating strategies into their instruction.
Highly trained teachers develop and implement extended learning opportunities.	For most teams, students who need extensions are working independently with little teacher support.	Teams have worked collaboratively to develop instructional materials, and a teacher is available to deliver initial instruction and answer questions as students complete their work.	Teams assign a teacher from the collaborative team or another specialist to teach the extended learning groups of students.	Teams work with a coach or specialist to develop a range of instructional materials for each of the three tiers of extension. A highly trained teacher plans and delivers units.

Figure 8.11: Continuum of practice for extended learning and enrichment.

Visit go.SolutionTree.com/PLCbooks for a free reproducible version of this figure.

Table 8.1: Team Needs and Leader Actions to Respond to Beyond-Proficient Students

Identified Need	Possible Action
• Teams need specific information about ways to find time for responses, write better assessments, or use data to plan their responses.	• Provide teams with opportunities to meet with other teams. • Brainstorm solutions with the team so that the final decision has buy-in. • Ensure that teams aren't waiting to begin until their plan is perfect. Encourage them to learn while doing. • Provide more extended-release time for teams to have sustained discussions about their plans.
• Teams are experiencing difficulty identifying students for either Tier 1, Tier 2, or both, or they seem to be putting all of their proficient students into the same group for response.	• Model effective ways to use the data they have. • Provide ideas about collecting better data for this purpose. • Suggest additional ways to group students using the results of their common formative assessments.
• Teams are limiting the opportunities they offer to students to skills taught in the regular curriculum.	• Ask teams to complete the diversity of opportunities matrix themselves and identify what they are providing students in each box. Help them choose one new area to explore. • Find quality resources (books, videos, and professional learning workshops) to suggest teams explore.

• Based on observation, teams are experiencing a lack of student engagement.	• Ask coaching questions:
	  – What resources (materials, time to plan, or access to professional learning) would you need to move forward with new ways to extend student learning?
	  – Would you like to visit (in person or electronically) a school or classroom that has tried out some of these strategies?
	  – If you had all the time in the world to plan projects and lessons, what would your Tier 2 time look like?
	  – Can we develop a plan with realistic time lines and specific next steps in mind?
	• Remind teams to dream big but start small.

• Teams are interested in using more engaging strategies but don't have all the information they need.	• Teams can build shared knowledge around new strategies by reading professional literature about engagement. See, for example, *The Handbook for the New Art and Science of Teaching* (Marzano, 2019). • Teams can learn from professional organizations such as the National Science Teaching Association, National Council of Teachers of English, and so on.
• Data suggest students aren't knowledgeable about extension and enrichment opportunities.	• Help teams determine if this is a perception problem or a real lack of quality experiences for students. • Suggest or brainstorm better ways to communicate directly with students. • Identify specific gaps in how teams are offering enrichment and extension and plan ways to correct these gaps.

Leaders can provide support in a plethora of ways. Some teams need more uninterrupted time to think more deeply about their work. Providing substitute teachers so that the team can meet together for a half or full day of work time may be an important solution. However, if teams don't have all of the information (capacity) that they need to solve an identified problem, leaders must consider who or what will help those teams move forward. Many schools have instructional coaches in their buildings to do this work. These coaches may be able to suggest another team in the building who has effectively solved the same problem, so that sharing information across teams would be a good solution. Locating and providing resources is another way to support teams. When teams are deep into the work of responding to already proficient students, they don't always have time to seek out good resources but are excited when someone is willing to do that legwork for them.

Consider, as well, how an outsider can help teams look at data without making excuses. This person might be another staff member not assigned to a team such as a guidance counselor, technology coach, instructional coach, or the like. When leaders can strip away the idea of blame, examining data can be extremely powerful. Each of the tools in this chapter is intended to help leaders gather information that allows teams to recognize issues and problems as well as possible ways to improve practices. We always start by asking teams to list the facts they see in the data. Often this first step allows teams to avoid being defensive about information they may perceive as negative. As we discussed earlier, the student perception survey in figure 8.9 (page 220) reveals what students believe is true but may not be the actual case. We believe that, especially in this instance, what students perceive to be true is important even if it's not accurate. For example, if students don't feel they have access to various levels of support or extension, is it because they don't understand how groups are formed, or is it because they've been at the same level for a long time and don't understand why? The team might deduce that it has to be more transparent with its students rather than concluding that it isn't reforming groups frequently enough.

As leaders work through the data analysis for critical question 4, we recommend they regularly ask teams, "What do you need to get to the next step in answering critical question 4?" If a team responds that it needs more ideas, more knowledge about differentiated instruction, or better program models, think about who has the ability to provide this to the team. Is there a coach who could support them? Is there someone outside the school at the district level (such as a science coordinator) who could provide support for them? Is there a similar school they can visit for ideas? Chris's teams at Woodlawn Middle School in Long Grove, Illinois, were visited all the time by teams from other schools that wanted to see how this could work in the real world. What other resources might be effective? We've been helped in our work by materials and ideas provided by professional organizations such as the National Science Teaching Association, National Council of Teachers of Mathematics, and National Council of Teachers of English. Need some ideas for extending engineering standards aligned to the Next Generation Science Standards? There's a book for that (Jones, Corin, Ennes, Clayton, & Childers, 2019)! Leaders must become comfortable with the notion that no one person has all the answers. Seeking out good resources may be the best support leaders can provide a team trying to get better at their work.

But what if the team is reluctant to move forward? Then the leader must ask whether it's skill or will holding the team back. Are the team members not confident they have the expertise to design these new experiences? Or, do they not believe beyond-proficient students need enrichment? In either case, leaders can help facilitate teams taking initial steps to get started. For teams who lack the skill (or perceive that they do), help them choose one specific area to start with by guiding them to secure the time and resources they need to successfully plan a lesson, a framework, or a unit of instruction. Don't try to plan everything at the start. Leaders should emphasize that this is a learning experience for everyone and that they're willing to provide necessary support. Help teams develop a list of steps they need to take and lay out the time line they want to use. Think gradual release of responsibility (Fisher & Frey, 2014)! Just as educators know that students need much more support early in a unit of instruction, consider what support collaborative teams need as they approach a new strategy. As they become confident in their work, leaders can allow them to become independent.

If, on the other hand, the team lacks the will to engage in this work, the leader will probably want to probe deeper into why team members are reluctant. Authors Anthony Muhammad and Luis F. Cruz (2019) explore three investments leaders need to make to motivate teachers to make changes: (1) cognitive investment, (2) emotional investment, and (3) functional investment. The first investment (cognitive) is about providing rationale for whatever change is being promoted. Make sure teachers understand the why and give them the data that lead them to see why the change is important. In the introduction of Marzano's (2017) *The New Art and Science of Teaching*, he makes the case for the importance of starting with why and calls the book "a framework for substantive change. Indeed, one might even consider it a manifesto" (p. 9). The subsequent chapters investigate effective instructional strategies. Muhammad and Cruz (2019) also make the case that leaders need to persuade teachers to engage in change and emphasize the importance of providing details to teachers about how to proceed. Often teachers feel overwhelmed at the start and need someone to help them determine the steps they will need to take. To circle back to the introduction, in which we discussed the stages of concern (see figure I.4 on page 10; Hall & Hord, 2006) that teachers typically go through when facing major change, by knowing what the concerns are, leaders can provide the support that best matches the needs of the team.

The second investment (emotional) leaders need to make is taking stock of whether prior negative experiences are influencing teachers' reluctance. Be cautious about asking teams to redo work they feel they've already completed. We see this happen in schools that hire a new principal or curriculum director who isn't familiar with the work teams have already done. Other times a need is uncovered when student achievement becomes stagnant. If teams must redo something, it's important for them to see the results (data) of their first attempt and use those data to determine how their work can be more effective. The key to emotional investment is that teachers need to trust leaders. Muhammad and Cruz (2019) discuss how leaders can establish trust in their book *Time for Change* and include a free reproducible (Establishing Trust Rating Scale, available at **go.SolutionTree.com/leadership**) to help leaders identify what their current reality around trust is.

The third investment (functional) leaders must make is to provide training and resources that teachers need to do the work of supporting beyond-proficient students. Leaders cannot assume that all teachers have the capacity to develop projects and plans to enrich student learning without training and support; rather, leaders need to see their role in providing the time, support, and resources teachers will need to be successful. The more diagnostic a leader can be about where a team is on the continuum of skill and will about a change, the better the action plan can be.

Sustain the Momentum

When schools decide to become professional learning communities, they usually do so because they want a process to guide their work as they take on the challenge of ensuring that all students learn at high levels. Frequently leaders and teams begin implementation feeling enthusiastic about the future and how these practices will impact their work. However, we know that this is hard work; a school can't just make a checklist of things to do, and quickly complete each step. Instead, we know that this is a process that encourages continuous improvement. Teams aren't finished until all students are proficient and even beyond. In chapter 1 (page 15) we introduced the importance of using celebrations around short-term wins to sustain momentum. As we come to the end of part 2, focused on the four critical questions, we urge leaders to extend school celebrations to collaborative teams, recognizing their short-terms wins and successes.

Epilogue

As we've worked with schools across the United States, we've seen how collaborative teams embrace the power of common formative assessments on student learning. We've also seen how, as collaborative teams become more confident and skillful assessment authors, they recognize the impact formative assessment can have on achievement both for students who need more time and support and for those who can benefit from extensions to the curriculum. In this book, we have tried to imagine what would and could happen when leaders apply the same principles of formative assessment and feedback to teachers and staff as they work with collaborative teams in their schools.

We advocate that leaders should work with teams to gather formative information that will provide the right feedback to teams as they work through the process of building a strong foundation, embracing collaborative practices, investigating and including the best instructional practices, creating a systematic response for students, and effectively answering the four critical questions. Working with teams to support their actions based on this feedback can provide teams with what they need to move forward. In some cases, this support might simply be the opportunity for more time together, coaching teams as they do their work, or offering expertise (external experts, professional learning experiences, or knowledgeable colleagues) to build shared knowledge with the team. Support can take the form of assisting high-performing teams in refining and expanding their own practices.

To this end, we encourage you to choose from the multiple tools we've presented in this book and use them to effectively gather information about teams' current reality and plan next steps in implementing the practices we know will improve student learning. Our hope for your school and your students is that these tools will allow you to provide the right support, whether a team is just getting started or is well on its way to showcasing premier practices for its colleagues. We have seen time and time again that when schools learn together, they consistently make a difference for their students.

References and Resources

Achieve the Core. (n.d.). *Mathematics: Focus by grade level*. Accessed at https:// achievethecore.org/category/774/mathematics-focus-by-grade-level on May 19, 2021.

AllThingsPLC. (n.d.). *See the evidence: Want proof that the PLC process is working for others and can work for you too?* Accessed at www.allthingsplc.info/evidence/ on May 20, 2021.

Ainsworth, L. (2004). *Power standards: Identifying the standards that matter the most.* Englewood, CO: Advanced Learning Press.

Ainsworth, L. (2010). *Rigorous curriculum design: How to create curricular units of study that align standards, instruction, and assessment.* Englewood, CO: Lead + Learn Press.

Bailey, K., & Jakicic, C. (2012). *Common formative assessment: A toolkit for Professional Learning Communities at Work.* Bloomington, IN: Solution Tree Press.

Bailey, K., & Jakicic, C. (2017). *Simplifying common assessment: A guide for Professional Learning Communities at Work.* Bloomington, IN: Solution Tree Press.

Bailey, K., & Jakicic, C. (2019). *Make it happen: Coaching with the four critical questions of PLCs at Work.* Bloomington, IN: Solution Tree Press.

Bailey, K., & Jakicic, C. (2020). *The collaborative team plan book for PLCs at Work.* Bloomington, IN: Solution Tree Press.

Boaler, J. (2015). *Fluency without fear: Research evidence on the best ways to learn math facts.* Accessed at www.youcubed.org/evidence/fluency-without-fear/ on March 25, 2021.

Brown, B. (2018). *Dare to lead: Brave work, tough conversations, whole hearts.* New York: Random House.

Buffum, A., & Mattos, M. (2015). *It's about time: Planning interventions and extensions in elementary school.* Bloomington, IN: Solution Tree Press.

Buffum, A., Mattos, M., & Malone, J. (2018). *Taking action: A handbook for RTI at Work.* Bloomington, IN: Solution Tree Press.

Bybee, R. W., Taylor, J. A., Gardner, A., Van Scotter, P., Powell, J. C., Westbrook, A., & Landes, N. (2006). *The BSCS 5E Instructional Model: Origins and effectiveness.* Accessed at https://media.bscs.org/bscsmw/5es/bscs_5e_full_report.pdf on July 19, 2021.

Colburn, L., & Beggs, L. (2021). *The wraparound guide: How to gather student voice, build community partnerships, and cultivate hope.* Bloomington, IN: Solution Tree Press.

Conzemius, A. E., & O'Neill, J. (2014). *The handbook for SMART school teams: Revitalizing best practices for collaboration* (2nd ed.). Bloomington, IN: Solution Tree Press.

Covey, S. R., Merrill, A. R, & Merrill, R. R. (1994). *First things first: To live, to love, to learn, to leave a legacy*. New York: Simon & Schuster.

D'Costa, K. (2018). *Why is cooperation so difficult in the workplace?* Accessed at https:// blogs.scientificamerican.com/anthropology-in-practice/why-is-cooperation-so -difficult-in-the-workplace/ on April 11, 2021.

Dean, C. D., Hubbell, E. R., Pitler, H., & Stone, B. (2012). *Classroom instruction that works: Research-based strategies for increasing student achievement* (2nd ed.). Alexandria, VA: Association for Supervision and Curriculum Development.

Donohoo, J. (2017). *Collective efficacy: How educators' beliefs impact student learning.* Thousand Oaks, CA: Corwin Press.

DuFour, R., DuFour, R., Eaker, R., Many, T. W., & Mattos, M. (2016). *Learning by doing: A handbook for Professional Learning Communities at Work* (3rd ed.). Bloomington, IN: Solution Tree Press.

DuFour, R., & Marzano, R. J. (2011). *Leaders of learning: How district, school, and classroom leaders improve student achievement*. Bloomington, IN: Solution Tree Press.

Dweck, C. S. (2016). *Mindset: The new psychology of success* (Updated ed.). New York: Random House.

Eaker, R. (2020). *A summing up: Teaching and learning in effective schools and PLCs at Work*. Bloomington, IN: Solution Tree Press.

Eaker, R., & Keating, J. (2011, March 4). *Prerequisites for standards-based reporting.* Accessed at www.allthingsplc.info/blog/view/120/prerequisites-for-standards-based -reporting on March 30, 2021.

Eaker, R., & Marzano, R. J. (Eds.). (2020). *Professional Learning Communities at Work and High Reliability Schools: Cultures of continuous learning*. Bloomington, IN: Solution Tree Press.

Eastside Elementary School. (n.d.). *Eastside: One team, one dream* [Newsletter]. Accessed at www.smore.com/qtm8p-eastside-one-team-one-dream on February 16, 2021.

Elmore, R. (2006). *School reform from the inside out: Policy, practice, and performance.* Cambridge, MA: Harvard Education Press.

Erkens, C., & Twadell, E. (2012). *Leading by design: An action framework for PLC at Work leaders*. Bloomington, IN: Solution Tree Press.

Ermeling, B. A., & Graff-Ermeling, G. (2016). *Teaching better: Igniting and sustaining instructional improvement*. Thousand Oaks, CA: Corwin Press.

Ferriter, W. M. (2020a). *The big book of tools for collaborative teams in a PLC at Work.* Bloomington, IN: Solution Tree Press.

Ferriter, W. M. (2020b). *Differentiating learning in a remote learning environment* [Online workshop]. Presented at the Solution Tree Remote Teaching Virtual Institute, Bloomington, IN.

Fisher, D., & Frey, N. (2014). *Better learning through structured teaching: A framework for the gradual release of responsibility* (2nd ed.). Alexandria, VA: Association for Supervision and Curriculum Development.

Friedman, R. (2014). *Why working together doesn't always work*. Accessed at www
.psychologytoday.com/us/blog/glue/201407/why-working-together-doesnt-always
-work on April 11, 2021.

Friziellie, H., Schmidt, J. A., & Spiller, J. (2016). *Yes we can! General and special educators
collaborating in a professional learning community*. Bloomington, IN: Solution
Tree Press.

Great Schools Partnership. (2013, November 25). *School culture*. Accessed at www
.edglossary.org/school-culture/ on January 22, 2021.

Guskey, T. R. (2000). *Evaluating professional development*. Thousand Oaks, CA:
Corwin Press.

Guskey, T. R. (2020). Flip the script on change. *Learning Professional, 41*(2), 18–22.
Accessed at https://learningforward.org/journal/beyond-the-basics/flip-the-script-on
-change/ on March 25, 2021.

Hall, G. E., & Hord, S. M. (2006). *Implementing change: Patterns, principles, and potholes*
(2nd ed.). Boston: Allyn & Bacon.

Hammond, Z. (2015). *Culturally responsive teaching and the brain: Promoting authentic
engagement and rigor among culturally and linguistically diverse students*. Thousand
Oaks, CA: Corwin Press.

Hannigan, J., Hannigan, J. D., Mattos, M., & Buffum, A. (2021). *Behavior solutions:
Teaching academic and social skills through RTI at Work*. Bloomington, IN: Solution
Tree Press.

Hattie, J. (2012). *Visible learning for teachers: Maximizing impact on learning*. New York:
Routledge.

Hattie, J., Fisher, D., & Frey, N. (2017). *Visible learning for mathematics, grades K–12:
What works best to optimize student learning*. Thousand Oaks, CA: Corwin Press.

Heath, C., & Heath, D. (2007). *Made to stick: Why some ideas survive and others die*. New
York: Random House.

Hoegh, J. K. (2020). *A handbook for developing and using proficiency scales in the classroom*.
Bloomington, IN: Marzano Resources.

Jones, A. (2019). The Tuckman's model implementation, effect, and analysis and
the new development of Jones LSI model on a small group. *Journal of Management,
6*(4), 23–28. Accessed at www.researchgate.net/publication/335176254_THE
_TUCKMAN'S_MODEL_IMPLEMENTATION_EFFECT_AND_ANALYSIS
_THE_NEW_DEVELOPMENT_OF_JONES_LSI_MODEL_ON_A_SMALL
_GROUP on April 11, 2021.

Jones, M. G., Corin, E., Ennes, M., Clayton, E., & Childers, G. (2019). *Discovery
engineering in physical science: Case studies for grades 6–12*. Arlington, VA: National
Science Teaching Association.

Kanold, T. D. (2011). *The five disciplines of PLC leaders*. Bloomington, IN: Solution
Tree Press.

Keating, J., Eaker, R., DuFour, R., & DuFour, R. (2008). *The journey to becoming a
professional learning community*. Bloomington, IN: Solution Tree Press.

Klein, G. (2007, September). *Performing a project premortem*. Accessed at https://hbr
.org/2007/09/performing-a-project-premortem on February 9, 2021.

Kotter, J. P. (2012). *Leading change*. Boston: Harvard Business Review Press.

Lencioni, P. (2002). *The five dysfunctions of a team: A leadership fable*. San Francisco: Jossey-Bass.

Lencioni, P. (2005). *Overcoming the five dysfunctions of a team: A field guide for leaders, managers, and facilitators*. San Francisco: Jossey-Bass.

Many, T. W., & Horrell, T. (2014). Prioritizing the standards using the REAL criteria. *TEPSA News, 71*(1), 1–2. Accessed at https://absenterprisedotcom.files.wordpress.com/2016/06/real-standards.pdf on March 25, 2021.

Marzano, R. J. (2003). *What works in schools: Translating research into action*. Alexandria, VA: Association for Supervision and Curriculum Development.

Marzano, R. J. (2017). *The new art and science of teaching* (Rev. and expanded ed.). Bloomington, IN: Solution Tree Press.

Marzano, R. J. (2019). *The handbook for the new art and science of teaching*. Bloomington, IN: Solution Tree Press.

Mathewson, T. G. (2016, July 5). *Teacher expectations top list of effects on student achievement*. Accessed at www.k12dive.com/news/teacher-expectations-top-list-of-effects-on-student-achievement/422029/ on January 22, 2021.

Mattos, M., & Buffum, A. (Eds.). (2015). *It's about time: Planning interventions and extensions in secondary school*. Bloomington, IN: Solution Tree Press.

McKibben, S. (2019). Carol Dweck on fixed mindsets in new teachers. *Educational Leadership, 77*(1), 12–13.

Muhammad, A. (2015). *Overcoming the achievement gap trap: Liberating mindsets to effect change*. Bloomington, IN: Solution Tree Press.

Muhammad, A. (2018). *Transforming school culture: How to overcome staff division* (2nd ed.). Bloomington, IN: Solution Tree Press.

Muhammad, A., & Cruz, L. F. (2019). *Time for change: Four essential skills for transformational school and district leaders*. Bloomington, IN: Solution Tree Press.

National Council of Teachers of Mathematics. (2014). *Principles to actions: Ensuring mathematical success for all*. Reston, VA: Author.

National Governors Association Center for Best Practices & Council of Chief State School Officers. (2010a). *Common Core State Standards for English language arts and literacy in history/social studies, science, and technical subjects*. Washington, DC: Authors. Accessed at www.corestandards.org/assets/CCSSI_ELA%20Standards.pdf on February 26, 2021.

National Governors Association Center for Best Practices & Council of Chief State School Officers. (2010b). *Common Core State Standards for mathematics*. Washington, DC: Authors. Accessed at www.corestandards.org/assets/CCSSI_Math%20Standards.pdf on February 26, 2021.

NGSS Lead States. (2013). *Next Generation Science Standards: For states, by states*. Washington, DC: National Academies Press.

Patterson, K., Grenny, J., McMillan, R., & Switzler, A. (2012). *Crucial conversations: Tools for talking when stakes are high* (2nd ed.). New York: McGraw-Hill Education.

Pearce, S. (2015). The FLEX schedule. In M. Mattos & A. Buffum (Eds.), *It's about time: Planning interventions and extensions in secondary school* (pp. 147–164). Bloomington, IN: Solution Tree Press.

Reason, C. (2018, May 28). *The gift of conflict in a PLC* [Blog post]. Accessed at www .solutiontree.com/blog/?s=conflict on May 14, 2021.

Roberts, M. (2019). *Enriching the learning: Meaningful extensions for proficient students in a PLC at Work.* Bloomington, IN: Solution Tree Press.

Sagie, A. (1997). Leader direction and employee participation in decision making: Contradictory or compatible practices? *Applied Psychology: An International Review, 46*(4), 387–416.

Saphier, J. (2017). *High expectations teaching: How we persuade students to believe and act on "smart is something you can get."* Thousand Oaks, CA: Corwin Press.

Schimmer, T. (2016). *Grading from the inside out: Bringing accuracy to student assessment through a standards-based mindset.* Bloomington, IN: Solution Tree Press.

Schmoker, M. (2004). Learning communities at a crossroads: Toward the best schools we've ever had. *Phi Delta Kappan, 86*(1), 84–89.

Senge, P. M. (2006). *The fifth discipline. The art and practice of the learning organization* (Rev. and updated ed.). New York: Doubleday.

Sinek, S. (2009). *Start with why: How great leaders inspire everyone to take action.* New York: Portfolio.

Soumeillan, B. (2018). Research-based tips to turn up math talk. *ASCD Express, 13*(22). Accessed at www.ascd.org/ascd-express/vol13/1322-soumeillan.aspx on March 25, 2021.

Spiller, J. (2020, August 1). *Ensure learning for all, no matter what* [Webinar]. Bloomington, IN: Solution Tree.

Stiggins, R. (2005). Assessment *for* learning: Building a culture of confident learners. In R. DuFour, R. Eaker, & R. DuFour (Eds.), *On common ground: The power of professional learning communities* (pp. 65–83). Bloomington, IN: Solution Tree Press.

Subban, P. (2006). Differentiated instruction: A research basis. *International Education Journal, 7*(7), 935–947. Accessed at https://files.eric.ed.gov/fulltext/EJ854351.pdf on March 25, 2021.

Theisen-Homer, V. (2018, September 3). *How can we support more empowering teacher-student relationships?* [Blog post]. Accessed at www.edweek.org/teaching-learning /opinion-how-can-we-support-more-empowering-teacher-student-relationships /2018/09 on January 22, 2021.

Timms, P. (2020). *The five dysfunctions of a team: Still applicable in 2020?* Accessed at www.makingbusinessmatter.co.uk/the-five-dysfunctions-of-a-team/ on May 13, 2021.

Tomlinson, C. A. (2017). *How to differentiate instruction in academically diverse classrooms* (3rd ed.). Alexandria, VA: Association for Supervision and Curriculum Development.

Tuckman, B. W. (1965). Developmental sequence in small groups. *Psychological Bulletin, 63*(6), 384–399. Accessed at https://doi.org/10.1037/h0022100 on July 12, 2021.

Tuckman, B. W., & Jensen, M. A. (1977). *Stages of small-group development revisited.* Accessed at http://faculty.wiu.edu/P-Schlag/articles/Stages_of_Small_Group _Development.pdf on April 11, 2021.

Visible Learning. (n.d.a). *Collective teacher efficacy (CTE) according to John Hattie.* Accessed at https://visible-learning.org/2018/03/collective-teacher-efficacy-hattie/ on January 22, 2021.

Visible Learning. (n.d.b). *Hattie ranking: 252 influences and effect sizes related to student achievement.* Accessed at https://visible-learning.org/hattie-ranking-influences-effect-sizes-learning-achievement/ on March 4, 2021.

Vogt, M., Echevarria, J. J., & Short, D. J. (2016). *Making content comprehensible for English learners: The SIOP model* (5th ed.). Boston: Pearson.

Vygotsky, L. S. (1978). *Mind in society: The development of higher psychological processes.* Cambridge, MA: Harvard University Press.

Webb, N. (1997). *Research monograph no. 6: Criteria for alignment of expectations and assessments on mathematics and science education.* Washington, DC: Council of Chief State School Officers. Accessed at https://files.eric.ed.gov/fulltext/ED414305.pdf on March 25, 2021.

Webb, N. (2002). *Depth-of-Knowledge levels for four content areas.* Accessed at http://ossucurr.pbworks.com/w/file/fetch/49691156/Norm%20web%20dok%20by%20subject%20area.pdf on April 27, 2021.

Wiliam, D. (2018). *Embedded formative assessment* (2nd ed.). Bloomington, IN: Solution Tree Press.

Wilson, D., & Conyers, M. (2020). *Developing growth mindsets: Principles and practices for maximizing students' potential.* Alexandria, VA: Association for Supervision and Curriculum Development.

Wolff, S. B., Druskat, V. U., Koman, E. S., & Messer, T. E. (2006). The link between group emotional competence and group effectiveness. In V. U. Druskat, F. Sala, & G. Mount (Eds.), *Linking emotional intelligence and performance at work: Current research evidence with individuals and groups* (pp. 223–242). Mahwah, NJ: Lawrence Erlbaum Associates.

Zwiers, J., & Crawford, M. (2011). *Academic conversations: Classroom talk that fosters critical thinking and content understandings.* Portsmouth, NH: Stenhouse.

Index

Make It Happen: Coaching With the Four Critical Questions of PLCs at Work®
Kim Bailey and Chris Jakicic

Ensure every team is engaged in the right work with a collective focus on improved student learning. Aligned to the Professional Learning Communities (PLC) at Work® model, this resource includes processes, protocols, templates, and strategies designed to support the multidimensional work of instructional coaches.
BKF840

The Collaborative Team Plan Book for PLCs at Work®
Kim Bailey and Chris Jakicic

Designed exclusively for teacher teams, this plan book provides practical PLC information and resources. Access forty weekly planning pages, in-depth examples, succinct summaries of PLC concepts, and many more tools that will help you and your team thrive throughout the year.
BKF981

Simplifying Common Assessment
Kim Bailey and Chris Jakicic

Discover how to develop effective and efficient assessments. The authors simplify assessment development to give teacher teams the confidence to write and use team-designed common formative assessments that help ensure all students master essential skills and concepts.
BKF750

Common Formative Assessment
Kim Bailey and Chris Jakicic

The catalyst for real student improvement begins with a decision to implement common formative assessments. In this conversational guide, the authors offer tools, templates, and protocols to incorporate common formative assessments into the practices of a PLC to monitor and enhance student learning.
BKF538

The Big Book of Tools for Collaborative Teams in a PLC at Work®
William M. Ferriter

Build your team's capacity to become agents of change. Organized around the four critical questions of a PLC at Work®, this comprehensive resource provides an explicit structure for learning teams. Access tools and templates for navigating common challenges, developing collective teacher efficacy, and more.
BKF898

Solution Tree | Press

a division of
Solution Tree

Visit SolutionTree.com or call 800.733.6786 to order.

Wait! Your professional development journey doesn't have to end with the last pages of this book.

We realize improving student learning doesn't happen overnight. And your school or district shouldn't be left to puzzle out all the details of this process alone.

No matter where you are on the journey, we're committed to helping you get to the next stage.

Take advantage of everything from **custom workshops** to **keynote presentations** and **interactive web and video conferencing**. We can even help you develop an action plan tailored to fit your specific needs.

Let's get the conversation started.

Call 888.763.9045 today.

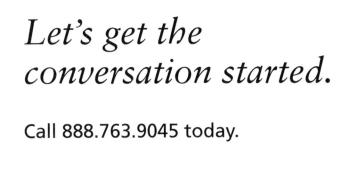

 SolutionTree.com